Desi Divas

Christine L. Garlough

Desi Divas

POLITICAL ACTIVISM

IN SOUTH ASIAN AMERICAN

CULTURAL PERFORMANCES

UNIVERSITY PRESS OF MISSISSIPPI / JACKSON

www.upress.state.ms.us

The University Press of Mississippi is a member
of the Association of American University Presses.

First printing 2013

∞

Library of Congress Cataloging-in-Publication Data

Garlough, Christine, 1967–
  Desi divas : political activism in South Asian American
cultural performances / Christine Garlough.
      pages cm
  Includes bibliographical references and index.
  ISBN 978-1-61703-732-0 (cloth : alk. paper)
ISBN 978-1-4968-5369-1 (paperback) —
ISBN 978-1-61703-733-7 (ebook) (print) 1. Performance
art—Political aspects—United States. 2. Performance
art—Social aspects—United States. 3. South Asian
American women—Social life and customs. 4. South Asian
American women—Ethnic identity. 5. Women in the
performing arts—United States. 6. Art and social action—
United States. I. Title.
  NX512.3.A83G37 2013
  792.089'914073—dc23   2012036106

British Library Cataloging-in-Publication Data available

✦   ✦   ✦

For Gabriel, Isabel, and Dhavan,
and for Don, Patsy, and Carrie,
with all my love

✦   ✦   ✦

Contents

Acknowledgments

Writing a book is always a collective endeavor. With this in mind, I would like to express my deep gratitude to those who have contributed to this work.

This book would not have come into being without the open and welcoming response of the South Asian American activists and performers whose efforts fill these pages: teachers and students at the School for Indian Languages and Cultures, the South Asian Sisters and *Yoni ki Baat* performers in San Francisco and Madison, and the Post Natyam Collective. Specifically, the relationships I developed with Vandana Makker, Ayeshah Emon, Preeti Mathur, Roopa Singh, Shyamala Moorty, and Cynthia Lee Ling leave me in their debt.

At the University of Wisconsin-Madison, I am fortunate to have exceptionally supportive colleagues in the Department of Gender and Women's Studies, the Folklore Program, the Center for South Asia, and the Center for the Study of Upper Midwestern Cultures. A special acknowledgment must be paid to Julie D'Acci, Jane Collins, and Myra Marx Ferree, who read the manuscript with care and offered astute comments. In addition, Tom Dubois, Jim Leary, Joe Salmons, and Rob Howard all offered guidance and support in the early stages of this manuscript. Feedback from colleagues outside these departments, such as Michael Hyde and Hemant Shah, helped to push this project forward. A special thanks to Erik Doxtader and the participants in the biannual Conference on Rhetorical Theory who listened carefully to my ideas about acknowledgment, care, and critical play as they were developing and offered excellent feedback.

I also wish to thank several research assistants and copy editors for their help, close reading, and meticulous comments: Paige Black, Paul Smaglik, Danielle Devereaux-Weber, Michelle Murray, Ryan Solomon, Ayeshah Emon, Manisha Shelat, and Carley Yuenger.

Funding for this book was generously provided by two University of Wisconsin-Madison Graduate School Research Competition Grants and a Vilas Lifecycle Grant.

I would like to thank my family who has encouraged and supported me during the research and writing of this book—most especially Dhavan, Gabriel, Isabel, and Carrie. You are dear to me, and this book is a testament to what a person can complete within a context of care and love. Lifelong friends like Beatriz Botero, Hernando Rojas, and Laura Seybold sustained me through laughter and companionship. To you, I extend a heartfelt thanks. I would also like to offer a sincere thank you to Craig Gill, editor-in-chief of the University Press of Mississippi, who embraced this interdisciplinary venture and took interest in its development. He has been a delight to work with.

Desi Divas

Shyamala performing as the goddess. Photo credited to Christine Nguyen, courtesy of Te Ada Productions.

◆   ◆   ◆

Chapter One

Toward Acknowledgment

Care in Diasporic Performances

◆   ◆   ◆

Shyamala Moorty sits on a cold, white toilet in the center of a bare stage. Her eyes move slowly across an audience that includes mainstream and South Asian American community members, war veterans, as well as university students and faculty. This diverse group has come together on a cold October night in Madison, Wisconsin, to participate in a 2005 performance called *Rise*. Hands shaking as she holds a newspaper, Shyamala listens to a cacophony of local and national media reports. Playing one over the other, each details the terrorist destruction of the World Trade Center in New York City and the Pentagon in Washington, D.C. Picking up a carefully folded American flag from the stage floor, she slowly opens it up for the audience to view and places her hand over her heart. Next, she begins to tell a story. It is an incident that occurred immediately after 9/11, while walking in her California neighborhood. She recalls:

> I walked through my neighborhood passing lawns bordered by the flags of blue with white stars and stripes of red. I came upon a plain white house and I saw a middle-aged white man with glasses watering his lawn. I prepared my friendly stranger smile, only to be met with a grotesque scowl making a gargoyle statue out of his still body. Suddenly, his arm jerked, spraying the water at me. I was far enough away that the droplets didn't physically touch me but I felt them pour down inside, flooding my lungs with shock. I struggled to breathe but he did it again. I turned to go in confusion. Only to see the same stars, brighter now against the red

of anger. Watching me. Lining the street like a regiment. Watching me. Monitoring me. Ushering me into the future of Homeland Security.

Of course, Shyamala's experience was not uncommon. Immediately following 9/11, South Asians experienced a record increase in incidences of bias, hate crimes, profiling, and discrimination. Indeed, in the first week following 9/11, hundreds of incidences of bias or violence against South Asians were reported in the United States (http://www.saalt.org).

However, what does make Shyamala's testimony in this public forum unique is its artistic and inventive form. While wondering aloud about the politics of "home" and identity politics within contexts that are characterized by violence, Shyamala enacts the outlines of her bicultural ethnicity, as her body gracefully combines ballet, a traditional Indian dance called Bharatanatyam, and contemporary dance movements. Moments later she plunges the newspaper and the American flag down the toilet.

In her performance of *Rise*, this South Asian American activist and feminist performance artist extends an invitation—a *call for acknowledgment*. Asking for more than mere tolerance or simple recognition, she weaves together personal testimony and traditional cultural forms in inventive ways, with the hope of generating concern, care, and compassion among her audience. In doing so, Shyamala adds a meaningful perspective to the public sphere in an alternative fashion. Politics, of course, has always had an element of performance, though attention toward its importance has arguably increased in recent years (Alexander 2010). However, what interests me about Shyamala's presentation is precisely the means by which her political performance persuades in unconventional ways. She relies less upon claims for recognition and more upon calls for acknowledgment that intertwine justice and care. She also embeds her testimony in traditional cultural forms to invite reflection and connection among those who gathered to witness it. That process encourages her audience to not merely think differently about citizenship, violence, and belonging, but also to feel differently about the plight of the South Asians she dramatized.

She uses this approach to explore a question that defines post-9/11 America: "What happens to a nation of individuals engrossed by constant ever-present threats to the home?" In doing so, she evokes inquiry into the experience of hate crimes and human rights offenses. How can people—citizens and immigrants, women and men, people of differing cultures and faithsdwell together in ways that address the complicated politics of our time, while simultaneously acknowledging that those marginalized and isolated by these complexities have disproportionately been victims of violence in their neighborhoods and their homes? These issues have been examined in political speeches and social protests; rational arguments have been made, and anger and outrage expressed. Yet when Shyamala invited consideration of them through the careful presentation of an eclectic mix of folk forms, classical dance, and dramatic narrative, she injected a new set of considerations into the public sphere. These considerations call for an emotional connection grounded in a "politics of care."

As the concerns of our local communities intertwine with those of our national or global existence, it seems crucial to ask how people can "be-with-others" in ways that reflect a concurrent political commitment to justice and care. Shyamala's questions point toward her specific experiences as a South Asian American woman, while also drawing attention to the problems of others who are situated in various ways across border lines. Her performance opens her audience to witness the challenges of diasporic life for those who are made to feel less than welcome while participating in the public sphere. This use of culture, or *cultural politics* as some have called it (Darnovsky, Epstein, and Flacks 1995), makes this sort of engagement more inviting for both the performer and the audience, enabling participation in policy debates, attempts at persuasion, and involvement in social protest.

Desi Divas is about performances, like Shyamala's, that are a form of grassroots activism. This book offers a multisited ethnographic account of

Post Natyam Collective members Shyamala Moorty, Cynthia Lee Ling, and Anjali Tata-Hudson. Photo credited to Andrei Andreev.

contemporary South Asian American women who participate in progressive politics and local community engagement. These women, in connection with feminist groups, human rights organizations, ethnic culture schools, and transnational art collectives, engage in the heart of contemporary controversies. Working through a variety of artistic media, they enter a dialogue and explore pressing questions related to immigration rights, ethnic stereotyping in the media, hate crimes, religious violence, educational policy, sex positivity, and gender identity. In doing so, they insert an often-marginalized diasporic perspective on current events—one that accounts for the ways in which the local and global intermesh in today's transnational world.

These South Asian American women are committed to arguing on behalf of social justice issues and the care for victims of violence—both social and domestic—and this is apparent in venues ranging from community theater spaces, folk festivals, poetry readings, to public blogs. Their performances often offer a social critique that risks public censure in the hope of spurring acknowledgment—for a chance to create a connection with others through a sharing of struggles and suffering. The use of political performance to engage with concerns and controversies is not exclusive to South Asian women in the diaspora, as illustrated by Kulich's (1998) research on Brazilian travesti and Rupp and Taylor's (2003) consideration of drag queens; nonetheless, immigrants from India, Pakistan, Sri Lanka, Nepal, and Bangladesh also use performance as a political tool.

Accordingly, in this book, I strive to understand the ways women from diverse South Asian communities in the United States offer personal testimonies and narratives in culturally inventive ways that grow from their experiences in the diaspora. Since 1990, the South Asian community has been one of the fastest growing immigrant groups in the United States, with a population of over two million. The South Asian community in America includes individuals whose familial heritage originates in countries such as India, Pakistan, Bhutan, Bangladesh, Sri Lanka, and Nepal, as well as other diasporic communities in the Middle East, Tibet, Afghanistan, Trinidad, Kenya, and beyond. Although the War on Terror has certainly increased suspicion and prejudice toward South Asian immigrants, violence against and within South Asian American communities has a long history, extending back to the turn of the twentieth century—a history that connects to complex debates surrounding labor, race, nationalism, and religion. South Asian Americans were the focus of intolerance in 1907, when mobs forced nearly seven hundred people of South Asian decent to flee across the Canadian border, and in 1923 when the Asiatic Exclusion League successfully pressured the Supreme Court to revoke the citizenship rights of South Asians. Today, a large majority of U.S. citizens indicate that they favor policies that restrict or curtail immigration from certain non-Western countries. Moreover, within the mainstream there is, of course, the hate speech, hate crimes, and social intolerance that had taken root in the "dot busting" climate of 1980s and has once again found fruit in the "fifth column" suspicions following 9/11.

Within this group, women face particular sets of challenges. Significant disparities are evident along several variables such as immigrant status, population size, English proficiency, presence in the workforce, and education level. Moreover, feminist scholars such as Shamita Dasgupta (2007) and Grace Poore (2007) concur that issues like domestic abuse, sexual assault, and incest become particularly problematic in diasporic contexts for a variety of reasons.

Here, I foreground how, through cultural performances, South Asian women raise awareness in their communities about these problems, advocate for civil and human rights, and enter into political partnerships with other marginalized people. These performances invite audiences to understand local and national rhetoric, as well as the challenges of negotiating self and Other in an increasingly transcultural world. Their performances, I argue, inquire into pressing contemporary social questions by creating opportunities for ethical listening and the possibility of social action on the part of diverse audiences. In the process, many of these performances appropriate, transform, and juxtapose texts from popular, folk, and high culture, gathering together fragments to articulate a gendered diasporic perspective.

Feminist Theory and Communication

To understand the South Asian women's performances at hand, I weave together two disciplinary lines of thinking—one in feminist theory and the other in communication theory—that point to the political legitimacy of using performance to seek a sense of connection and mutual understanding with others (Butler 2004; Dolan 2005; Hamera 2002; Madison and Hamera 2006; Hyde 2006; Noddings 2000; Oliver 2001; Robinson 1999; Sevenhuijsen 1998; Tronto 1993). At the most basic level, this perspective critiques the Habermasian view that the only legitimate speech in the public sphere is based on unemotional, neutral argumentation, as opposed to communication that employs sentiment and persuasion to achieve a goal. As Pajnik (2006, 394) argues, "the separation of the rational from the irrational in Habermas pushes aside emotion, imagination, and playful forms of action, which are regarded as not worthy of attention." Political performance and the opportunity for acknowledgment that it creates counters this Habermasian view with the feminist critique of communicative rationality and other tenets of his public sphere theories (Fraiser 1990).

This perspective is grounded on the belief of the interdependence and relationality of all individuals, and thus, the moral obligation to advocate on behalf of those who are vulnerable. It also raises a series of deeper questions and intriguing possibilities for those interested in the intersection of politics and performance: What happens when an ethic of care puts compassion, empathy and presence into dialogue with the civic values of rights, duties, and justice (Sevenhuijsen 1998)? Moving beyond colloquial and romanticized notions of "care," how can we understand care as a critical social practice? How might an ethic of care that manifests in performance contexts serve as "an act of acknowledgment"—a communicative effort that encourages a sense of connection and compassion? How might the act of acknowledgment provide an ethical response to suffering or injustice and lead us to perceive and judge political problems in innovative ways? In asking these questions, I am not simply calling attention to the ways everyday citizens engage in public debates in culturally inventive or artistic ways. Instead, I invite readers to look closely at the conditions under which care is provided when performers and audiences interact with each other.

The book, then, is concerned with engaging with debates over what constitutes legitimate discourse in the public sphere, and providing a feminist communicative perspective that centers on the ethics of care and acts of acknowledgment. As noted above, my examples that exemplify this approach focus on South Asian American women's performances. I approach them as a form of grassroots advocacy that grows from public acts of acknowledgment. These small South Asian American community organizations and their critical use of cultural forms are a counterpoint to large nationally recognized groups and their conventional use of platform oratory. By paying attention to the ways in which political performance groups engage in the public sphere, I turn attention from political centers to peripheries, looking at critical communication from the margins of the margins.

This book also attends to the movements between ethnic and diasporic communities, publics and counterpublics, vernacular and high culture, as well as national and transnational ways of being. In short, this focus on political discourse, grassroots activism and cultural acts seeks to engage with discussions about the public sphere, question essentialized representations of South Asian Americans (especially women), redirect attention to intercommunity diversity, and offer a critical analysis of the conditions for ethical speaking and listening that exist in performance.

Performance and Politics

To understand the significance of these performances, this book takes a decidedly interdisciplinary approach. The topic—grassroots progressive performances by South Asian American women—has required me to draw upon and extend a well-developed body of scholarship that makes many important connections between performance and politics. The multisited fieldwork method I have used to gather material for this project grows primarily from the disciplines of anthropology and folklore.

To complement this approach, my readings of these performances combine theory from the areas of women's studies, folklore studies, performance studies, political science, and communication. This decision to take a multidisciplinary approach signals a broader commitment to critically theorizing connections between art, inquiry, and activism across academic boundaries (Bauman 1977a; Conquergood 1992; Dolan 2005; Mills 1993; Pezzullo 2007; Pollock 1999; Rupp and Taylor 2003).

Scholars from these disciplines share a common interest in testimony, oral history, community building, citizenship, and social transformation. Whether through popular, folk, or high cultural forms, or an eclectic mix of the three, there is a growing appreciation of the ways that people can construct and participate in public life through voicing a critical perspective in cultural performances. Since the eighties, many scholars in communications and performance studies have found points of commonality through work in cultural studies (Brummett 1991; Gronbeck 1979; Madison and Hamera 2006; Rosteck 1999). Recent work has attempted to explicitly theorize connections between communications, the study of folk or vernacular culture, and performance studies (Abrahams 2005; Del Negro 2004; Dolan 2005; Garlough 2007; Hauser 1999; Howard 2005; Oring 2008; Pezzullo 2007). When studying women's political performances, these connections are precisely what concern me the most.

Within this book, I understand performance in two intersecting ways. First, it is conceived of as theatrical practice, even though the political performances I focus on do not necessarily occur within a formal theatrical space. In particular, I am interested in exploring performances as a communal experience. It is both an embodied practice and a process of critical inquiry through which individuals engage in imaginative acts of social change. Moreover, I understand performance to be an intrinsic element of the customs, rituals, and practices of everyday culture—a part of the vernacular.

In this sense, performance is both a way of being and of becoming in social contexts (Madison and Hamera 2006; Markell 2003; Pollock 2005). It

Shah family sangeet at wedding. Author photo.

is relational, and arises in the stories we tell one another around the dinner table, on a community stage, or on internationally available Web sites. It is also potentially transformational and can move performers and audiences closer to a sense of "emancipatory potential" (Zipes 1983). The transformational power of performances includes, yet goes beyond, theater productions. Puberty rituals, ethnic festivals, folk dramas, inauguration ceremonies, holiday parades, storytelling—as well as everyday symbolic acts—all fall under the category of performance (Bauman and Briggs 1990; Madison and Hamera 2006; Richman 1991; Turner and Schechner 1987). Focusing on the political and democratic potential of these performances, I illustrate the ways they may hold the possibility for facilitating deliberation and debate, constituting identities, and broadening critical consciousness. I suggest that performances are a powerful means of community and political participation that encourage a range of conventional and progressive forms of engagement in the public sphere. Consequently, building upon the work of Abrahams (1968), Conquergood (2002), and Dolan (2005), among others (Garlough 2008; Oring 2005; Richman 1991), I trace new connections between performance and politics.[1]

In this book, I explore performances that invite audience members to participate with one another and the topic at hand—to sing, dance, listen, discuss, and imagine together. As forms of historical intervention, they sometimes ask us to critically engage with the ways the past has been represented. They also address the politics of including marginalized narratives. These performances, each particularly situated within contexts of power, are characterized by an atmosphere of debate and offer a diverse range of strategies for civic engagement in local and global politics. They often offer oppositional or resistive perspectives or make the misuse of institutional power visible. They are rhetorical, seeking to influence or persuade audiences about an exigence as much as to entertain. These performances provide audiences ways of being together and create what Jill Dolan (2005) has called "audiences as participatory publics" (10).

South Asian American women from diverse backgrounds and cultural contexts have responded to experiences of violence, exclusion, and prejudice through such critical performances in the public sphere. These performances share a fundamental feature: they are political in nature. By this I mean that these performances artistically address and guide judgments about matters of civic importance, often encouraging engagement on these topics and participation in the public sphere. In some ways all politics is performative, yet not all political performances center on the use of art for political ends. When art is deployed in this way, the potential appears for broaching issues that would otherwise go unacknowledged in ways that engage cultural traditions in innovative and imaginative ways.

The performers and performances considered in the pages that follow speak to the possibility of dissent within climates of fear, where social differences challenge the limits of what can be said and the ways South Asian American women can appear as speaking subjects. In this and the following chapters, I explore how experiences of social intolerance and suffering can be expressed through performance in ways that represent the very differences that put diasporic individuals at risk. In doing so, I inquire into the cultural barriers and political challenges of protesting violence and loss— especially when there is pressure to stay silent or to voice one's opinion in a solitary political idiom, shared community perspective, or singular epistemological account (Butler 2004).

These pressures are particularly acute in times of crisis. In such moments, minority voices are often deterred from publicly denouncing injurious, hateful, and harmful practices and policies. This problem directly speaks to debates concerning what constitutes nation and citizen, home and foreign, self and Other, and sparks related questions. Who should feel "at home" speaking about violence? Who has the right to speak and in what mode? What is one's ethical responsibility, despite the costs, to participate in critical discussion and debate about violence in civil society?

And there are often costs to the expression of dissenting views in climates of fear. As Michel Foucault (2001) argued in *Fearless Speech*, artistic opposition requires the courage of a *parrhesiastes*—the ancient Greek name for one who speaks her mind and heart, despite social censure and the potential of physical retribution. In the tradition of *Antigone*, such citizens put themselves at risk in order to publicly protest in the face of hegemonic national and community unity. To a great extent, their strength resides in the ways in which they make themselves vulnerable to others, as they open a space for the questioning of law, cultural norms, and established reified social practices.

The use of artistic means to engage in acts of *parrhesia* embraces the obligation to speak the truth, even at great personal risk, on behalf of the greater good. Unlike such expression in political speeches and protests, the deliberate presentation of these arguments through cultural forms, movements, and narrative invites attention to a new set of considerations, ones that encourage an emotional connection to the issues.

Understanding performance in this way counters the view that the public sphere should be characterized by dispassionate, balanced exchanges (Pajnik 2006). Performance, by employing sentiment and relationality to evoke emotion and a sense of emancipation, provides a feminist critique of conventional notions of the public sphere (Fraiser 1990). As Pollock (2005) astutely notes,

> Performance—whether we are talking about the everyday act of telling a story or the staged reiterations of stories—is an especially charged, contingent, reflexive space of encountering the complex web of our respective histories. It may consequently engage participants in new and renewed understandings of the past. It may introduce alternative voices into public debate. It may help to identify systemic problems and to engage a sense of need, hope, and vision. As live representation, performance may in effect bring imagined worlds into being and becoming, moving performers and audiences alike into palpable recognition of possibilities for change. (1)

Oppositional Political Performance and Cultural Action

For many years, minority leaders and activists have reminded their communities that such oppositional political performance may take a variety of forms. Today, the use of traditional cultural forms as potential vehicles for persuasive messages is apparent in the work of Chicano/as, Native

American, African American, and Asian American groups. Indeed, anthropologists, folklorists, and communications scholars have spent decades documenting the innumerable ways in which community members use culture to persuade one another. This phenomenon, which I term "cultural action," is a powerful means of social change.

For example, folklorists have developed a lasting interest in the power of strategic interpretation and appropriation to sustain, revitalize, and critically transform cultural traditions and communities. The work of Richard Bauman (1977, 1990, 1992, 1993), Giovanna P. Del Negro (2004), Deborah Kapchan (1996), Barbara Kirshenblatt-Gimblett (1983), Wolfgang Mieder (1987), John Radner and Susan S. Lanser (1993), and Jack Zipes (1983) all speak to the ways that individuals purposively (re)make socially accepted folk forms to communicate marginalized or potentially threatening social perspectives. Indeed, it has been many decades since folklore has been conceptualized as a set of timeless, static traditions or remnants of a long vanished past. This we know: on an everyday basis, people in all corners of the globe work to create communities, think through their problems, make sense of their lives, and find new meaning through folk practices and performances.[2]

This work clearly demonstrates the need for scholars, government agents, business people, and others to enhance their understanding of other cultures and their methods of effective expression and communication. It also highlights the importance of understanding cultural forms found within particular ethnic groups. While some communications scholars focused on oratorical performances (Balgooyen 1968; Camp 1978; Ek 1966; Jones 1965; Prosser 1978; Smith 1971; and Starosta 1979) others are more firmly grounded in cultural ritual (Abbott 1987, 1989, 1996; Bahr 1988; Blythin 1990; Flores 1996; Hammerback and Jensen 1994), whereas others provide extensive research upon the historical significance of performative acts (Kaiser 1987; Lyons 1997; Morris and Wander 1990; Suleri 1992).

Research related specifically to women's political performance also is robust. Feminist researchers, including Sue-Ellen Case (1990), Elin Diamond (1997), Jill Dolan (2005), Lynda Hart and Peggy Phelan (1993), and Vivian Patraka (1993) explore issues of gender, sexuality, feminism and patriarchy through the performances of everyday women. Some cases focused on the connection between performance and political demonstrations, considering the explicitly partisan aims of some performances. For example, as Case (2001, 146) notes, in the 1970s:

Even the protests themselves were theatrical. As Abbie Hoffman, one of the leaders of the Free Speech Movement, put it: "Free speech is the right to shout theatre in a crowded fire." Campus protests joined other protests in the streets to represent rebellion against dominant codes of citizenship, national policy, and oppressive morality through activism and acting. Costumes visualized issues: the bathing suit composed of slabs of raw meat, which was worn in protest against the Miss California beauty contest, literalized the sense of the display of women's bodies as meat. The burning of bras staged a revolt against restrictive fashion. A woman in an evening dress sitting in the midst of a garbage heap imaged the discounting of her body through the fashion of objectifying gowns. These political events were not functional so much as theatrical in their efficacy. "Demonstration" came to mean a performance of oppression and liberation through gesture and deed, forming both political action, through disruption, and a pedagogical device.

This can be seen in my research in Gujarat, India, where I have worked with grassroots feminist groups that conduct political outreach campaigns through street plays that use familiar cultural forms, such as songs, dance, and street theater, as a means to raise critical consciousness and mobilize groups of women.[3]

The performances that are the center of this book—whether in everyday life or on the stage—hold the potential to create a public forum for audiences

Sahiyar's street play on sex-selection abortion. Author photo.

to come together for a moment in time, feel allied with one another, and find a place to scrutinize public meanings important to the community (Farrell 1993). In some cases, performances also show audiences how they might become more active citizens by portraying potential means of participation to audiences who might not see themselves as agents in their own lives or political systems (Dolan 2005). As such, they are not simply ceremonial spectacles but demonstrate a "radical performance pedagogy" that create profoundly deliberative occasions and model the ways one might engage in a participatory democracy through attentive listening and dialogic reciprocity (Denzin 2006).

These performances are intensely reflective. They serve as mirrors for individuals and communities to view themselves, enacting narratives that create social solidarity, provide a place for critique that widens community borders, and make public what has been veiled (Conquergood 2006). Certainly, as Pollock (2005) notes, this approach does not always work.

> As oriented as performance may be toward change, performance does not work instrumentally. In the symbolic field of representation, effects are unpredictable, even uncontrollable. They may be fleeting or burrow deeply, only to emerge in an unexpected place, at another time. They may unfurl slowly, even invisibly, on affective currents that may compete with what we think a given performance is or should be doing. Or they may refuse to come out altogether, preferring instead to rest in the discourses of "mere" entertainment or passing pleasure. (2)

Yet, the potential exists. In performing a desire for acknowledgment and by making claims of vulnerability, a petition for future relations and a stake in one's own being is made. These diasporic performances by South Asian American women—what I will call diasporic performances—keep trauma visible and testify to the suffering of others. They participate in the rhetorical work of listening, speaking, deliberating, and knowing together. They "offer an opening for talk (or meaningful silence)—a creation of space and time that is personal, interpersonal, and significantly political" (Garlough 2008, 369).

Diasporic Performance and Rhetoric

I conceptualize "diasporic performance" as the practices and aesthetic acts of migrant, immigrant, and exiled peoples that address rhetorical situations from global, transnational, and postcolonial perspectives and negotiate exigencies in ways that are marked by hybridity and polysemy.

To understand what I mean by diasporic performances, it seems fruitful to explore the boundaries of the concept "diaspora." In recent years, diaspora has been a hotly debated concept in disciplines like anthropology, English, folklore, and cultural studies. Generally it refers to communities of individuals who have been displaced from their indigenous homeland due to colonial expansion, immigration, migration, or exile.[4] In this way, diaspora suggests an awareness of belonging that is global or transnational in nature. However, as Janna Evans Braziel and Anita Mannur (2003) observe in their influential research in this area, while diaspora certainly may be characterized as transnationalist, it is not synonymous with transnationalism:

> Diaspora refers specifically to the movement—forced or voluntary—of people from one or more nation-states to another. Transnationalism speaks to larger, more impersonal forces—specifically those of globalization and global capitalism. Where diaspora addresses migration and displacements of subjects, transnationalism also includes the movements of information through cybernetics, as well as the traffic in goods, products, and capital across geopolitical terrains through multinational corporations. While diaspora may be regarded as concomitant with transnationalism, or even in some cases consequent of transnational forces, it may not be reduced to such macroeconomic and technical flows. It remains, above all, a human phenomenon—lived and experienced. (8)

Diaspora describes experiences of living across borders, within diverse cultural traditions, and through disparate desires that complicate processes of translation and understanding. Yet it also attends to the ways immigrants cultivate and nourish social relations that connect places of settlement to places of origin. Taken together, it denotes a way of life, a hybrid culture, or perhaps, a third space between home and somewhere new that characterizes the diasporic experience.

Like all other aesthetic forms, diasporic performances offer an interpretive understanding of the world, mining its materials from the everyday lives of people. Appearing as public speeches, as well as stories, songs, dance, corporeal presentation, poetry, and material art, it deals with matters that are contingent, contestable, and multiply situated. Consequently, this book stresses rhetorical performances where South Asian Americans are actively engaged in their marginality by "protesting, reinterpreting, and embellishing their exclusion" (Tsing 1993, 5). Drawing from the work of anthropologists like R. K. Narayan (1993) and Anna Tsing (1993), my approach employs ways of thinking that are responsive to particularities, oddities, discontinuities, and contrasts; that is, to the "deep diversity" that characterizes these diasporic lives. As Clifford Geertz (2001) rightly noted, this creates "a plurality of ways of belonging and being, that yet can draw from them—from it—a sense of connectedness, a connectedness that is neither comprehensive nor uniform, primal nor changeless, but nonetheless real" (224).

Accordingly, I focus on the *diversity* of perspectives articulated by South Asian American women that relate to differences in religion, region, caste, and class, while recognizing women as individual commentators of their culture. In this way, my work draws heavily on and extends the body of feminist scholarship in folklore and anthropology that focused on the everyday resistance of South Asian women (Raheja and Gold 1994; Hansen 1992; Mills 1985; Narayan 1986; Richman 1991). Rather than focusing on women in positions of power—the exemplary women in history books or female political leaders—I look to everyday women and their vernacular ways of engaging politically. In doing so, I draw my cases from a variety of contemporary performance genres and locations. This allows me to explore the features and functions of diasporic performances that demand rhetorical acts of acknowledgment. In particular, it permits me to consider how calls for care and justice appear in these artistic renderings.

Performing an Ethic of Care

In *Desi Divas*, I am particularly interested in reflecting on how diasporic performances, like Post Natyam's, make *calls for acknowledgment* that grow from an "ethic of care." So just what is an "ethic of care?" For the past few decades, "ethics of care" has been an important focus of theory and method for feminists, moral philosophers, communication studies scholars, and political scientists (Engster 2007; Gilligan 1993; Held 2006; Tronto 1993). These scholars draw from a range of philosophers, including Aristotle, Heiddeger, Arendt, Levinas, Foucault, and Ricoeur, to make a varied set of claims about how we might understand the concept of care, its function, scope, practical manifestations, and political purposes in public spheres.

At its core, this body of scholarship argues that care is important to everyone (Clement 1996; Held 2006; Larrabee 1993; Robinson 1999; Sevenhuijsen 1998; Slote 2007; and Tronto 1993). It is a fundamental social good. In our daily lives, "care is both a value and a practice" (Held 2006, 9). That is, care is more than a moral ideal; rather, it is a moral orientation that guides individuals toward considering people's needs and finding ways those needs may be addressed. As a value, care relates to issues of morality, focusing on aspects

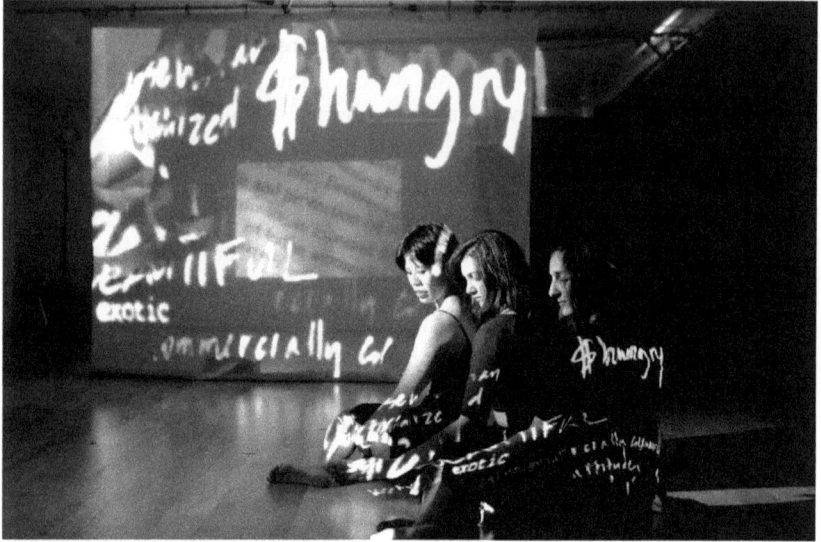

Post Natyam members Cynthia Lee Ling, Shyamala Moorty, and Anjali Tata Hudson.
Photo credited to Andrei Andreev.

such as responsibility, vulnerability, and trust. As a practice, caring, in all its stages, entails relationality (Tronto 1993). As Held (2006) observes, "Even when one is just beginning to understand another's needs and to decide how to respond to them, empathy and involvement are called for" (34).

For many scholars, their interest in an ethic of care reflects a concern with the traditional distinctions made between the concepts of "care" and "justice." As Virginia Held (2006) remarks, an ethic of justice, such as Kant's moral theory, often "focuses on questions of fairness, equality, individual rights, abstract principles, and the consistent application of them" (16). In contrast, an ethic of care often concentrates on "attentiveness, trust and responsiveness to need" (Held 2006, 15). Working from this set of oppositions, care seldom figures into a conceptualization of citizenship that is most understood in the terms of justice, rights, and judgment associated with distance and impartiality.[5]

Put another way, care is more than a moral concept. It is a political concept as well. The ethic of care calls into question the universalistic and abstract rules of dominant moral theories, in order to revalue emotion and relationality when confronted by the claims of others in the public sphere. Care helps us to understand humans as fundamentally interdependent beings. Caring relations extend to the social ties that bind groups together and include the foundation on which political and social institutions can be built. It touches upon even global concerns that citizens of the world can share.[6]

Robinson suggests that a critical ethics of care:

> [This conception] starts from the premise that people live in and perceive the world within social relationships; moreover, this approach recognizes that these relationships are both a source of moral motivation and moral responsiveness and a basis for the construction and expression of power and knowledge. The moral values of an approach to international ethics based on care, then, are centered on the maintenance and promotion of good personal and social relations among concrete persons, both within and across existing communities. These values, I argue, are relevant not only to small-scale or existing personal attachments but to all levels of social relations and, thus, to international or global relations. (2)

A critical ethics of care, in the context of social and political relationships, aims to reveal the relationships that exist among and within groups. At the same time, it maintains a critical stance toward those relations. Understood this way, the ethics of care can be seen to relate not only to personal relationships among particular individuals. It also extends to a diverse set of institutional and structural relations in and across societies.

Selma Sevenhuijsen (1998), for example, also conceptualizes care as a critical practice that serves the goals of citizenship. Her work addresses what happens when we "entangle values derived from an ethic of care (attentiveness, responsiveness, responsibility) into concepts of citizenship" (iii). In this process, we reach toward a concept of citizenship that is enriched and better able to cope with diversity and plurality. Care is de-romanticized, enabling us to consider its political virtues. In particular, Sevenhuijsen argues that care is a form of social agency that can inspire careful judgment—and judging is a principle task of citizenship and collective action within a democracy.

Acts of Acknowledgment

Building from this theoretical base, the question Robinson (1999) and Sevenhuijsen (1998) approach but do not answer is what communicative strategies might such a critical ethic of care entail? I argue that one such communicative strategy is the *act of acknowledgment*. This leads me to

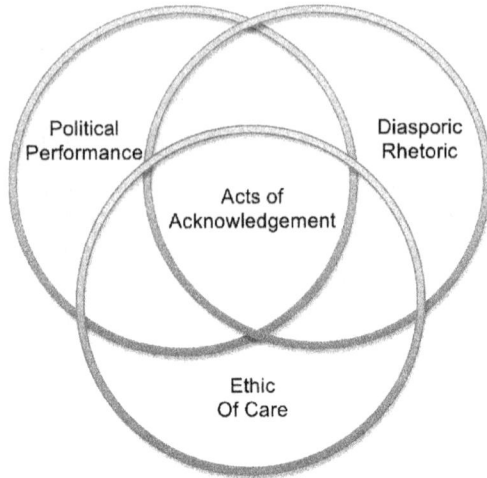

explore three key questions within performance contexts characterized by an ethic of care. Through acknowledgment, how might one "judge with care" in performance contexts? How might performers facilitate the creation of participatory publics through an ethic of care in performance? Moreover, how does self-care manifest in performance? We take up these questions through an explication of the notion of "acts of acknowledgment," the synthesis of these perspectives.

These three dominant strands of theorizing—the first, which expands and politicizes the notion of performance; the second, which connects this to rhetoric from the margins and the issues of hybridity; and the third, which considers the moral and political conceptions of an ethic of care—can be wound together to situate the rhetorical performances of South Asian American women considered in these pages. Indeed, I contend that it is at these concepts' intersection that the notion of acknowledgment resides, a rhetorical manifestation of the ethic of care in a performative context.

To illustrate this, I offer the following visualization while at the same time recognizing that doing so simplifies a complex set of interrelationships. Nonetheless, it is important to understand how these three strands, and the three field spaces that they represent, come together. Contemporary research on the concept of "acknowledgment" often appears in literature at the intersections of rhetoric and philosophy, specifically ethics. It also is typically referenced in conjunction with a substantial and growing body of literature on recognition studies (Cavell 1987, 2005; Markell 2003).

For example, in the disciplinary area of rhetorical studies, Michael J. Hyde (2006) recently published an influential book, *The Life-giving Gift of*

Acknowledgment. Hyde's orientation on acknowledgment grows from an engagement with the work of Heidegger and Levinas, with an eye toward Aristotle and the Sophists (Garlough 2007). He offers a rhetorical orientation toward acknowledgment that reflects an abiding concern with human contingency, civic responsibility, rhetorical competence, and social well-being. Here, Hyde argues that acknowledgment is a way of "being-for-others." It is deeply relational, a means of giving attention to others in our lives. It is a form of communicating care. For this reason, he explores a phenomenology of acknowledgment, not only to understand the existential nature, but also its connection to rhetorical performances in heightened moments of crisis and in the realm of the everyday.

Acknowledgment, Hyde (2006) argues, embraces both humanity's vulnerability and our strength as individuals to address that fragility. In acknowledgment, there is the potential for healing and hope essential to communal spirit, social activism, and the moral well-being of humankind. Conversely, a lack of acknowledgment is a fundamental precondition for suffering. The result is often a social state of being marginalized, ignored, or forgotten. There are, of course, innumerable local, national, and global ramifications for such a lack—all of them forms of "social death," according to Hyde. This state of being appears, for example, in institutionalized forms of negative acknowledgment like racism or sexism. In particular, Hyde's Levinasian sense of acknowledgment and "the Other" lays the groundwork for how we might more ethically acknowledge those who are "foreign" or "a stranger" to us in increasingly globalized contexts.

In these moments, Hyde (2006) argues, acknowledgment, as a way of being-for-others, shows itself to be "more than recognition." This statement gestures toward a larger scholarly debate, spanning across disciplines, that has attempted to differentiate the connections and distinctions between the terms "recognition" and "acknowledgment." That is, although etymologically both sets of terms find their root in the concepts of *anerkennung* or *anerkennen/erkennon*, many believe that the conflation of the two in everyday language is deeply problematic. Indeed, Calvin O. Schrag (2002) argues that "the blurring of the grammar of acknowledgment with the grammar of recognition is one of the most glaring misdirections of modern epistemology" (117–18).

So what characterizes the distinction between the two? Patchen Markell (2003, 1), in *Bound by Recognition*, suggests that,

Life is given texture by countless acts of recognition. From everyday interactions to the far-reaching deliberations of legislatures and courts, people are constantly asking the interconnected questions: Who are you? Who am I? Who are we? In answering these questions, we locate ourselves and others in social space, simultaneously taking notice of and reproducing relations of identity and difference. And in this way, we orient ourselves practically: we decide what to do and how to treat others, at least partially on the basis of who we take ourselves, and them, to be.

This accords with Paul Ricoeur's (2005) sense of recognition, in *The Course of Recognition*, where he outlines three major senses of the word: "(1) To grasp (an object) with the mind, through thought, in joining together images, perceptions, having to do with it; to distinguish or identify the judgment or action, know it by memory; (2) To accept, take to be true (or take as such); and (3) To bear witness through gratitude that one is indebted to someone for (something, an act)" (12). Recognition involves the difficult practice of seeing something within the terms of something else. We recognize a thing *as* a thing (Markell 2003). We attempt to recognize the strange, so that it becomes identifiable. And as Gadamer (2004) aptly notes, there is a joy in recognition—in making meaningful associations, even when regarding unpleasant subjects of the association (17). In sum, recognition provides our lives "depth and continuity" (Markell 2003, 2). Without markers of identity, we would be unable to find our way in such a complicated and chaotic world.

Some would assert that such recognition is a matter of discourse. That is, when recognition is at stake, justice is provided when people are well represented in print, in media, and in everyday speech. That is why, in educative settings, "through literature, art, pictures, historical accounts, food, dress, student genealogies, days of cultural recognition and many other practices, teachers embrace the folk paradigm of recognition either implicitly or explicitly" (Bingham 2006, 328). However, there also can be significant costs associated with struggles for recognition. As scholars like Arjun Appadurai (2003), Homi Bhabha (1980), and Charles Taylor (1994) have argued, recognition also serves to institute and then sustain relations that are characterized by inequity, prejudice, or discrimination. Building from this scholarship Markell (2003) contends, "If recognition makes the social world intelligible, it often does so by stratifying it, subordinating some people and elevating others to positions of privilege or dominance" (2–3). In this sense, recognition may be a "medium of injustice," as seen in acts such as racial profiling.[7] Kelly Oliver (2001) argues that the very emphasis upon "struggle" is the problem. She says within the "pathology of recognition" the struggle to become objectified, in order to be recognized by the sovereign subject, is part and parcel of the dehumanizing practices of the dominant culture.

Perhaps we should, as a first step, refuse to "struggle."[8] Alternatively, it may be that we need to move beyond the language of recognition to the more promising and meaningful term of *acknowledgment* and the acts that call for it.

Looking beyond Recognition

Theorized in this way, acknowledgment is not interchangeable with recognition. Rather, I would suggest that it refers to a related but distinct set of behaviors and practices. To begin, building from the work of Michael J. Inwood (1992), it is important to note that often recognition may be private—as when one realizes one's error or a truth. When recognition is private, the concept of acknowledgment cannot be substituted because one may recognize an error but not acknowledge it publicly (245). Also, when we identify a thing or a person as a particular individual, recognition is not necessarily replaceable by acknowledgment. That is, one can recognize someone without acknowledging them (*erkennon*). In contrast, acknowledgment (*anerkennon*) goes further to include the following practices: "(1) To admit, concede, confess a thing or person to be something, (2) to endorse, ratify, sanction, approve or take notice of something or a person, and (3) to take notice of someone in a special way or to honor them" (Inwood 245). This exceeds my intellectual identification of a thing or a person. The bigger question is how I should *behave* toward others. All this goes beyond simply seeing the other as a person; instead, one must become aware of and confirm the other. As Hyde (2006) states, "the act of acknowledgment is a communicative behavior that grants attention to others and thereby makes room for them in our lives . . . . There is hope to be found with this transformation of space and time as people of conscience opt to go out of their way to make us feel wanted and needed, to praise our presence and actions, and thus to acknowledge the worthiness of our existence. Offering positive acknowledgment is a moral thing to do when approaching the Other" (1).

I believe a focus on acts of acknowledgment is significant to understanding the diasporic performances of South Asian American women featured in this book. I would argue that the concept of acknowledgment may be useful precisely because it highlights where the feminist debates on care and justice intersect. Put differently, through a feminist reading of the performances in this book, it becomes clear how especially in times of crisis an "ethic of care" and the "ethic of justice" are fundamentally interlaced within acts of acknowledgment. These performances inspire moments in which audiences begin to care for and feel themselves allied with one another, as well as with a wider, more diverse sense of a public.

This seems particularly important with respect to critical scholarship that seeks to understand subaltern and counterpublic spheres and modes of enacting resistance and citizen exchange. As Raka Shome (1996) noted more than a decade ago, we need more critical scholarship that addresses "how rhetoric functions in hybrid borderlands and cultural spaces, as well as how rhetoric aids in the creation of diasporic disjunctured identities" (601). There is very little work of this kind in rhetoric or performance studies that focuses specifically on South Asian Americans, let alone South Asian American women. In most cases, research on South Asian Americans' political performances tend to grow out of the disciplines of anthropology, folklore, or political science (Mills 1985; Mohanty 1993; Shukla 2003). These scholars are more likely to draw on postcolonial theory or work in recognition studies to construct their analyses (Hegde 2005; Mookherjee 2005; Shome 1996).

My insights in this book are informed by these perspectives as well. However, I also hope to contribute to these discussions by focusing specifically on the rhetorical work that acknowledgment accomplishes for particular South Asian American women who engage with issues of social justice, violence, and suffering. In taking this approach to the study of acknowledgment in diasporic performance, I am able to look closely at the intersection between gender and wider political relations, particularly transcommunal and global/local connections. This allows exploration of the cultural heterogeneity within and relationships among South Asian American communities, in terms of religion, regionality, nationality, caste, and class differences.

Dialogic Fieldwork and Feminist Ethnography

My understanding of the diasporic performances explored in this book grows from a decade of interviews and ethnographic fieldwork with a diverse range of South Asian American community groups, from feminist collectives in San Francisco to secular ethnic schools in Minneapolis. In this sense, *Desi Divas* is a multisited feminist ethnography. I use traditional fieldwork methodology in a variety of locations both spatially and temporally to follow exigencies and conflicts related to women's issues that transcend boundaries (Behar 1995; Marcus 1995; Minh-ha 1989; Visweswaran 1994).

Without question, it has been a humbling experience. In these contexts, these women often operate in a volunteer capacity with few economic resources. Consequently, they strategically use the cultural resources they have at hand in order to raise awareness, form alliances, and create constitu-encies. They make impressive personal sacrifices, in terms of time, economic gain, and personal risk, to create valuable opportunities for people in need, from women who have experienced domestic abuse to communities torn apart by religious intolerance.

My methodological approach for this research was triangulated. It included arranging focus groups after performances and conducting sur-veys with organizational members. To uncover "lost" documents about early South Asian and South Asian American performance, I engaged in archival research at the British Library, U.C. Berkeley's South Asian Library, Wiscon-sin and Minnesota's Historical Societies, the University of Iowa's Redpath archive, and the International Institute of Minnesota. With an eye toward online presence, I studied the blogs and Web sites associated with the per-formers and activists and corresponded regularly with them over e-mail.[9]

In addition, so that I could understand their efforts, these women gener-ously included me in their grassroots activities and performances, sharing their sense of the world around them. In the process, I have had the opportu-nity to speak, listen, and learn with women from diverse backgrounds—all positioned differently with regard to nationality, immigration status, sex-ual orientation, age, education, and economic privilege. We asked difficult questions of one another and shared personal stories. We sat in silence and thought together. We wrote together. There were conversations that twisted and turned. Some led to understanding, others not. All required trust. And, as such, trust became a topic of conversation to be continually revisited.

In my experience, trust often emerged from exchanges in which I acknowledged my own privilege and positionality. Consequently, I believe discussions of privilege or positionality should not come after six months of interviews or as a brief aside within a personal conversation. They should not happen as one is writing up the ethnography, to function as context for the reader. Moreover, they should not appear as an apology for difference, for we are all positioned in particular ways along axes of power. Rather, they should be a means of honestly addressing power within relationships, while simultaneously communicating care. They are a way to acknowledge the risk people take when sharing with another. These discussions can be messy, uncomfortable, and even unpleasant, as well as filled with moments of con-nection and self-reflection. Most important, they provide the potential for acknowledgment that exceeds intellectual recognition.

I had a good deal in common with the women I worked with—sharing a passion for grassroots volunteerism and activism, theater, and dance. However, with each unique person, there were power issues to consider that included privilege associated with race, class, academic positioning, and so on. Consequently, in my account of our interactions I take very seriously feminist critiques regarding antiessentialism and endeavor to pay close attention to historical and social context, as well as intersectionality. Yet, in my writing I certainly can't escape my own positionality, as well as the tasks of evaluation and interpretation (Behar 1995). This text is written in my voice and structured to address my own research interests. We are colleagues, friends, and allies—and our dialogues together have taken a form that was co-created and bound by ethics that have been explicitly discussed over many years. But, of course, sometimes words fail. Sometimes people fail us or we fail others. However, I believe by disclosing something of ourselves and openly addressing the exploitation that is possible within the fieldwork and ethnographic process there is a will to hope.

Does such acknowledgment overcome all the concerns about ethnography that feminists have highlighted (Stacey 1988)? I'm sure it does not. But then again, I'm not sure that any relationship can overcome such potentialities. Fieldwork is inevitably risky business. People may reveal things they wish they had not. People may be disappointed when what they have revealed is not published. But oftentimes there is potential for good as well. We can learn to care about each other's lives in long-term ways and maintain relationships across time and space. We can listen attentively when one person offers a delicate performance of the self—a sense of self that is multiple, shifting, messy, contradictory, and relational. We can keep promises about secrets, even at cost to ourselves. We can bear witness to loss. We can decide not to give up because there are issues of privilege to address or power dynamics to negotiate. I believe it is in these relationships where our humanity emerges—when we care even though we will never care perfectly.

In these ways, my role as a researcher has been characterized not just by observation or participation (although these are important parts of my approach), but also by conversation. At the center of this approach is an abiding dialogue with the people I have collaborated with over the years. In sharing time and space with others, this dialogic approach is, in many ways, an exercise in mutual acknowledgment. That is, I have strived in each encounter to do ethnography *with* the people at field sites and not *of* them (Conquergood 1992; Das 2007; Fabian 1983; Madison 2005).

I believe strongly in the ethical potential of these conversations among researchers and those with whom they collaborate. Such dialogue "involves participants in a heightened encounter with each other and with the past, even as each participant and the past seem to be called toward a future that suddenly seems open before them, a future to be made in talk, in the mutual embedding of one's vision of the world in the other's" (Pollock 2005, 3). Careful fieldwork conversations have provided opportunities for me to "be-with-others" in ways that allow for a puzzling through of what is known, not known, and may never be understood.

In this process, I pay particular attention to the silences, as well as the inconsistencies and gaps that gesture toward a nuanced sense of individuals and their everyday lives. The ethical potential of ethnography, to me, has a good deal to do with how we struggle together to make ourselves known to others. This is sometimes characterized by playful ways of thinking and speaking, a movement that nurtures understanding and creates, for a time, a sense of connection among participants. The idea here is not necessarily to gain information, but to experience together the movement of words in a genuine dialogue. What continues to interest me about these moments is the heightened awareness of giving itself—the rising up and flowing of thought, an experience of revealing and concealing. The value of this process, fraught as it can be with confusion and misunderstanding, is the inter-subjective struggle—the communication that occurs among people engaged in a process of giving. Such moments elevate observers and participants above the present and add to a deep and abiding dialogue that creates meaning. To my mind what this means, above all, is that we must embrace our own and other's vulnerability within this fieldwork process and attend to this with the appropriate care and ethical considerations.

As must be clear, this book is strongly influenced by feminist critiques of ethnography, although I certainly do not take feminism as a stable refer-ent for my readings of these performances (Abu-Lughod 1986; Tsing 1993). Women everywhere are not the same. Nor do women always speak from the gender identity of "woman." The task of this book is to attend to local cri-tiques of prevalent gender norms and work to expose the gender dynamics in which "official stories" of culture are told, invoking and criticizing domi-nant representations of culture. To do so, I focus upon men and women as individual commentators of their culture(s). As a consequence, this book resembles critical ethnographies found in anthropology, while providing the deep textual analysis typical of many critical rhetorical studies. In each chapter, I weave together rhetorical theory, performance and folklore stud-ies theory, and critical feminist theory with interviews and thick descrip-tion of political cultural performances by South Asian women. Like many other rhetorical scholars and critical ethnographers, I share with the soph-ists "a commitment to particular practices, pluralism, unpredictability, local performances, playfulness, and partial truths" (Schiappa 2001). I attempt to foreground many voices to provide a complex sense of the South Asian

American community, to ensure their performances live beyond the immediate moment, and to "preserve the pleasure of the affective gifts these moments share" (Dolan 2005, 9).

A Trip Homeward

This approach to research is rooted in my own positionality as a researcher, as my interest in South Asian American communities and women's performance is both scholarly and personal. That is, although I am not South Asian American, in a sense, I am implicated in the diasporic experiences I describe. My early experiences growing up in a small Protestant family, in a house next to a cornfield and across a gravel road from a rock quarry in rural Illinois, certainly limited my early sense of the global. For my early schooling, I walked to a six-room schoolhouse that lacked a library, gym, cafeteria, music or art room, as well as diversity.

However, when my family moved to Madison, Wisconsin, I began a relationship with Dhavan Shah, a first-generation South Asian American whose parents had immigrated from Gujarat, India, in the late 1960s to work as scientists at the University of Wisconsin. His suburban home—often filled to capacity with aunties, uncles, cousins, and close family friends—was a vibrant place that smelled of turmeric and peppers and was filled with engaging conversations spoken in Gujarati. This was my first long-term

Family photo of wedding in Houston, Texas. Author photo.

The Garlough-Shah family. Author photos.

experience with another culture. When I reflect on it, this experience also provided my first informal "training" in ethnographic methods. In many ways, I was "hanging out" in the Geertzian sense (Geertz 1973): watching the ways cultural practices changed over time and in different contexts, depending on the positionality of the performer—be it auntie, sister, cousin, or friend; learning to listen closely and quietly in an engaged way to what I did not understand and to what some might not explain to me.

Eventually, Dhavan and I traveled to India together. There, I began working with two South Asian feminist organizations in Gujarat, studying the ways women appropriate folk practices and use them in street theater performances and political protest contexts (Garlough 2007).

My daughter with her cousins. Author photo.

Some years later, we began our own family, in which we have tried to maintain a dynamic interplay between cultural traditions. We live in a small town in Wisconsin, and from the outside, our life together likely appears somewhat provincial, filled as it is with soccer games, fishing, dance lessons, and family trips to the Wisconsin Dells. However, sometimes people simply are not what they initially appear to be in the local grocery store aisle or academic conference. And in the latter case, I am often surprised at how quickly the jump is made to conclusions about my positionality. Although it is not immediately visible, I also am embedded in tight networks that tie me to a home in Gujarat, India, nearly 7,800 miles away. We travel regularly to this place in India, participate in ethnic schools, take part in South Asian American community organizations, support local cultural events, and worry greatly about racism, hate speech, and other forms of violence after the Gulf War and 9/11.

My children have grown up with their grandfather living just a few miles away and our luck is such that he enjoys cooking homemade Gujarati meals for us each week. Large family events and holidays with relatives provide my children with opportunities to be at home with diverse ways of being "Indian American." It is in these same familial and larger community networks, I first learned about women's performances in India. At wedding celebrations—including my own—Dhavan's aunts took the time to teach me women's folk songs, folk dance, and rituals for luck in the future. Today, when I complain of a sore throat, friends in the community ply me with folk remedies using ghee, warm milk turmeric, and other herbs. I offer these examples, as a way of making clear that these performances have become an important part of my daily life.

In this way, though my positionality is "Other" (Abu-Lughod 1986), I have been close to the experiences and events that I explore in this book. I trace an exploration that has spanned more than twenty years and deepened my understanding of South Asians in America as much as it has contributed to a changing understanding of rhetoric, ethnography, gender studies, and folklore. In a sense, doing fieldwork for this book was not so much a trip to an exotic location but a trip homeward.

My interest in acknowledgment began during fieldwork with the San Francisco feminist collective called South Asian Sisters. In particular, it was after witnessing a spoken-word performance by Shyamala Moorty at an event called a Day of Dialogue that I began thinking through these issues. As I watched her performance, I was fascinated by her eclectic approach to addressing the social problems facing her community—locally, globally, and transculturally. Her performance was generous and emotionally open, as well as aesthetically and intersubjectively powerful. It connected diverse audience members and challenged them to acknowledge not only issues of violence, but also her experience of suffering.

Here, the power of bearing witness through such testimony was not simply located in the "proof" that Shyamala provided. Rather, it came from a sense of "singularity" that her words evoked, the sense of presence, of having experienced it yourself (Derrida 2005). Such a process of witnessing is often painful, requiring one to relive moments of suffering, creating a sense of isolation (Nancy 2002). Yet, at the same time, to know oneself through this pain is to be in relation to the Other—to all others who have suffered and are still suffering. In this sense, she is both an eyewitness to historical facts and a witness to a truth about humanity and suffering that transcends those facts (Oliver 2004). Her testimony is a poetic and deeply personal account of the issues of the day. It is the first of many accounts that will appear in this book concerning the feminist performances imagined and enacted within contemporary South Asian American communities as acts of acknowledgment.

I recount this performance to illustrate at the outset what is at stake in this book and what I hope to accomplish by its end. To begin, this personal account demonstrates the wide swath of discourse and performance I consider important to attend to for scholars interested in South Asian American activism by women. It also provides evidence of my conviction that performance studies, folklore studies, and women's studies have something crucial to contribute to one another. My sense of the important connections among these disciplines will become clearer in the chapters to come, as I explore the political and playful dimensions of South Asian American performances in cultural festivals, performance art events, Web pages, and spoken-word pieces. In these performances, I trace how violence against South Asian Americans relates to naturalized notions of the American "nation." I consider how the interplay between "foreign" and "home" bears on our willingness to embrace those unlike ourselves—the Other. I explore how essentialism and stereotyping—especially within the context of identity politics—work to marginalize individuals not only within mainstream society, but also within their own communities.

The aim of this book is not to offer a complete presentation of community identity. Rather, it showcases South Asian American women's performances that are not readily categorized and, indeed, may be characterized by self-contradiction. The burden of this book is to maintain the complexity of these performances, as well as the exigencies, contexts, and South Asian American communities they represent. Doing so also involves bringing these performances together and critically examining each of them in relation to the Other. The subsequent chapters take the form of overlapping conversations that seek to understand the interrelationship of acts of acknowledgment, exceptional violence, and the subtle forms of hostility perpetrated by institutions.

Chapter Outlines
Chapter 2: Performing South Asian American Histories

Performance has always held a prominent place in political movements for social justice. From AFL-CIO ballads about the burning of textile mills to the use of satirical anecdotes in soapbox speeches by the NAACP, everyday people have used the cultural resources available to them in order to comment upon the political, social, and economic issues they face. Like other marginalized groups before them, South Asian Americans have performed their desire for social justice and compassion in the public sphere through many different modes, from folk songs and speeches at political protest rallies to ethnic pride parades. Protest performances often take on elements of the "theatrical" as diasporic community members addressing exigencies within their communities through both words and bodies. Indeed, there is a long tradition of political performances by South Asian American grass-roots actors, although some of the early history is not well documented. This chapter seeks to fill this gap and provide context for the ideas that will guide my ethnographic cases of "acts of acknowledgment" that are a part of art and not always sought out or allowed in politics.

From platform speeches to theater pieces, South Asian Americans have addressed issues such as immigration, citizenship rights, and human rights violations in a variety of ways over the last two centuries. Some of these early examples provide instances of more explicitly political performances in the service of issue advocacy. Understanding this overlooked activism offers a crucial context for understanding the contemporary women's performances discussed in later chapters. For example, few know the work of Indian activist and early feminist Pandita Ramabai Saraswati, who traveled in the United States in 1886 to raise awareness and money to build homes for child widows in India. By contrast, more people are familiar with the oratorical performances by her contemporary Swami Vivekananda at Chicago's 1883 Parliament of World's Religions. Yet few are aware of the controversies that ensued over his speeches, due to their perceived "erotic" effect on white, female audience members.

There are, of course, other important examples of political performances by women and men throughout the early decades of South Asian American immigration, particularly within the highly controversial Gadar movement (1912–1919). Individuals involved in this grassroots movement for Indian independence worked from American shores to support fledgling nationalist struggles against British colonialism. To support this effort, activists wrote protest songs based on Indian folk music and performed them at political events, a practice similar to many marginalized groups in American history, such as African Americans during the civil rights movement or union laborers with the AFL-CIO. Twenty years later, South Asian American political activists, like Sudhindra Bose, performed on the popular Chautauqua circuit across the Midwest to speak about Indian cultural heritage and immigration rights in response to anti-Indian sentiments stirred up by critics, like Katherine Mayo, who were supporters of the Asian Exclusion Acts.

These early performances offer an interesting contrast with the contemporary political performances that are the focus of this book. Yet they also contain elements that herald what was to follow. After the "brain drain" in the 1960s, a new influx of immigrants organized ethnic parades and cultural heritage events to rally against hate crimes like "dot busting" in their neighborhoods. Soon after, women's activism emerged from within local South Asian American communities that grew out of broader national, transnational, and global contexts. Today, a second generation of South Asian immigrants is voicing its political opinions through popular culture forms like Bhangra and hip-hop, spoken-word poetry, or political blogs (Sharma 2010). Understanding this history provides the background for appreciating the three case studies this book highlights and the acts of acknowledgment of featured performers.

Chapter 3: National Recognition and Community Acknowledgment

Public expressions of ethnic culture, such as parades, pageants, and festivals, are often enjoyed by mainstream citizens as a way of consuming symbolic aspects of multiculturalism. Certainly, they provide a means of virtual tourism and an opportunity to experience the carnivalesque. However, between the performance of folk songs or dancing, there are always exigencies to be addressed, social critiques to be explored, as well as constraints and limitations to be negotiated based on mainstream or in-group values and norms (Prasad 2000; Purkayastha 2005; Sharma 2010). Chapter 3 presents the first of three ethnographic case studies that grow out of my decade of fieldwork studying such artistic political performances. Here, I explore "ethnic cultural performances" by progressive South Asian American activists at the Minnesota Festival of Nations in 1999 and the resulting tensions between acknowledgment and recognition at this event. Folk festivals have long been understood as important sites for performances that constitute local and national community identities, as well as political agendas. This is undoubtedly true of the Festival of Nations, one of the largest annual folk festivals in the world.

This event was originally imagined by Alice Sickels, who served as the director of the International Institute of St. Paul, Minnesota, from 1931 to 1944 and was a nationally renowned grassroots community activist for immigrant rights. Unlike proponents of more conservative "Americanization" efforts who sought to expunge "ethnicity" and encourage total immersion into mainstream society, Alice emphatically argued for the value of cultural differences. Consequently, as part of her grassroots political efforts, she created a public festival to bring together strangers from different ethnic communities to celebrate what a tolerant and inclusive America might look like—simultaneously supportive of both American citizenship and ethnic cultural heritage. This folk festival, she believed, needed to be characterized by an "acknowledgment" that supported a politics of difference, while addressing the challenges of national solidarity and the rise of immigration. Rather than putting ethnic identities on display for the consumption of a disengaged public, she argued that the festival should be organized in ways that encouraged interaction, dialogue, and friendship among individuals from different cultural groups.

I examine the legacy of Alice Sickel's commitment to the potential of acknowledgment, focusing on specific South Asian American folk performances that take place within the context of an "India" cultural booth designed to appear as a "village home" by volunteers from the School for Indian Languages and Cultures (SILC). I argue that the progressive political potential of this performance becomes complicated when SILC's commitment to educating people about India's internal cultural, religious, and linguistic diversity or its colonial, global, and transnational histories is put into dialogue with the American nationalist agenda of the Festival of Nations. The conflict emerged when, in order to demonstrate the ways "India" and "Indian immigrants" fit into the American mosaic, the performers from SILC were enjoined to enact cultural practices in ways that foreground a reified sense of "Indian-ness" that was at odds with the multicultural vision of their progressive grassroots school. Given this, I engage with the work of Elizabeth A. Povinelli (2002) and Colin Bingham (2006) to ask how liberal discourses of multiculturalism may become forms of domination by calling on South Asian Americans to perform an "authentic" and recognizable difference in exchange for the good will of their fellow citizens. I argue that these sorts of demands for recognition—for the recognizable—impede acts of acknowledgment that may require more complex, contradictory understandings.

At the same time, I offer a parallel feminist reading of this performance that points toward the ways acknowledgment might surpass these demands for recognition. To do so, I examine the ways that the booth produces yet another set of tensions—those between performances of "high" Brahmin culture and local women's "folk" culture. These tensions, I argue, become visibly productive in the performance by one particular South Asian American woman—Sheela Roy. Sitting on the floor of the "village home," Sheela performs a daily ritual of creating rangoli, a folk art form of sand painting typically done in the doorways and courtyards of Indian homes. As she uses colored powder to make the geometric designs, she weaves for festival audiences a life-narrative. In the process, she engages particular audience members in conversation about her early experiences learning "women's folklore," the ways her folk practices have changed as a result of immigration, and the limitations of performing them within the festival context.

In doing so she creates *a women's space for performance.* This performance, I contend, is one characterized by an act of acknowledgment—creating a performance both dialogical and intimately political. I argue that through these claims for acknowledgment, Sheela refuses the constitutive and identitarian violence of the festival discourse. Her encounter with the audience creates space and time that allow the performance to exceed recognition. This case provides the first evidence that the language of actors and agency, of communicative rationality, and traditional notions of the public sphere are insufficient to encompass the political work of those whose messages are artistic and cultural, those who employ acts of acknowledgment in their efforts.

Chapter 4: A Future in Relation to the Other

In many ethnic communities, the performance of "tradition" is often a gendered activity; frequently women in ethnic or diasporic contexts are expected to take on the responsibility of maintaining the vitality of cultural heritage for their families and communities (Dasgupta 1996). Through weddings, festivals, ethnic pageants, and school events, women are asked to not just preserve and teach valued cultural forms to in-group members but also to perform them for mainstream audiences as evidence of a thriving community presence. Ironically, for some young women, this pressure to perform their culture "traditionally" can lead to personal feelings of inauthenticity. Ironically, women who are repeatedly asked to perform an "authentic" ethnic identity at public events are sometimes left with a profound feeling of unease, as they seek to reconcile their own sense of intersectional or diasporic ways of being with community or familial expectations. For some of these women, a means by which to connect "authentically" to their cultural heritage becomes available through political action. By appropriating and critically playing with traditional cultural forms as a means to address issues of importance in their communities, these women simultaneously renew their connection to their cultural heritage and create the potential for social change.

Growing from this set of concerns, in chapter 4, I reflect upon Shyamala Moorty's October 2005 performance of *Rise* in Madison, Wisconsin. Moving from the festival context to a theatrical one, this performance elides some of the more conventional practices of the previous case in favor of a more radical, explicitly political perspective. A member of Post Natyam, a Web-based "grassroots" performance collective, Shyamala works through community theater to create sites of political activism across national, transnational, and global contexts. Experimenting with aesthetic form, narrative, and media, her work often calls for acknowledgment. To this end, she has performed *Rise* in venues throughout the United States and Europe.

In this semiautobographical piece, Shyamala focuses on two important periods of hostility, violence, and confusion for many South Asian Americans, drawing interesting parallels between them: first, within the United States, racism against South Asian Americans in the days following the September 11, 2001, terrorist attacks; and, second, in India, violence between Muslims and Hindus following the February 27–28, 2002, Godhra train burning and communal riots throughout Gujarat. In *Rise*, these two periods of violence are read together and through the situated perspective of a second-generation biracial woman, using dance and drama to draw the audience into the conflicted and complicated experience of these two events. Her performance plays with and effectively blurs the lines between here and there, citizen and exile, self and Other, Indian and American.

My analysis of this performance begins with questions about the viability of representations of suffering in political performances. I explore the political potential that exists in these representations beyond voyeurism and the relationship between truth and invention in such testimony. I ask how might the relationship between memory and public mourning, dissent and acknowledgment, appearance and absence be viewed through this performance. To this end, I consider the manner in which representations of suffering find their way into the public sphere—arguing for the legitimacy of these moral and emotional considerations—and reflect on how they may move us to action and renew our sense of collective responsibility for the lives of others, especially those whom we view as foreigners.

I contend that the viability of representation also leads to a concern with the limits of acknowledgment. This, of course, raises other questions: if I cannot know the pain of the Other, what is it to relate to such suffering (Butler 2004)? Does our personal experience of traumatic images and stories encourage acts of identification or illuminate encounters with ourselves? What would it mean to endure the suffering of others—to hold them in our minds and remain open to the suffering—to let them haunt us and move us toward compassion toward the Other?

I argue that, in her performance of *Rise*, Shyamala not only communicates what is important and injurable, she also enacts calls for acknowledgment that simultaneously awaken awareness, communicate care, and make claims for justice. To ask for such acknowledgment is to solicit a future in relation to the Other in a way that affirms the viability of difference—accounting for the fault lines that run through nations, races, religions, classes, and sexualities. Consequently, in my reading of Shyamala's performances, I pay close attention to the ways Shyamala presents both her narrative and body eclectically, as a transcultural site of suffering, in order to both "answer" moments of social violence and demonstrate the limits of language in these instances. Appropriating and transfiguring Indian and American cultural forms—from traditional folk dances to religious narratives—Shyamala simultaneously recognizes and refuses borders in order to enact a feminist critique of violence and argue for an ethic of care. Some of the resulting representations are readily identifiable, such as the Goddess Ganga, while others remain strategically open to interpretation, inviting negotiation and acknowledgment.

Of particular interest to me, building from the work of feminist performance studies scholar Jill Dolan, are the ways in which Shyamala explicitly asks the audience to take on the role of witness and to participate in the political work of ethical listening. This request is first issued at the beginning of the performance when Shyamala asks participants to envision themselves as *rasikas*—ideal audience members in South Asian performance traditions who are active, alert, and able to reflectively experience emotion. In a different mode, her request for audience participation is also offered at the conclusion of her performance. At this moment, she engages her audience in a question-and-answer session, conducted in the same manner that some feminist groups in India do when concluding a political street play (Garlough 2008). In these ways, I contend that the piece enjoins the audience to engage in acknowledgment that transcends deliberation. Shyamala's actions point toward the notion of *critical play*. This goes beyond the various conceptions of play as occupying oneself in amusement, free invention, dramatic production, creative speech, or the pursuit of fantasy; it extends these conceptions to play that engages in social critique of power relations and political relations.

Chapter 5: Cultural Activism and Sexuality in Feminist Performance

In the United States today, mainstream consumerism often drives multicultural interest in ethnic performances. Nose rings, henna tattoos, belly chains, salwar kameez tunics, and other women's fashions can be found in most mainstream shopping centers as "fun" accessories. In my interviews, many women expressed that this experience of having one's culture co-opted can be deeply disconcerting, leaving one feeling as if one's cultural tradition has been turned into a fad. In stark contrast, however, across the United States a growing group of progressive South Asian American women are finding ways to critically engage with cultural tradition in order to participate in important debates about sexuality, ethnic essentialization, and sexual violence.

In chapter 5, I draw from my ethnographic fieldwork with a San Francisco-based grassroots feminist collective called South Asian Sisters. Shifting from the more formal presentation of performance art to less formal sharing in community theater, this performance seeks to question the boundary between public and private spheres. Members of South Asian Sisters see their mission as empowering South Asian American community members to address social violence through art, dialogue, and grassroots political action. To this end, in annual performances of *Yoni ki Baat*—a South Asian version of the *Vagina Monologues*—women are encouraged to speak out against domestic violence, sexual abuse, and demeaning representations in mass media and to talk openly about sex-positive attitudes. This is accomplished through autobiographical monologues about topics often considered taboo in the South Asian American community, crossing the line between public and private. These issues include incest, menstruation, rape, masturbation, sexual pleasure, and sexual orientation.

Many of these monologues embed personal testimony in folk narratives, figures, tales, songs, and jokes to address topics in a culturally salient and sensitive way, adding to their impact. I provide an account of the South Asian Sisters' grassroots political work, their innovative *Yoni ki Baat* events. Next, I focus on the increasing number of young South Asian American women in the Midwest, from Chicago to Ann Arbor to Madison, who are now producing and participating in versions of *Yoni ki Baat* in their own local communities. In doing so, I discuss the wide range of narratives that offer feminist critiques and commentaries about mainstream American and South Asian culture, such as *Kama Sutra* stereotypes and the "exotic Indian woman" in mainstream media.

In particular, I offer a detailed account of one autobiographical performance by the feminist activist and media scholar Roopa Singh that addresses the experience of childhood sexual abuse—a topic often considered unspeakable in the South Asian community. In my analysis of the performance, I explore how Roopa's claims for acknowledgment gain force by appropriating folk traditions associated with the *Mahabharata*. In doing so, she draws on a long tradition of women's folklore, in which songs, stories, and material culture are used to constitute an ethical dialogue in which kinship and gender identities are created and negotiated in daily life (Hansen 1992; Mills 1991; Narayan 1986). In this *Yoni ki Baat* context, the *Mahabharata* traditions become a location from which to explore South Asian and South

Asian American kinship traditions within the diaspora, personal memories, and social perspectives of sexuality related to incest.

During her performance, Roopa also engages the audience in a "call-and-response" exchange that draws upon her background in hip-hop, spoken-word performance, and interest in African American folk culture. For example, at emotionally intense points in the performance she calls out to the audience, "Are you with me?" and they are asked to respond, "Yes I am." This dynamic, I argue, does not only reflect connections between racialized identities and realities. It also does not simply function as a form of self-care. Through performative acts, this presentation engenders a sense of "passionate acknowledgment" that strives to awaken a sense of community, care, and connection between diverse audience members. This form of acknowledgment attends to the pathos through which audience members are gathered, so that ethical relationships might be forged, constraints may be overcome, and work toward social change may begin.

Chapter 6: Intertwining Folklore and Rhetoric:
Cultural Performance, Acknowledgment, and Social Justice

The book concludes by returning to the political purpose that prompted it. First, it highlights the examples of political performance that encourage acknowledgment, moving us beyond simply deliberation. That is, each of the ethnographic cases illustrates the limits of communicative rationality as an approach to public sphere discussions. Moreover, these efforts make accessible the experiences and voices of South Asian women whose stories contribute to contemporary discourses of social justice. My goal is to take readers beneath surface appearances, illuminate operations of power, address instances of injustice in the public sphere, and question assumptions about deliberation, acknowledgment, and the ethics of care. However, given this focus, I want to stress that this is not an ethnography filled with "authentic voices" of an excluded minority. Instead, I seek to acknowledge the unique, lived experiences of individuals in specific contexts through their expressions and performances. As Clifford Geertz (1973) reminds us, often "small facts speak to large issues" (59).

In particular, I am interested in reflecting upon how acknowledgment in diasporic performances may rely, in part, on the inventiveness or playfulness of the discourse created by performers and audiences. How might we characterize play within a performance that engages the political? Is *critical play* an effective strategy to engage audiences with political considerations through amusement, free invention, dramatic production, or creative speech? How does this approach embrace uncertainty and through this create the potential for care? I argue that this play works to refuse unified messages and invite multivalent readings, potentially disrupting the claims of dominant forces and their authority. In this way, the work of play and acknowledgment are fundamentally intertwined.

In order to understand how critical play functions rhetorically in diasporic performances to facilitate claims for acknowledgment, I suggest a three-pronged framework: First, I consider the ways that critical play in diasporic performances may pose important problems of interpretation in the name of creating contexts for acknowledgment. This is particularly the case in contexts driven by concern for authenticity, traditional rhetorical competence, and synthesis. Second, I seek to understand the ways in which critical play within these diasporic performances is constrained by cultural translation, appropriateness, incommensurability, and diverse audiences. Here I am concerned with how and where constitutive power unfolds within performances and how this is achieved through certain rhetorical strategies. Along these lines, I consider the ways that such power might function as a form of violence itself. Third, I explore the ways in which critical play may overcome these constraints to provide the conditions for the "gift" of acknowledgment. I look to diasporic performances as sites of critical play that may operate productively to judge with care, create participatory publics, create conditions for self-care, and work toward social change.

This framework places an emphasis on performance as a way of exploring and expanding the acceptable modes of engaging in the public sphere. As such, social activists play through their performances, learning about themselves at the same time they are connecting with their audiences. By examining these issues through these cases, this book traces the range and strategies of critical play in South Asian American diasporic performance. It also further develops the notion of play as an important concept, crucial for understanding the political performances of marginalized groups, the ethics of care, and the work of acknowledgment.

Chapter Two

❖   ❖   ❖

Performing South Asian
American Histories

❖   ❖   ❖

Stay in the harness and work for justice and the betterment of your country, the maintenance of its flag and the protection of its white people, and let it not be said of us that there
is a streak of yellow or brown in the American flag.

—Delegate C. O. Young, Representative of the American Federation of Labor, February 1908

We have not only a Hindu prayer being offered in the Senate, we have a Muslim member of
the House of Representatives now, Keith Ellison for Minnesota. Those are changes and they
are not what was envisioned by the Founding Fathers. The principles that this country was
built on, that have made it great over these centuries, were Christian principles derived from
Scripture. You know the Lord can make the rain fall on the just and the unjust alike.

—Representative Bill Sali, Republican congressman from Idaho, July 2007

One hundred years separate these evocations of flags and founding fathers
in the name of minority exclusion.[1] Taken together, however, they reveal a
good deal about the central dilemmas facing South Asian American community members today. In both moments, South Asian Americans have
found themselves characterized as perpetual strangers at the door of
American democracy. By raising the specter of the Other and promising
protection from their fearsome "foreignness," these appeals to the majority
do not recognize the legitimacy of South Asians as citizens or neighbors.
This long history of discrimination against South Asian Americans, firmly
rooted in colonialism and global economic movements, goes relatively unacknowledged in the public sphere.[2] Even less familiar to most is the history

of political activism by South Asian Americans who use performance to address issues related to citizenship, social justice concerns, and human rights issues (Dasgupta 2006).

In this chapter, I draw from archival research at the University of California Berkeley's South Asian Library, the British Library, the University of Iowa Library's Chautauqua Archives, and the Minnesota and Wisconsin State Historical Societies, as well as fieldwork with progressive activist groups like SAALT (South Asian Americans Leading Together) to unearth a range of such performances directed at and produced by South Asian Americans— both men and women. These case studies explore South Asian Americans' histories, the tensions and ties that characterize them, and the identity-driven struggles that continue to dominate their discourse and practices. This chapter is about the fundamental problems and concerns that motivate South Asian American individuals to take action in their communities, creating spaces for discussion, debate, and education. Given that less attention has been devoted to the rhetorical work of those whose messages take the form of artistic cultural performances, the first task is to provide a historical overview of such performances and political practices by South Asian Americans, focusing on 1850 to the present. These historical case studies will do the work of foregrounding the issues at stake (i.e., citizenship or justice) and the concepts at hand (i.e., intersectionality or hybridity) that will guide the analysis of performances in later chapters.

A truly diverse array of performances and practices have been employed by South Asians—including speeches, parades, songs, storytelling, and theater events, all of which are considered here. Many people, even those within the South Asian American community, are unaware of this rich legacy. Indeed, few American histories mention the political performance traditions of South Asians in the United States. A vast majority of current South Asian immigrants to this country arrived after 1950, during the so-called brain-drain period, when large numbers of highly educated South Asians relocated to the United States. Even today, the majority of South Asians (75 percent) who live in the United States are foreign born. This earlier history is not their history, per se, as many of the original South Asian immigrants to North America returned to their natal home after a term of labor or education. As a consequence, unlike immigrants of many other nationalities, it is not the direct ancestors of most South Asian Americans who engaged in the first fights for immigrant rights. Moreover, it should be noted that these early efforts often met with unsuccessful ends, which may be one reason this history has remained largely unwritten and misunderstood. Yet, we know that the social violence of today is linked to that of the past. Consequently, the tracing of South Asian American history provided here also is intended to supply a framework for gauging the significance of the case studies and analyses that constitute the remainder of this book.

The "Orient" and the Politics of Colonial Folk Parades

As was discussed in chapter 1, performances are an intrinsic element of the customs, rituals, and practices of everyday culture. They are an aspect of the vernacular. Consequently, paying attention to local performances is a way to understand how people make culture, work within power dynamics, and create identity (Madison 2005). The earliest known American performances about India appear in the late 1700s, as a result of the growing trade of Indian goods between Britain and New England[3] and the activities of a handful of Indians settling in Salem. Some were able to marry African American women and blend into this community as they made new lives for themselves.[4] However, by far, most of the earliest South Asians in America worked as indentured servants. Local townspeople often appeared intrigued by their everyday encounters with these people from "the East," their traditional customs and everyday performances. Prashad (2000), for example, recalls an account of one Yankee trader who "enjoyed the services of 'a tall, black-bearded Sikh who stalked around town in the turban and white woolen coat and red sash of his sect'" (14). In addition, the representations of "the mysterious Orient" that they encountered through traded textiles or stories were cause for wonder as well.

As a result of this curiosity, these same traders organized an East India Marine Society parade in 1804. The performance event showcased stereotypical folk costumes and material arts of the "East." The highlight of the march was a masked "Chinaman" and four African Americans dressed as East Indians who carried an ornate palanquin. The rest of the parade participants marched two by two, each carrying an 'East Indian curiosity'" (Prashad 2000). These parades were popular entertainment for the townspeople, creating a performative context in which they publicly celebrated their economic ties to the "Orient," as well as engaged in a carnivelesque manner with the "mystery of the exotic Other" (Davis 1986). During this time period, South Asians participated in American patriotic festivals as well. Consequently, archives show that in 1851 there is another record of a half dozen South Asians participating in a Fourth of July holiday celebration of the East India Marine Society in Salem (La Brack 1988). In the next decades, as immigration opportunities expanded, a handful of South Asian

HINDU STUDENTS AT WISCONSIN

First "Hindu" students at University of Wisconsin-Madison. Photo credited to University of Wisconsin Madison, Records Management Services.

political exiles and students also arrived to pursue educational opportunities at Berkeley, Cornell, Harvard, Stanford, and progressive midwestern state schools like the University of Wisconsin-Madison[5] (Jensen 1988). These students were often asked to share their "exotic" customs in campus-organized performance events.

However, the most significant influx of South Asian immigrants to the Americas came in the early 1900s, after they were recruited to work for Canadian railroads, lumber mills, and mines. Most were young, unmarried men from rural villages in the Doaba and Malwa regions of the Punjab province in northwest India that had been economically devastated by British colonialism and the feudal zamindar system. Others had previously worked overseas, "usually for the British government in police and army stations in Singapore, Shanghai, and Hong Kong" (Hays 1974, 578). These immigrant men found work on the farms, ranches, lumber camps, and railroads of the Pacific Northwest. Despite poor pay, deplorable working conditions, and isolation from familiar, everyday cultural practices and performances, they attempted to forge communities in Canada, which, like India, was part of the British Commonwealth.

Oratorical Performances for Social Justice and Recognition

The absence of women among this early group of immigrants is striking and has been the focus of numerous studies in the historiography of U.S. migration (Mazumdar 2003). By some accounts, the number of women coming to the United States from Punjab during this time period never exceeded more than two hundred—only 1 percent of the new arrivals. Even when employers in California sent bulletins to Punjab urging families to migrate to the United States, few took up the offer. As Sucheta Muzumdar (2003) notes, reasons for this vary; cultural explanations tend to focus upon morality or taboos about travel, while legalist explanations concentrate on the role of the U.S. state and exclusionary laws.[6] In contrast, feminist scholars interested in the intersections of gender, labor, class, and transnationalism argue that the women's work on these farms was simply too valuable to lose to migration, although this value was not always made evident in public discourses.

While most women did not choose to migrate, some like Pandita Ramabai Saraswati traveled temporarily to the United States on their own accord and participated in the public sphere. Ramabai, an Indian social activist, was influential in laying the foundation of women's liberation in India. After putting forward her views on women's poverty, social disenfranchisement, and lack of education to the colonial Hunter Commission, she was invited to give oratorical addresses in England and published books, such as *The High Caste Hindu Woman* and an autobiography titled *My Testimony*. Prestigious newspapers, like *The Statesman*, reported on her speeches, praising her ideas and acknowledging her eloquence. Her performative skills were an invaluable asset to possess during this time period. As D. Soyini Madison and Judith Hamera (2006), drawing on Dwight Conquergood (2000), point out,

Elocution or the "art of public speaking" was of major importance in the nineteenth-century United States and Europe. In an age where telephones, television, movies, CD players, and the Internet were non-existent, it was the art of public speaking that became the powerful communicative and entertainment medium of public life and thereby influencing central aspects of community and nation . . . The elocutionary speaker was a performer who could leave his audience on the edge of their seats with the turn of an imaginative phrase or compelling anecdote. The speaker could build the story or the argument to a peak that held the audience captive to the spoken word that was filled with varying registers of a performing presence wrapped in dramatic gesture and utterance. The public speaker was a performer whose work was to make the audience listen and learn through a drama of communication. Elocution was a social event. The audience gathered to witness the speaker through a collective that brought friends and strangers together to meet and greet. This event was a moment of communal experience, listening and watching together, but also responding together to what they heard—from reserved claps of appreciation to uproarious laughter, to the insulting taunts of hecklers—they listened and responded together. The event was also a ritual with its customary beginnings and endings; it was a ritual of information gathering, persuasion, affirmation, and change. (xiii)

In 1886, Ramabai traveled to the United States to see the graduation of her cousin, Anandibai Joshi, who was the first Indian woman physician to be educated abroad. She also used this opportunity and the public platforms available to her to advocate on behalf of child widows in India. Ramabai's public speaking engagements were filled to capacity with audiences who listened with rapt attention to her life stories detailing an impoverished and unorthodox childhood. Living in the wilderness she managed to avoid the social discrimination that faced most Indian women at the time. Ramabai's father and mother taught her Sanskrit and encouraged her to pursue all forms of higher learning. When they passed away, she went out into the world with the intention of improving the lives of women.

Once in America, Ramabai made the acquaintance of Caroline Dall. Dall (1888) was present for some of Ramabai's speeches and wrote about their relationship in her book, *The Life of Dr. Anandabai Joshee: A Kinswoman of Pundita Ramabai.* In it Dall recalls the first time Ramabai spoke in this country.

> For an hour before this began, we received in an ante-room about eighty ladies of the highest social position . . . The audience in the Hall itself was estimated at about five to six hundred. Ramabai spoke . . . as if English were her native tongue, but there is a certain piquancy and originality . . . The audience was reverant, struck by the speaker's beauty and awed by her enthusiasm and elequence. Never shall I forget the hush which followed her appeal when, after clasping her hands in silence for a few moments, she lifted her voice to God in earnest entry for her country-women. The whole city echoed the next day with wondering inquiry and explanation. (135–36)

These positive reactions to her claims for acknowledgment continued throughout her speech circuit. Unfortunately, copies of those addresses have disappeared from the historical record. While Ramabai eventually returned to India, her visit to the United States was an eventful one, exposing many citizens to ideas and humanitarian causes they had not previously considered or cared about, as well as a new sense of Indian women's activism.

Parables and Political Discourse

Beginning in the late 1800s, businessmen, students, and laborers were joined by Hindu religious leaders associated with the Vedanta movement.

The Vedanta movement had begun as a social response to Western critiques of Indian culture. The British, in order to establish their hegemony in the early nineteenth century, had taken great pains in colonial documents and missionary reports to portray India as a land economically stagnant, politically bereft, culturally depraved, and overrun by crime and thuggery (Garlough 2007). The vast majority of this institutional discourse focused upon sensational and often exceptional practices, such as the burning of widows (sati) or "the worship of stone lingas (stone pillars venerated by Shivites erroneously identified with the phallus) claiming that such 'perversions' defined Hinduism's true spirit" (Jackson 1981, 2). This discourse contemptuously regarded India's religions as degraded faiths or base superstitions. Hinduism—even the ancient philosophies of the *Upanishads* and *Bhagavad Gita*, both basic texts of Hinduism—was reduced to idol worship and dismissed as barbaric and backward.

The Vedanta movement was part of the "Hindu Renaissance" that simultaneously accepted and rejected Western critiques, with the aim of championing the reform and renewal of Hinduism. Sri Vivekananda, a disciple of Ramakrishna (considered by many to be a modern saint or avatar), was one of the most famous advocates of this movement. In India, Vivekananda defended Hinduism against outside attacks and embarked on humanitarian projects. In the West, he instituted the first Vedic societies in Europe and America in order to communicate a sense of Hinduism based on ancient Vedas and *Upanishads* and to act as a cultural ambassador.

Interest in this movement gained momentum in September 1883, at the first World Parliament of religions held in Chicago. The event was organized in conjunction with the Chicago Columbian Expo and attended by thousands. It was a watershed moment in religious history and rhetoric in the United States, providing the first large-scale public speaking opportunity for religious representatives from India, Sri Lanka, Japan, and China that included various sects of Hinduism, Jainism, Buddhism, Shintoism, and Confucianism.

Here, Swami Vivekananda, just thirty years old, delivered twelve historic speeches that popularized Hinduism and earned him fame as the "lightening orator" (Mumukshananda 1979). As Jackson (1994) notes, "Vivekananda's very first words on Parliament's opening day, 'Sisters and Brothers of America,' attracted much comment, seeming to capture the spirit of the occasion" (26).

I will quote to you, brethren, a few lines from a hymn which I remember to have repeated from my earliest boyhood, and which is every day repeated by millions of human beings: As the different streams having their sources in different places all mingle their water in the sea, so, O Lord, the different paths which people take through different tendencies, various though they appear, crooked or straight, all lead to Thee. The present convention, which is one of the most august assemblies ever held, is in itself a vindication, a declaration to the world of the wonderful doctrine preached in the Gita: Whosoever comes to Me, through whatsoever form, I reach them; all are struggling through paths which in the end lead to Me. Sectarianism, bigotry, and its horrible descendant, fanaticism, have long possessed this beautiful earth. They have filled the earth with violence, drenched it often and often with human blood, destroyed civilization and sent whole nations to despair. Had it not been for these horrible demons, human society would be far more advanced than it is now. But their time is come; and I fervently hope that the bell that tolled this morning in honor of this convention may be the death-knell of all fanaticism, of all persecutions with the sword or with the pen, and of all uncharitable feelings between persons wending their way to the same goal.

In this opening speech, and those thereafter: "Swami Vivekananda revealed unusual talents. Demonstrating a fluent command of English, an impressive stage manner, and a gift for the memorable phrase, the Hindu spokesman was a sensation from his first address. His blunt rejection of the stereotypical view of Hinduism raised the hackles of mission-minded Christians but attracted wide public attention" (Jackson 1981, 249). Indeed, people flocked to see him and the other Asian representatives. Tracy Fessenden quotes Charles Little, a Methodist speaker at the event as saying, "People expected pagans. And pagans they thought were ignorant and impotent of mind, with no reason for their worship and no brains in their theology. To them, the Parliament was a stunning revelation" (Fessenden 194). Indeed in an 1897 interview it is clear that Vivekananda was aware that the event was designed to be something of an Orientalist spectacle. He says, "The Parliament of Religions, as it seems to me, was intended for a 'heathen show' before the world but it turned out that the heathens had the upper hand and made it a 'Christian show' all round" (Fessenden 194). In addition, a sexual element manifested itself in the oratorical relations between the Asian speakers and the Christian female audience. For many, it seems, the oratorical sway of the Asian delegates was portrayed as a form of interracial seduction. For example, Mrs. S. K. (Roxie) Blodgett, wrote, "When that young man got up and said, 'Sisters and Brothers of America,' seven thousand people rose to their feet as tribute to something they knew not what. When it was over I saw scores of women walking over the benches to get nearer to him and I said to myself 'Well, my lad if you can resist that onslaught you are indeed a God'" (Fessenden 201).

Over the course of the week, his speeches, such as "Religion Not the Crying Need of India" and "The Essence of the Hindu Religion," outlined the teachings of his faith and countered British claims that India's degraded social condition served to justify colonial presence. During the course of his speaking sessions Vivekananda often used folklore to engage his audiences.[7]

For example, in a short speech titled "Why We Disagree" given on the fifth day of the Parliament, Vivekananda adopts an eclectic style in his telling of an Indian parable about a frog in a well, which he uses to illustrate an important contributing factor to social violence:

> A frog lived in a well. It had lived there for a long time. It was born there and brought up there, and yet was a little, small frog. Of course the evolutionists were not there then to tell us whether the frog lost its eyes or not but, for our story's sake, we must take it for granted that it had its eyes, and that it every day cleansed the water of all the worms and bacilli that lived in it with an energy that would do credit to our modern bacteriologists. In this way it went on and became a little sleek and fat. Well, one day another frog that lived in the sea came and fell into the well. "Where are you from?" "I am from the sea." "The sea! How big is that? Is it as big as my well?" and he took a leap from one side of the well to the other. "My friend," said the frog of the sea, "how do you compare the sea with your little well?" Then the frog took another leap and asked, "Is your sea so big?" "What nonsense you speak, to compare the sea with your well!" "Well, then," said the frog of the well, "nothing can be bigger than my well. There can be nothing bigger than this. This fellow is a liar, so turn him out."
>
> That has been the difficulty all the while. I am a Hindu. I am sitting in my own little well and thinking that the whole world is my little well. The Christians sit in their little well and think the whole world is their well. The Muslims sit in their little well and think that is the whole world. I have to thank you of America for the great attempt you are making to break down the barriers of this little world of ours, and hope that, in the future, the Lord will help you to accomplish your purpose.

Here, Vivekananda evokes a simple folk parable or "teaching story" as a rhetorical strategy to challenge the audience's beliefs about territory, oppression, and dwelling. This narrative type, common to many religious traditions, was meant primarily to instruct or influence listeners, rather than entertain (Kirkwood 1983; Korom 2006). The parable celebrating tacit Hindu worldviews about the value of pluralism serves to move listeners to acts of self-reflexive confrontation, helping them to recognize obstacles to their humanitarianism. It also sought to involve audience members in a new sense of relationality that moves beyond local community identity to address something more global in nature. At the same time, he modernized his story by referring to evolutionary science and bacteriology, cutting-edge conceptions of the world at that time, and directly at odds with the British depiction of Hindus as backward and primitive.

By 1896, Vivekananda's reputation was firmly established. He filled Madison Square Garden for a series of Sunday lectures titled "Bhakti-Yoga," "The Real and Apparent Man," and "My Master, Sri Ramakrishna Paramahama." Later that year, in March, he was invited by the Harvard Graduate Philosophy Club to speak on "The Vedanta Philosophy" to an audience filled with distinguished thinkers, such as William James, George Palmer, and George Santayana. His ideas were well received, so much so that he was offered the chair of Eastern Philosophy at Harvard, which he respectfully declined. Instead, Vivekananda focused his efforts upon social reform and religious dialogue, using his abilities as an orator to facilitate the development of the Vedanta movement.[8]

A Long History of Intolerance

However, just as American intellectuals began developing an interest in India and Hindu philosophy, the first communities of Punjabi Hindus, Sikhs, and Muslims in the Pacific Northwest started facing rampant racial intolerance (Varma 1995). Concerned with the increase of Asian immigrants in low-wage labor positions, Canada began passing discriminatory immigration laws and several bills limiting the civil rights of Indians. These included the rights to vote, to hold public office, to serve on juries, and to practice as pharmacists, lawyers, and accountants. In order to fight these injustices, South Asian immigrants founded the Khalsa Diwan Society in 1907, with branches in Stockton, Victoria, Abbotsford, New Westminster, Fraser Hill, Ducan Coombs, and Ocean Falls (Hess 1974, 584).

Despite the work of this organization, many were forced to migrate to Washington, Oregon, and California in search of low-wage jobs in the lumber mills and farm fields. Labeled the "Tide of Turbans" and "The Yellow Peril," this migration was viewed unfavorably by many Americans. In that same year, on September 14, race riots broke out in Washington in Seattle, Everest, and Bellingham. In Bellingham, homes of South Asian immigrants were burnt to the ground, workers were beaten, and their possessions stolen. Four hundred Hindus and Sikhs were placed under police guard in the city hall, while mobs rioted outside and forced more than seven hundred individuals to escape across the border from Bellingham to British Columbia, beaten, half-clothed, and fearful for their lives.

Asiatic Exclusion League

This violence was, in part, fueled by the political speeches of groups like the Asiatic Exclusion League (AEL). This group, formed in 1905 in San Francisco by sixty-seven labor unions, was responsible for organizing racist parades, instigating riots, spreading anti-Asiatic propaganda, and influencing anti-immigration legislation. In 1908, the Asiatic Exclusion League established a Lecturers' Bureau, "for the benefit of organizations and associations desiring to bring the subject of immigration before their members"[9] (1908, 13). This bureau included influential politicians, such as state senators Frank McGowan and A. Camminetti, congressmen E. A. Hayes and Julius Kahn, and California secretary of state Charles Forrest Curry, who wrote, "as an American citizen, I am unalterably opposed to any and every association which assumes the equality of Asiatics with ourselves. We have dismissed even the suggestion of an assimilation of the two races as a monstrous impossibility involving inevitably our voluntary degradation."[10]

He was not alone in this opinion. Indeed, in the proceedings of the Asiatic Exclusion League, an unattributed published speech states,

> The Asiatic race and the Caucasian race never could and never can exist in the same territory. Their morals, their philosophy, their religion, their education, their standard of living are reversed, and as far apart as the two poles. They can never blend, harmonize, commingle or live together in peace. The welfare of both races will be best served and their happiness effectively advanced if they confine their operations and efforts to that portion of the earth given to them as a home by God. (Proceedings of the AEL, February 1909, 11)

This discourse about home and strangers, peace and violence, reflects a profound sense of anxiety about the loss of an imagined homogeneous public.[11] This rejection of peaceful dwelling is paired, not surprisingly, with an "aggressive blaming of immigrants for their resistance and inability to assimilate" (Hegde 2005). The "Hindus" were characterized as the most objectionable of all the eastern Asiatic races; "herding together in miserable hovels which if permitted to exist will soon invite disease and epidemic"[12] (Proceedings from the AEL 1910, 10–11).

Similar to most British colonial literature at the time, the AEL's discourse also abounds in fear appeals and degrading animalistic imagery, claiming the "brown and yellow races are coming like a swarm of maggots, worming and burrowing and eating the substance of the land" (Proceedings of the AEL 1909, 12).[13] These representations played a double role, justifying British colonial rule while providing a rationale for keeping South Asians from gaining citizenship in the United States. It was argued that South Asians, like savages, were not only unfit and incapable of discharging the duties of citizenship but, further, were also alien to American ideas of patriotism and morality. Figuring themselves as loyalists, members of the Asiatic Exclusion League argued that their work was a "crusade, in which we, with the helmet of truth and clothed in the armor of righteousness and with a desire to maintain the liberty of this country, armed with the weapons of knowledge, are driving from this country hordes of Asiatics back across the ocean whence they came" (Proceedings of the First International Convention of the AEL 1909, 9).[14]

Calls for Freedom and Democracy

The Asiatic Exclusion League's racist claims that South Asians could not understand the sentiments of freedom, democracy, and citizenship were nothing short of ironic. In reality, during this same time period, these very ideals were being evoked by South Asian students and political dissidents to foster feelings of Indian patriotism and to gain support for overthrowing the British Raj.

Basanta Koomar Roy and the Friends of Freedom for India

Particularly relevant, from the situated position of this author, is an interesting example of "on the ground" political resistance by Basanta Koomar Roy at the University of Wisconsin-Madison during the early part of the twentieth century. A student from Calcutta, India, Roy took advantage of the institutional forums available to him while a student at the UW. For example, he participated in the annual oratorical contests and spoke eloquently about

Poster for speech by Basanta Kumar Roy, delivered at Gadar movement rally. Photo credited to University of California, Berkeley's South Asia Digital Collections.

Basanta Koomar Roy, activist. Photo credited to University of Wisconsin Madison, Records Management Services.

the oppression of the British Raj, as well as the need for democratic reform in India. One such speech, titled "English Rule in India," won first place in the "Oratorical Contest of the Senior Class of 1911."[15] Described in testimonials as an "ardent believer and enthusiastic worker in the cause of human liberty," Roy exhibited "humanitarian passion" when he spoke in front of audiences. Later, in 1912, while pursuing a graduate degree in journalism and political science, he wrote an article in the *Wisconsin Alumni Magazine* titled "Wisconsin and the Hindu Student,"[16] where he argued eloquently for the cultural importance of democratic education for Indians and the United States' potential role in that process. He wrote:

> As a result of the studious application of the British stifling instinct on the educational system of the country, we find ourselves face to face with the grave problem of educational dearth in India, the enormity of which is enough to amaze any human being, of course with the honorable exception of the imperialistic. It is indeed a pity that over and above the perennial food famines the Hindus have to suffer from educational famine as well. (378)[17]
>
> The Hindu, realizing the seriousness of the backward conditions of India are getting restless to arm themselves with all the strength of modern education; and when they cannot get it at home, they must come out and get it anywhere at any cost. . . . A great many of those students come to America; and it is quite natural that they should. The opposite poles do attract. America's democracy cannot fail to attract those that are smarting under the galling yoke of an absolute despotism; nor can America, a student's paradise, with all its educational opportunities, fail to draw the hearts of those that suffer under India's educational disabilities . . . we can safely hope that as long as there is no direct law against it the Hindu students will continue to come to America in ever increasing number. (381)

In this article and others, Roy drew attention to the ways in which British colonialism had systematically dismantled and destroyed indigenous economies and institutions to disastrous ends. Repeated famine, he argues, murdered thousands of innocents. Meanwhile, the dearth of educational opportunities available to the vast majority of Indians further tightened the shackles of servitude, despite British claims that social progress justified their colonial presence. In contrast, America provided democratic educational opportunities that held the potential to liberate minds and ultimately free a homeland in bondage.

Later, Roy became associated with the Friends of Freedom for India (FFI) in New York City, serving as their foreign correspondent. This grassroots political organization was primarily concerned with protecting the rights of diasporic Indians to protest against British colonialism. Therefore, they dedicated themselves "to maintaining the right of asylum and to see that Hindu political prisoners and refugees in America get justice in the light of American traditions" as well as "To assist in fair, frank, and open discussion that

𝕿𝖍𝖊 𝕻𝖑𝖆𝖙𝖋𝖔𝖗𝖒

Senior Open

Main Hall, March 8, 1911

Prof. Rollo LuVerne Lyman
President of the Evening

Basanta Koomar Roy

Program

Basanta Koomar Roy	*English Rule in India*
Samuel Lyman Barber	*The Reawakened South*
Fred Merk	*Industrial Diseases*
Ralph Sherman Hoyt	*The Service of the Engineer*
Charles Henry Velte	*Chinese Gordon*

Judges

Maxwell Charles Otto
Miss Grace O. Johnson
William Henry Lighty

First three places arranged according to rank.

Yearbook page to Roy's speech competition victory. Photo credited to University of Wisconsin Madison, Records Management Services.

truth about India may be ascertained" (Heading on unpublished letterhead). While with the Friends of Freedom, he collaborated with a host of notable historical figures such as Dr. Gertrude Kelly (feminist activist, labor radical, and medical doctor); Margaret Sanger (feminist social reformer and birth-control advocate); Agnes Semdley (revolutionary and labor radical); Sara Bard Field (suffragette, poet, and orator); Franz Boas (anthropologist and human rights activist) and W. E. B. Du Bois (American civil rights activist).

Meanwhile, Roy also continued on the public lecture circuit, drawing upon South Asian culture for motifs and figures while speaking on topics such as "women's suffrage," "the worldwide emancipation of womanhood," "the feminist movement in the Orient," "Human Brotherhood and World Peace," and "The Awakening of India." He also authored a well-regarded book titled the *Woman Question* that illuminated what he saw to be the feminist nature of the poet and social activist Rabindranath Tagore's work.

The Gadar Party and the Political Potential of Folk Song

On the West Coast, undergraduate students like Taraknath Das at the University of Washington were active in campus life and worked for Indian independence by organizing campus forums. In particular, Das was instrumental in founding the Hindusthan Association of America and its journal the *Hindustanee Student* to document the activities of Indian students in the United States, as well as to provide news and opinion about the potential for Indian independence.[18] After graduation, Das was admitted as a research fellow in International Law at the University of California, Berkeley. During this time, he helped to found the Gadar party (1913).[19]

Gadar, a San Francisco–based South Asian political party, comprised anti-colonialist Bengali intellectuals and Punjabi laborers, many of whom had served in the British army. Scholars like Ramnath (2005) have argued that the Gadar movement represented a type of hybrid radicalism perhaps possible only in the context of diaspora. Physically and ideologically, it exceeded national boundaries in an eclectic combination of nationalism, left-wing radicalism, and religious and ethnic revivalism.[20]

This group formed its own speakers' bureau to create forums for informing the general public about the oppressive policies of the British Raj in India. These speaking tours included prominent South Asian scholars and activists, such as Stanford professor Har Dayal, who had recently resigned a scholarship at Oxford University to protest against the British educational system in India. Another core participant was Berkeley student Kartar Singh, who worked among the South Asian immigrants in the agricultural fields while attending school. These two leaders, and others involved with the group, used this bureau to articulate their plans for social reform and deliberate the possibilities for creating a national democratic government in India.[21] Indeed, the Gadar party slogan was "Put at stake everything for the freedom of the country."[22]

In addition to articles and editorials, the paper also published revolutionary poetry and songs, composed in a direct folk style well known in India, that were often performed during rallies and speaking tours. For example, Kartar Singh at a meeting in Sacramento on October 31, 1913, jumped to the stage and began to sing *"Chalo chaliye desh nu Yuddha Karen, eho aakhiri vachen to farmanho gaye"* (Come! Let us go and join the battle of freedom, the final call has come, let us go!).[23] Performed in the manner of Punjabi folk song, the style and content were similar to protest songs sung in the pre-Independence period in India. In this way, these protest songs were not unique. Rather, as Ved Prakash Vatuk (1969) aptly notes, "They belong integrally within what may be called the Indian rural popular tradition" (68). Although they were not folk songs by traditional definition, they were songs "concerned with the interest of the folk and in complete possession of the folk" (67). The songs, created to "intensify patriotism among Indians living abroad," were sung in a variety of contexts: public meetings, gatherings in Indian homes, living quarters. The performers ranged broadly, from talented singers to groups of small children.

Audience members were encouraged to participate as well. For example, if a song had a repeated refrain, the assembled group would join in after each verse was sung by the performer. As Vatuk notes, some songs described significant historical events like the Revolt of 1857 or the fate of a shipload of Indian migrants who, in 1914, tried to gain entry into Canada. Most portrayed the conditions in India and made appeals for freedom, revolution, and personal sacrifice. Other songs described "Mother India" as being a nation of past glories before British colonialism and glorified the deeds of heroes like Tilak, Ghosh, or Bhagat Singh. At heart, these folk songs were rhetorical. This poetic form functioned as a creative response to the social constraints faced by many minority groups speaking against the rule of an oppressor. This allowed sociopolitical protests to remain somewhat veiled in colonial and diasporic situations, blurring lines between official and vernacular political discourse. The popularity of these songs and poems was such that they were eventually compiled, printed, and distributed numerous times in a book titled *adar-Di-unj*. Many of Gadar's publications, targeted at sympathetic Americans, were in the form of handbills, posters, and limited-run pamphlets. The publications served as both historical record and propaganda.

In 1913, following a speech given at an anarchist rally in San Francisco, Har Dayal was arrested as an undesirable alien and ordered deported. He escaped to Europe and from Germany and Sweden continued his work for Indian independence from the British Raj (Hess 1974, 585). The Gadar party continued its work in his absence and on August 5, 1914, the leaders published the *Decision of Declaration of War* against the British that was modeled after the American *Declaration of Independence*. Thousands of copies were distributed, leading the British government to pressure the United States to prosecute members of the group and limit immigration from India. By 1915, 79 percent of Indians who applied for admission to the United States were

refused. Later that year, the British government launched the first crimi-
nal inquiries against Gadar members in India and other British colonies.
The Lahore Conspiracy Case sentenced to death more than two dozen Gadar
revolutionaries. This included Kartar Singh, who was arrested while in India
trying to gain support for revolutionary action. Singh reportedly died singing one of the revolutionary songs he had written.

> *Sewa desh di jinddhiye badhi aukhi*
> *gallan karnia dher sukhalliyan ne,*
> *jinha desh sewa 'ch pair paya*
> *ohna lakh museebtan jhalliyan ne.*
> (Serving one's country is very difficult
> It is so easy to talk
> Anyone who walked on that path
> Must endure millions of calamities.)

America's entry into the war in 1917 sealed the fate of the Gadar party.[24]
The leaders of Gadar, such as Taraknath Das, were deemed to be criminals.
Indeed, Das was considered the "most dangerous" and the all-white jury
proposed to withdraw his American citizenship and surrender him to the
British police (Mukherjee 1998). Instead, in a gesture of leniency, he was
sentenced to twenty-two months in Leavenworth federal penitentiary. After
his release, Das left for Europe and married his longtime friend Mary Keat-
ing Morse, a founding member of the National Association for the Advance-
ment of Colored People and the National Women's party (Mukherjee 1998).
He returned to the United States several years later and was appointed professor of political science at Columbia University and a fellow of Georgetown
University.[25]

Anti-Immigration Sentiment and Arguments for Rights

At this time, owing also to the beginning of World War I, anti-immigration
sentiment was running high in the United States. The controversial Bur-
nett Immigration Bill was advanced in 1914 and ultimately passed in 1917.[26]
This severely restricted Indian immigration on the basis of race-based quo-
tas. In 1923, the Asiatic Exclusion League brought further pressure to bear
upon the Supreme Court to revoke Indians' citizenship rights. In January
1923, the landmark case *United States v. Bhagat Singh Thind* (261 U.S. 204,
January 11–12, 1923) was decided before the U.S. Supreme Court.[27] Despite

Thind's history of service to the United States (and in seeming contradiction with the prior decision in *Takao Ozawa v. United States*, in which the same Court had ruled that a light-skinned native of Japan while "White" was not "Caucasian" in terms of racial classification), the Court decided to reserve naturalized citizenship rights for whites only.[28] This was despite the fact that a majority of contemporary anthropologists defined most of the people of India as part of the Caucasian race.[29] Instead, it was interpreted that the 1790 law that barred nonwhites from citizenship applied to Indians as well. This ruling also justified revoking the status of Indians who had previously been naturalized as U.S. citizens. In the following years, despite challenges to the legislation by the Hindu Citizenship Committee, only a handful of wealthy, well-positioned Indians were able to retain their citizenship.

In addition, Indians now had to contend with the Alien Land Law that prohibited noncitizens from purchasing or leasing land (Lal 1999). This left them legally defenseless against those like Attorney General Ulysses S. Webb, who actively set about revoking Indian land purchases. As a result of these oppressive legal sanctions, many Indian immigrants returned to India.[30] Following the closing of legal immigration channels, a second period of covert immigration commenced. Conservative estimates place the number of illegal South Asians entering the United States between 1923 and the early 1930s at around three thousand, most of whom came through Central America and Mexico via the Panama Canal. During the height of the Depression, this flow was drastically curtailed as immigration officials cracked down on illegal immigrants and deportations increased (La Brack 1988, 6).

Sudhindra Bose and Cultural Performances on the Chautauqua Circuit

In India, 1925–1935 marked a crucial period in pre-independence. In 1927, the annual conference of Congress in Madras began serious consideration of complete independence from Britain. Later, in 1929, this resolution was included in the official platform of the Congress in Lahore. In the face of this resistance, the British sought to find support for their colonial regime in the United States. One such piece of propaganda was the book *Mother India* (1927) written by the U.S. journalist and historian Katherine Mayo. The polemic travelogue, financed by the British government, hoped to counter a growing approval of Indian philosophy by detailing a variety of social ills, especially those related to "perverse sexuality" and the mistreatment of women, particularly child brides.

DR. SUDHINDRA BOSE
"Messenger of Brotherhood"

Pamphlet for Bose's speech on Chautauqua circuit. Photo credited to University of Iowa's Traveling Cultures Digital Archives.

According to Mayo, the roots of these social problems "lay in an irredeemable Hindu culture that rendered Indians unfit for political self-government" (Sinha 2006, 83). The book was reprinted many times in the United States, Britain, and India, and translated into more than a dozen languages. It was hotly debated in a variety of public platforms. In all, more than fifty books and pamphlets were written in direct response. Tension ran so high that a handful of South Asians gathered to burn the book in a protest outside town hall in New York City.[32] The foregrounding of race in these rhetorical situations clarified for many in the general public the shared agenda between South Asians' fight for freedom in India and for social justice in the United States (Gould 2006).

An acknowledgment of this shared agenda is clear in the political writings of public intellectual Sudhindra Bose, a Ph.D. and lecturer in political science at the State University of Iowa. During his time in America, Bose maintained a visible presence in India, contributing regularly to the *Modern Review*, a monthly magazine published in Calcutta that provided a crucial forum for Indian nationalist intelligentsia. In the United States, he served as a spokesman for Indians in America during the administration of Woodrow Wilson when the first Indian Exclusion Bill was introduced to Congress (Gould 2006). In order to further influence the public, Bose wrote popular books such as *Some Aspects of British Rule in India* and *Fifteen Years in America* in which both American and Indian audiences alike might bear witness to political struggle, violence, and social oppression. Written with the eye of a critical ethnographer, Bose conducted "fieldwork" in the United States and reported upon his observations on daily life and political climate back to his readership.

In addition, he delivered lectures such as *Musings on Race Prejudice* or *A Plea for Broader Outlook* in churches and community centers, as well as on the radio and the Chautauqua circuit, which was a popular adult education movement. Called "the most American thing in America," Chautauqua was considered an awakening of American culture. As Charlotte M. Canning (2005) describes, the circuit was performed almost solely in rural areas to thousands of audience members. "It promised to inspire cultural, community, and individual improvement through performances of various kinds . . . audiences could expect musical groups, lectures, elocutionary readers, specific programming for children, and leisurely socializing with other members of the community" (1). At Chautauqua, "foreign" performers abounded, from Ng Poon Chew (the Chinese Mark Twain), Yutaki Minakuchi (speaking on friendship between Japan and the United States), and Bagdasar Baghdgian (the American for Armenia).

Indian American orators were highly acclaimed on the circuit. Sakharam Pandit lectured in the Wisconsin Dells Chautauqua Circuit as early as 1910 on topics such as "Oriental Psychology and Applied Philosophy." Chandra Dharma Sena Gooneratne, a graduate from the University of Chicago, spoke on "Indian Poetry" and "Mahatma Gandhi" in lectures across the Midwest, including Sparta, Kenosha, and Fon du Lac, Wisconsin. Nirmal Andra Das was represented by the Redpath Bureau in New York and Chicago. In addition to delivering speeches on "Why Hindu Philosophy is so Inspiring," he directed a number of Indian plays in English and organized a group called the "Hindu Orchestra and Dancers." Bhaskar Hivale, a Ph.D. student at Harvard University, was credited with 831 paid speaking engagements since his start in 1922. He, along with many others, spoke often on "The New Woman of India."

Sometimes these performances reinforced notions of "foreign inferiority, " such as the performances of love songs, tattooing rites, and ritual chants by Dr. Wherahiko Rawai, who was billed as "Portraying the Rise of a Primitive People from Savagery to Culture" (Canning 86). In other cases,

Announcement

DR. SUDHINDRA BOSE is a man with a message which never fails to interest and thrill an American audience. Political reasons having made it impossible for him to return to India, he is devoting his life to the interpretation of the spirit and life of Hindustan. He has lived in this country for nearly ten years, and speaks the American language with the ease and clearness of a born American citizen. Dr. Bose has traveled extensively, and has given lectures in many parts of the United States. He has interested hundreds of Americans, he will interest you. Give him a hearing.

+   +   +   +   +

Lecture Subjects

INDIA AND ITS AWAKENING
THE COMING WOMAN OF INDIA
THE SOUL OF THE INDIAN ART
WOMEN OF THE ORIENT

N. B. Special lectures will be arranged to suit special audiences

Announcement for Bose's Chautauqua lecture subjects. Photo credited to University of Iowa's Traveling Cultures Digital Archives.

equality and tolerance were the focus, as with Bose's performance of *The Awakened Orient*. One can imagine the complexities and difficulties of being an "exotic" performer in the context of Chautauqua. However, Bose fared well, often because he framed his rhetorical message through broad themes of patriotism, democracy, and human compassion. In a speech titled "Gandhi's India," Bose wrote: "The Indian nation is greatly moved by President Roosevelt's Gospel of Four Freedoms. It wants these freedoms and the means to have them on some not distant tomorrow." Bose also responded to Mayo's *Mother India*, in his book *Mother America: Realities of American Life as Seen by an Indian*.[33] Here, in addition to other socially relevant topics, he specifically addresses the issue of race- related hate crime. In a chapter titled "Horrors of Lynching," he details the murder of an African American man named Jim McIlherron perpetrated by twelve masked men and witnessed by thousands.[34] McIlherron, in his last moments, was chained to a hickory tree, tortured with an iron bar, and then burned alive while he begged to be shot (66). Bose dwells upon this gruesome scene in order to testify to the violent realities of hate crimes in America. Tellingly, he also uses this example to support his claim for Indian equality and refute Mayo's assertion that Hindus, unlike Americans and Europeans, are barbaric in their cultural practices. He writes: "All I have been endeavoring here to do is to indicate . . . America cannot afford to assume a self-righteous air. Indeed, it comes with ill grace for Americans to condemn other people as 'vicious,' 'inferior' or degradingly 'Asiatic'" (68–69). In a later section of the book he goes on to write, "The Yellow Peril! I think of the irony of the situation. I reflect on the worth of the 'sense of white superiority.' The Yellow Peril? It does not exist! The White Peril? It is a reality!" (285). These words were further supported by commentary made by Bose's friend, Dr. Arthur Weatherly, a contributing editor of *The Unity*. Weatherly severely critiques Mayo's book stating:

> But far worse is Miss Mayo's indictment of the people of India as unfit to find for themselves a way of development of their own life and culture. The only possible excuse for such an indictment is an ignorance of history. It is the language that has been used during all the ages by dominant peoples. They have always insisted that the people they have crushed under their heels were so crushed because of their own unfitness. And they have triumphantly exhibited the mangled forms of their victims as a decisive proof of their own superiority. This has always been a very satisfactory conclusion for the ruling class. Abraham Lincoln answered it when he said that no man was born who was fit to rule another. If the experience of mankind reveals anything at all, it surely makes clear that both master and slave are corrupted morally and spiritually by their relationship. Miss Mayo's contention as to what will happen in India in the event of the cessation of British rule is a denial of the principles of the Declaration of Independence and the principles which animated the lives of every heroic character in American history, and for that matter, in the history of mankind. (Weatherly in Bose 1923, 57)

During this time period, the Indian Welfare League and the India League of America also renewed their efforts to obtain citizenship rights for Indians and increase the support for Indian demands for independence from Britain (Lal 1999). In addition, the writings and speeches of Anup Singh, Krishnalal Shridharani, Kumar Goshal, Shiva Rao, Syud Hassain, and Haridas Muzumdar helped to reinforce sympathy for the South Asian cause (Hess 1974, 592). South Asian Americans refocused their lobbying attempts in response to U.S. Government requests for Indian assistance in thwarting the creation of a Japanese-German military axis in Asia. Led by J. J. Singh, the president of the India League of America, and with support of prominent public figures like Pearl S. Buck and Albert Einstein, they argued that it was incongruous to expect the people of India to fight on the U.S. side of this struggle and to simultaneously deny them access to immigration (Lal 1999). Nearly two dozen years after *U.S. v. Thind*, on July 2, 1946, this lobbying resulted in President Truman signing the Luce-Cellar Act that reversed the Thind decision and allowed Indians the right to naturalization, as well as a small number of Indians to immigrate per year.

The "Bindi" as Cultural Performance and Protest

It was not until 1965 that U.S. immigration law truly began to loosen for South Asians. During this time, the U.S. Government sought to attract and retain highly skilled scientists, engineers, medical professionals, and scholars from Asia. The "Brain Drain," as it was called, allowed up to twenty thousand individuals to emigrate from India annually. As many have noted, the context of this immigration significantly altered the nature of the diasporic South Asian experience (Prashad 2000).

Previous diasporas were often a result of a forced immigration, due to religious, political, and social persecution. However, South Asian immigrants in this wave relocated primarily for economic reasons and, unlike their predecessors, many brought families with them. Moreover, a good number adopted the status of NRIs (nonresident Indian); this designated them as Indian nationals and allowed them to keep their citizenship and thus receive benefits not typically given to those living outside the nation state, such as owning property.

By 1980, the Indian immigrant population reached more than 387,000 and displayed a greater diversity in region of origin and religion, as well as higher levels of economic success than ever before, promoting the term "model minority." This success, however, did not exempt them from the hate speech and hate crimes experienced by their predecessors. To address these acts of violence, Indian Americans not only used traditional media outlets or community forums; they also engaged in political performances.

For example, in August 1987, a group calling themselves the "Dot-busters" began sending letters to Hudson County, New Jersey, newspapers threatening violence against South Asian Americans in an effort to purge Jersey City of their presence. One of the letters received by the newspaper outlined the "Jersey City Dot-busters'" plan:

I'm writing about your article during July about the abuse of Indian People. Well I'm here to state the other side. I hate them. If you had to live near them you would also. We are an organization called dot busters. We have been around for 2 years. We will go to any extreme to get Indians to move out of Jersey City. If I'm walking down the street and I see a Hindu and the setting is right, I will hit him or her. We plan some of our most extreme attacks such as breaking windows, breaking car windows, and crashing family parties. We use the phone books and look up the name Patel. Have you seen how many of them there are? Do you even live in Jersey City? Do you walk down Central avenue and experience what its like to be near them: we have and we just don't want it anymore. You said that they will have to start protecting themselves because the police cannot always be there. They will never do anything. They are a week race Physically and mentally. We are going to continue our way. We will never be stopped.[34]

During this time, South Asian Americans—often visually identified by a *bindi* (a cosmetic dot worn in the center of the forehead by women), garments, accents, or names—were verbally harrassed and, in certain cases, physically attacked, and their homes and businesses were vandalized. It was a series of attacks in late 1987 that resulted in the mobilization of the Indian American community. On September 27, 1987, four young men from Hoboken, New Jersey, attacked Navroze Mody, an Indian Citicorp manager, with bricks while shouting, "Hindu, Hindu!" He died after three days in a coma.[35] Four days later, Dr. Kaushal Sharan also was assaulted and beaten into a coma, causing permanent brain damage.

In response to these attacks, many South Asian Americans reported changing their everyday habits. Many no longer walked the streets alone or left home after dark. Some women and men felt compelled to stop wearing traditional adornments and clothing, and opted for Western-style dress in public. Yet, for others, the everyday performance of a South Asian identity became a point of pride as they continued in their traditional modes of dress.[36] *Bindis*, *saris*, and turbans—marks of distinction from the mainstream culture—were strategically figured as points of departure for how to deal with questions of difference and inclusion in America's multicultural society as the bodies of South Asians themselves became sites of dissent, community identity, and rhetorical performance.

This was notable, for instance, during a peace parade performance dedicated to mark the anniversary of the birth of Mohandas K. Gandhi. In the days before the event, the parade was reimagined as a rally for ending violence against Indians. More than 650 Indian immigrants marched to protest racial intolerance, chanting, "We want peace. We want justice." During this event, many chose to wear traditional clothing and shout political slogans in Hindi, performing modes of embodied citizenship that tested the limits of liberal discourses of freedom. The very "dots" that were the targets of violence became material for public argument and collective action concerning the conditions for South Asian Americans. Such actions call into question "the conditions under which the gendered transnational immigrant body will be accepted as a legitimate actor in the public sphere" (Hegde 2005, 2).

An analysis conducted as part of the Pluralism Project at Harvard University (pluralism.org) found that these attacks brought together different groups of South Asian immigrants for the first time in ways that "transcended intra-Indian ethnic affiliations, as well as class, religious and economic differences" (Williams et al. 2004). This violence against South Asian Americans has remained an important touchstone in the recent civil rights discourse of this community. Unlike in previous generations, it also has served to connect the South Asian American community with other minority groups facing social violence in America. For example, in a speech given by community activist Jeet Bindra to the South Asian Political Awareness Conference on January 29, 2000, he stated:

> Yes, it's a great country, but it's not a perfect country. We've got a way to go before we can say that. We've got a way to go when an African-American is brutally murdered in Jasper Texas, just for the "fun" of it. We've got a way to go when a white man kills a Japanese American grocery store owner in the suburbs of Chicago just because he looks "foreign." We've got a ways to go when "dot busters" can roam the streets harassing Indian American women with Bindi on their foreheads, and Sikhs are publicly ridiculed and denied their right to wear a turban. And we've a way to go when the number of violent acts against South Asians in this country increased nearly 2000 percent between 1997 and 1998.

As such, the contemporary rhetoric of South Asians in America is marked by calls of consciences directed at the mainstream society and calls for unity directed at those within the complex array of communities that define the South Asian diaspora. This largely untold history has nonetheless permeated the consciousness of many Indians, Pakistanis, and Bangladeshis living in the United States, who implicitly refer to it in their conventional engagement at community events, their media advocacy in documentary films, and the radical action of their political performances.

Contemporary Performances and Communal Fractures

This book relies on an understanding of this rhetorical and social history to provide context for the contemporary performances that follow. In the rhetorical efforts analyzed in the subsequent chapters, this rich history is meant to help the reader situate these accounts in relation to the examples that precede them and in some ways structure them. Nonetheless, shifting dynamics within the South Asian community in the United States coupled with America's experience with terrorism have further shaped how the cases considered in this book must be understood.

By 1990, the South Asian American population reached more than 815,000 and in 1995 it crossed the 1 million mark. According to 2008 census data, about 2.7 million South Asians live in the United States. South Asians were the fastest-growing Asian American ethnic group in the United States between 1990 and 2000. During this time, anti-immigration sentiment rose dramatically.[37] These anti-immigration sentiments found fruit in the "fifth column" suspicions of the War on Terror following September 11, 2001.[38] Since this time, Middle Eastern and South Asian communities in the United States have faced challenges ranging from hate crimes to employment discrimination, from racial profiling to neglectful inattention. Indeed, all immigrants are under close scrutiny.[39] South Asians are mindful of these historical milestones and attuned to the tenor of discourse in the public sphere.[40]

Some of these same divisions and forms of violence trouble relationships within South Asian American communities as well. In part, this manifests in the exclusion and repression of fellow South Asian Americans on the basis of religion, caste, class, and sexual orientation. While this was undoubtedly also the case in earlier periods of South Asian immigration, it is increasingly problematic as South Asian American communities face the challenge of actively negotiating the escalating diversity of their own composition.[41] That is, while the South Asian American immigrants during the "Brain Drain" were often bound together by high levels of class and economic achievement, today's communities are much more diverse and contain a complex array of national and regional histories, customs, and traditions, all with colonial and postcolonial manifestations.[42]

Internally, communities actively struggle with reconciling conflicts of interest. A powerful example of this was raised when members of the South Asian community lobbied President George W. Bush to celebrate Diwali at the White House. Within the South Asian community, questions arose about the orientation of this event. As a religious holiday, with attending secular traditions, should the festivities foreground religious or secular elements?

Should it honor the Hindu tradition that it originates within? Should regional practices be represented or should a more pan-Indian approach be taken? Should this event speak to the need for cultural representation, particularly after the events of September 11? How should it comment upon the identity struggles within the South Asian community? This complexity and fracturing are recurrent themes in contemporary South Asian American rhetoric. While it is no surprise that the internal politics of South Asia is echoed in the politics of South Asian American communities, it is to the disappointment of many that in recent decades, religious violence abroad has found purchase in South Asian diasporic communities.

Progressive Activism and South Asian American Performance

In contrast, in recent years many progressive South Asian American groups have developed and are filled with young activists working to affirm the rights of cultural, religious, and ethnic minorities both within the mainstream and within the South Asian American community. Their work provides an interesting rebuttal to the charges of apathy against South Asian American youth by critics who have argued this ethnic group is less politicized than other ethnic minorities—more interested in joining organizations that "promote cultural awareness" and traditional heritage than those that create social change (Maira 2002, 88).

The range of grassroots activism and community networking is impressive and growing (Dasgupta 2006; Gopinath 2005). For example, *Samar* (South Asian Magazine for Action and Reflection) is a progressive online magazine based in the United States. This group very consciously chose to provide discourses that work to connect the diverse communities that make up the South Asian collective, explaining their mission in the following way: "We choose to use the term 'South Asian' because we feel it is important to bring attention to the fact that South Asians are a group of people with a shared history and that this history provides a common basis for understanding our place in the contemporary world."[43]

Along similar lines, SAALT is a national, nonprofit organization "dedicated to fostering an environment in which all South Asians in America can participate fully in civic and political life, and have influence over policies that affect them. SAALT works to achieve this goal through advocacy, community education, local capacity-building, and leadership development." SAALT builds partnerships among South Asian organizations and individuals, amplifies the voices of disempowered members, and collaborates with civil and immigrant rights movements to address political, social justice, and quality-of-life issues facing South Asian Americans, especially the marginalized segments of the community.[44]

Progressive groups, like the South Asian Sisters in San Francisco, focus upon issues of social, domestic, and sexual violence directed at South Asians, with particular attention to oppression based on race, gender, class, and sexual identities.[45] Their friends involved in *Trikone* focus upon LGBTQ issues that remain relatively unaddressed in mainstream media and attempt to bring the community together through dances, film festivals, blogs, and conferences. Both groups also use performative contexts—from theater to parades—to make claims for acknowledgment and recognition of human rights and social justice concerns. And they are not the only ones. For instance, in Chicago the *Mango Tribe* has sponsored "queering the night" where LGBTQ performers provide testimonies for social justice through song and spoken word. This group shares members with groups like *Khuli Zaben*, a West Asian/South Asian LGBTQ network. In Minneapolis, Minnesota, Ananya Chatterjea has created stunning dance performances through *Ananya Dance Theater* that foreground the potential of social justice through art.

Along these lines, the contemporary case studies that are presented in the following chapters provide a set of portraits of the potential of performance activism. These performances grow out of this history of prejudice and tolerance, acrimony and belonging, silence and outspokenness. South Asians in America now explore a much wider array of rhetorical strategies to convey their experiences to argue for a more just state, a more welcoming community. Some, like the parents and teachers involved in the School for Indian Languages and Culture considered in the next chapter, employ performance within contexts of conventional engagement, such as large-scale community events. Events such as the Festival of Nations in St. Paul, Minnesota, are a rallying point for collective activity and a site of strategic self-presentation. And further still along this continuum is the radical art and political performances of those on the margins of the margins. Minorities within the South Asian community also employ the performative as a tool for contestation and negotiation. This is particularly true for those speaking from outside of conventional communal and caste boundaries, as well as those representing the voices of sexual minorities like those considered in chapter 5 through an analysis of the radical performances found within *Yoni Ki Baat*. These performances strive to make the invisible visible through an "unruly politics" that is an important but largely understudied part of diasporic rhetoric emanating from South Asian communities (Dasgupta 2006).

These case studies, then, provide a portrait of contemporary activist performances within the South Asian community, updating this hidden history of immigrant rhetoric in America. Although many still see themselves as "strangers at the door," the emergence of these forms of political action and rhetoric emanating from South Asians in the United States demands attention at this critical stage in our society.

Chapter Three

❖   ❖   ❖

National Recognition and
Community Acknowledgment

❖   ❖   ❖

And if it is good to be recognized, it is better to be welcomed, precisely because this is something we can neither earn nor deserve.
—**Hannah Arendt** (1969, Speech to American Academy of Arts and Sciences, 1)

Performances at folk festivals have long encouraged community members
to engage in imaginary travel, drawing attention to the tension between us/
them, here/there, and then/now, while also collapsing these divides (Bauman and Sawin 1991; Kirshenblatt-Gimblett 1991). Growing out of colonial
discourses of the eighteenth century, they implicitly address questions such
as: what does "foreign" or "foreigner" mean? Where is home? Or, who are
strangers or aliens? In this way, festivals like the Festival of Nations have
always broadly involved "struggles for recognition." These struggles center
around how people make cultural, political, or social claims that involve
gaining equal respect for diverse identities within a pluralistic society. Moreover, these struggles for recognition are most often grounded in concepts
of justice that place a strong emphasis on mutual dignity and appreciation.

Through folk performances in festival contexts, ethnic groups hope to
gain positive recognition for what their heritage has contributed to the
"American tapestry." Implicitly, their involvement also addresses concerns
about the social outcome of continuous "misrepresentation." As Charles
Taylor argued, "Our identity is partially shaped by recognition or its absence,
often by *misrecognition* of others, and so a person or group of people can suffer real damage, real distortion, if the people or society *mirror back to them* a

Festival of Nations banner.
Author photo.

confining or demeaning or contemptible picture of themselves. Nonrecognition or misrecognition can inflict harm, can be a form of oppression, imprisoning someone in a false, distorted, and reduced mode of being" (Taylor 1992, 25). Within community festival contexts, the question becomes: "are 'we' fellow community members, or, are 'we' alien to one another?"

Scholars studying such struggles for recognition have typically focused upon discourses that can be seen in courtrooms, mass media, cultural centers, political speeches, and school curriculum that celebrate the traditional dress, food, art, and local histories of students (Bingham 2006, 327–28). I believe this emphasis upon discourses of social justice and recognition has overshadowed how cultural performances, characterized by rhetorical claims for acknowledgment, may facilitate an ethic of care. These performances, I argue, must be attended to as we parse out the tensions between recognition and acknowledgment that I have outlined in chapter 1.

To explore these issues, I focus on women's folk performances at an "India" culture booth at the Festival of Nations in 2000. This booth, designed to replicate an idealized "village home" was created by members of the School for Indian Languages and Cultures, a grassroots nonprofit ethnic school that provides secular education about India and its diverse multicultural population. My understanding of the performances at this event grows from nearly two years of fieldwork with SILC that included participant-observation, interviews, formal and informal interviews, surveys, and archival research at the Minnesota Historical Society and the International Institute of Minnesota.

The Festival of Nations offers a myriad of folk demonstrations, from African American doll making to Iranian rug weaving. It is a rich fieldsite that has provided me opportunities in the past to think and write about issues of immigration and ethnicity and engage with scholarly critiques of multiculturalism in festival contexts. I have also interpreted performances at this site through a postcolonial feminist critique, focusing on the ways that women have often been constructed through ideas of family and home, within Indian nationalist discourses (Garlough 2011). In this chapter, however, I revisit this site to reflect upon a previously unexplored question. Through the enactment of women's folk art, how did SILC's "village home" emerge as a women's performative space that facilitated acknowledgment?[1] I argue that through spontaneous conversations within this gendered space, an invitation for meaningful interaction emerged. This playful discourse—fueled by the dynamic interactions between audience members and performers—allowed for the performers to strategically represent themselves in ways that transgressed the essentialized representations of "ethnic people" that festival goers have come to expect. Instead, the booth drew together a diverse group of women who offered personal narratives that provided a more complex understanding of the opportunities and challenges facing Indian American women as "tradition keepers" in their communities. Audience members responded to these more complex representations in ways that exceeded intellectual recognition; instead, they engaged in public acts of acknowledgment that took special notice of the performers, their personal narratives, and the folk practices that were shared.

I believe that it was not serendipity that this women's performative space facilitated the potential for acknowledgment; indeed, the Festival of Nations was designed, from the very first, to create occasions for such social intervention. The brainchild of Alice Sickels—a progressive community advocate for immigrants in the 1930s, social critic, and the first director of the International Institute of Minnesota—the festival was never meant to be simply entertaining or merely informative of Midwestern immigrant culture. Responding to the twentieth-century "Americanization" movement (an effort by both government agencies and private citizen organizations to coerce immigrants into adopting the English language and abandoning the cultural practices of "foreign places"), Alice envisioned the Festival of Nations as a means to counter prejudice against immigrants and advocate pluralism within American culture. In the process, she argued something quite innovative: in the public sphere, meaningful recognition often begins with practices of "acknowledgment" (Sickels 1945, 183–84).

In taking this perspective, Alice's progressive notions about the role of acknowledgment in folk festivals and the political ends they might accomplish seem to foreshadow the very arguments Fiona Robinson and Selma Sevenhuijsen (as described in chapter 1) advanced regarding the importance of establishing caring relations "with not so distant others" (Robinson 1999; Sevenhuijsen 1998). Within the Festival of Nations context, Alice hoped that preparations for the performances at the cultural booths might inspire conversation among diverse ethnic participants that would act as rehearsals for democratic discussion in the public sphere. Interestingly, from its inception in 1932, women played a prominent role in this effort. According to Festival of Nations records and Alice's writings, activities were primarily managed by local women who organized and inspired people in their communities to design and construct exhibits, donate local folk items to display, sew ethnic clothing, choreograph dances, and cook traditional foods. Women from different communities—initially strangers to one another—would spend the days leading up to the festival helping one another to set up booths and to prepare the event arena for audiences. In the process, they engaged in conversation, gained knowledge about one another's cultural traditions, and made friendships that transcended the festival boundaries and overflowed into everyday life.

Alice also hoped this "ethic of care" that characterized the preparation for the festival would then manifest in the performance context as well, as ethnic performers interacted with festival audiences and engaged in rhetorical acts of acknowledgment (Sickels 1945). This chapter considers the possibility that even within today's more complicated performance setting, Alice's commitment to the rhetorical potential of acknowledgment might still effectively facilitate community work toward liberal democratic goals. This exploration begins with a discussion of two specific ethnographic sites: the School of Indian Languages and Cultures and their work at the Festival of Nations.

SILC and Ethnic Schools in the United States

SILC, a "Saturday only" ethnic school, was founded by five women—Neena Gada, Usha Kumar, Rita Mustaphi, Rujuta Pathre, and Prabha Nair—in

1979. An offshoot of the Bharat School, established in the late 1970s by K. P. S. Menon, these women designed SILC to be a non-for-profit grassroots community project. This volunteer organization immediately caught my attention because of its reputation in the South Asian American community as an unusually progressive place for young people to learn about South Asian history, language, folklore, and classical culture. Ethnic schools have a distinguished history in American cultural life. Since the early colonial period, these schools have played a vital role in ethnic community creation and maintenance, communicating a group's conscious perception of itself and providing a cultural legacy to be given to subsequent generations (Mohl 1981). As Joshua A. Fishman notes, "we're dealing with an old and deservedly proud American tradition in education . . . the ethnic community school is American from the very beginning of the country and a constant theme in the history" (1980, 10). Yet, aside from the pioneering study conducted by the American Folklife Center in 1982, very little research has been done to explore the role these schools play in constituting identities for participants or the importance of community-based ethnic schools in helping the United States retain its multicultural profile. To some, it may seem unlikely that these schools have remained a permanent part of our educational landscape. In the past when immigrant neighborhoods disintegrated, ethnic schools often were disbanded as well; however, today it seems that they do not disappear easily. In fact, modern advances in transportation and communication technology—like the Internet—seem to be facilitating the development of these institutions, despite the challenges of grassroots organizing. Indeed, as ethnic communities continue to grow and coalesce, voluntary organizing efforts and grassroots subsistence for these institutions have intensified. Like most forms of grassroots social action, these ethnic schools arise when an underprivileged section of the local population becomes organized around specific issues and demands a more equitable distribution of power or resources for decision making. As Neena, a former SILC principal stated, "In other parts of the USA, many Indian provincial language and culture groups had been started and are working well toward limited objectives. However, we felt the need for an organization which can maintain an overall Indian cultural identity through the strength of our regional languages and cultures."[2]

In comparison to many language or culture schools for Indians in America it was envisioned as a progressive grassroots organization that would support the needs of South Asian American kids and parents from diverse social classes and regions, from Gujarat to Kerala. For SILC volunteers, this commitment goes beyond mere multiculturalism. Rather, its secular orientation speaks to a commitment to keeping the heterogeneity of their Indian American community visible and active. Consequently, SILC is open to all people, regardless of race, religion, or ethnicity and, as such, it provides a unique space in which to voice opinions, impart values, and teach cultural practices. It is not only a space of care where I saw examples of teachers interacting with students patiently, attentively, and empathetically. It is also an enclave in which community members can informally discuss frustrations and deliberate upon issues and exigencies within the local South Asian American community, mainstream America, or international contexts. Students here are enabled to develop a multicultural voice through which they can express their lived experience (Darder 1991).

The School for Indian Languages and Cultures is located in Minnesota, a state known more for its German, French, Norwegian, Swedish, or even Ukrainian immigrant communities. Indeed, for many people, Minnesota still epitomizes the culturally homogeneous or "white" agricultural interior of the United States, despite sizable diasporic movements of Mexican and Hmong individuals, and indigenous populations of Native Americans. The first substantial group of Indians in Minnesota did not arrive until the 1950s—primarily a group of professors, scientists, and graduate students enrolled at the University of Minnesota. Indeed, the bulk of the Minneapolis Indian immigrant community was created primarily as a consequence of the brain-drain 1965 immigration legislation.[3] Like many of the larger South Asian communities in the United States located in urban centers, such as New York, Chicago, Houston, or San Francisco, the Twin Cities community began as a small and regionally diverse group. As Neena Gada has commented, "Actually, for quite a few years it was just 'you were Indian'; you weren't Gujarati or Marathi and there weren't that many people. And in those days we did a lot of dinner parties, because people were homesick, so you would have dinner parties. And you were walking in the shopping center and you see someone from India, you will just go up to that person and say hi and introduce yourself and get their name and exchange telephone numbers and have them to the next party you have. Because there weren't that many people so everybody sought out everybody else."[4] However, today the cities contain plentiful Indian regional concentrations and is heterogeneous in terms of religious and ethnic traditions, as well as social class, education, occupation, and linguistic groupings.

Initial Fieldwork Encounters

I began my fieldwork at the School for Indian Languages and Cultures on a chilly Saturday morning in the fall of 1997. As I walked up the sidewalk to

Garlough and husband at an SILC dinner event. Author photo.

Como Park High School, I watched groups of South Asian American parents, teachers, and students make their way into the main hallway and heard Preeti—SILC's principal—ringing her handbell to signal the beginning of the school day. I wondered to myself, as I heard the general assembly of students singing "Jana Gana Mana," "Vande Mataram," and then the "Star Spangled Banner," how, I could balance the roles I hoped to play at this site.

A month before, I had met Preeti for the first time in the hopes of gaining permission to do ethnographic research at SILC. At the time, I was not sure how she would react to my proposal to participate in more than one capacity. First, as a scholar, I was interested in understanding how this grassroots ethnic school had developed within the broader context of the Minnesota South Asian American community. On first glance, it seemed to me to be unique in comparison to the rest of the South Asian American schools in the area that featured a rigorous religious or specifically regional emphasis. In particular, I was curious about the educational philosophy that fueled their mission and the grassroots volunteers whose efforts drove the activities. I wondered how this school might support members of the South Asian American communities by connecting local, global, and transnational concerns. In addition, I wondered whether this school and their performances, operating from outside of mainstream educational institutions, was part of broader grassroots struggles for recognition and justice. These concerns grew from my experiences as a teacher in alternative educational contexts,

as well as my interest in the work of educational theorists such as Paolo Frei-
ere and John Dewey. My research methods, I told Preeti, would be ethnographic—including formal and informal interviews, focus groups, surveys,
and participant-observation in various classrooms and the school cafeteria.
While I would schedule times for longer, more private conversations, there
was much to be learned by simply "hanging out" in the hallway between
classes with students and listening to them talk about their lives or chatting
with the parents at a lunchroom table while they waited for their children.
Indeed, I knew that from the earliest days of SILC, the "waiting area" for
parents had been an important and vibrant site for interpersonal community building.

By frequently being available and open to conversations in these spaces,
I hoped that, over time, a trust would develop between myself and the SILC
members, our talk would deepen, and I would begin to understand how individuals within this context struggled and strategized with the cultural traditions that connected them and the interests that divided them. I wanted to
get past the polite formalities that often characterize the early months of
forming relationships and learn about their struggles as well as their suc-
cesses. And, in the process, I wanted to share my own struggles and suc-
cesses, so that something more than a "working relationship" might develop.

Given this desire, the second request was somewhat easier to ask of Preeti, yet harder for me to imagine carrying out. As a first-time parent, and the
mother of a biracial child of Indian American origins, I was hoping to participate in SILC as a parent as well. Gabe, my first child, was growing up far away
from grandparents, aunties, uncles, cousins, and friends who could help us
to raise him within a rich set of Indian—specifically Gujarati—family traditions. As a small family unit of three, we were finding it difficult to create the
everyday context for living through and within the Indian American culture
we wanted Gabe to experience. Nevertheless, I also felt uneasy about bringing Gabe, afraid that it might compromise my role as a researcher. That is,
ironically, I was concerned about being misrecognized as simply a parent
and not as a professional as well. Preeti, who was herself pursuing a graduate degree and had children attending SILC, offered good advice about how
to balance roles within the SILC content and was enthusiastic about Gabe
attending. Indeed, many of the women I encountered at SILC had experience with this "balancing act" and found that this space provided not simply
a site for student learning but also a valuable support system for parents'
care-giving responsibilities. As Preeti has noted, "I feel like my 'Indianness'
is something like a springboard from which I have to feel my sense, my place
in this world. You can't deny your heritage, so SILC allowed me to embrace

Gabriel and friends at SILC. Author photo.

my Indian heritage. It kind of affirmed it, and it helped me with raising my kids. Like when I had my daughter's graduation. I had a big board with pictures of all the friends who helped me raise her. You know, I said, 'It takes a village to raise a kid' and to me, SILC in some ways, was a village really. I felt it strongly."[5]

And to my surprise and pleasure, in responding to all my requests, Preeti also added a third role that she wanted me to play on occasion—SILC volunteer teacher. In this capacity, she asked me to lecture on the subject of folklore, substitute for her art class, assist in other classrooms, and participate on the Festival of Nations committee. Not surprisingly, over the course of time it became clear that in many ways Gabe's weekly attendance actually helped me to do my job as a researcher. At the time, SILC did not have preschool for children his age and he was too young to attend classes. Nevertheless, Gabe bonded with the older kids, aunties, and uncles, as they helped to take care of him during class time. With the help of the teenage students, Gabe was also able to participate in school performances such as SILC Day.

Indeed, my dual roles as researcher and parent became a crucial part of how I was welcomed into this school context. It is through this lens that I began to understand the role of care in this ethnic school and the need for acknowledgment when you are initially in a position to be misrecognized in a social space.

SILC School: Philosophy and History

SILC is a nonprofit grassroots project and consequently has never had its own facilities. It runs entirely on the efforts of its staff of approximately thirty that is still composed exclusively of volunteers who are willing to make the significant time commitment required to attend teacher-administrative meetings, prepare curriculum, instruct class each Saturday, organize and facilitate field trips, or coordinate other extracurricular activities.[6] As Preeti Mathur, SILC's former president, wrote in the Twentieth Anniversary Commemorative Yearbook, "SILC has had and continues to draw some very dedicated volunteers who are its backbone. It is their hard work and diligence that sowed the seeds and nurtured it to where it is today. Many individuals put in countless hours and through their selfless service and enthusiasm have created an environment that has taught our students something no textbook could ever cover" (1997, 9).

The staff and students possess very diverse cultural backgrounds and there are representatives from many parts of India (Kerala, Gujarat, Andhra Pradesh, Bihar, Maharashtra, etc.), as well as other South Asian diasporic locations. The teachers display a range of economic levels and education, although most are middle class and college educated. However recently, as the community itself begins to diversify and highly educated first- and second-generation Indian Americans help their less educated relatives immigrate, the teachers are beginning to show a greater degree of occupational and educational diversity. This influx of new participants, recently arrived from India, has provided the school with important perspectives upon what cultural or linguistic practices are currently in vogue in India. For individuals who have immigrated thirty years or more ago, or perhaps have never lived in India for an extended period of time, this information is quite valuable.

Clearly SILC provides a "dwelling place" that supports a particular Indian American ethos—one that creates a pluralistic understanding of what it might mean to be Indian American. Thus, according to former principal Chitra, "SILC has been a bridge to connect first-generation Indian-American children to their Indian heritage. It has been a center for education and knowledge over the past twenty years. It has been a link between two worlds that are so very different" (SILC Yearbook 1997, 9). Moreover, it is a transnational venture that takes into account that many South Asians live their lives across borders and maintain their ties to home, even when their countries of origin and settlements are geographically separate.

According to many of the teachers and parents I spoke with each week, SILC's focus upon creating an Indian American community school "unified in diversity" not only addresses the potential for regional fragmentation within the Indian American community, it also called attention to the problems resulting from fragmentation in India as well. This fragmentation, of course, is not surprising given the fact that India was composed of separate princely states prior to and during British colonization and did not become a nation until just fifty years ago. Indeed, India is still developing a sense of what it means to be "Indian." Most individuals connect much more closely with regional or religious identities, rather than some national loyalty. Given this, it is relatively easy to understand how developing an Indian American identity might be challenging for some immigrants, particularly those in the first generation.

Consequently, during my time at SILC, I observed and participated in many performance events that address the delicate balance of the regional with the national. For example, students begin each school session by singing the American and Indian national anthems, but they also celebrate their regional Indian identities through language and cultural activities, such as regional folk dancing performances, storytelling performances that feature regional folk tales, or the regional dress pageant where students exhibit the traditional apparel from their Indian state. As Vishant, a SILC school student noted, "I think the beauty of SILC is that you go to school with kids from all around India. It is an experience that you could not easily have in India because of conflicts and tension. At SILC you work with people who come from many parts of India" (SILC Yearbook 1997, 9). Indeed, unlike other Indian American community groups I have worked with over the years, the very composition of the student body simply makes it impossible to forget the heterogeneity of India's citizenry. Needa Gada adds, "a lot of times—at least I remember twice—two different ambassadors visited over the years. And they told us that they didn't even think there's something like this in India, but in the United States, wherever they visited, they have not seen an experiment of something like this happening anywhere else, under one roof, all these languages. See usually, people have a tendency to have a Gujarati school or a Marathi school or religious school but nothing like actually having all different languages under one roof. That credit really goes to Dr. Menon for coming up with the whole concept."[7]

SILC's commitment to represent the diverse regional cultures of India is also apparent in their curriculum design. While some teachers base their curriculum choices upon students' interests, others focus upon their own areas of expertise. Over the years, offerings in languages have included Hindi, Kannada, Malayalam, and Gujarati—an impressive representation of the twenty-three languages and sixteen hundred dialects of India, especially given that many university campuses are unable to offer such a variety. In recent years, electives have included instruction on instruments like the tabla, regional Indian cooking, vocal performance, folk and classical dance, yoga, and folk art. These electives tend to focus upon "hands-on learning" that is then enriched by short lectures about the historical or cultural significance of the topic. The regular curriculum focuses upon subjects such as history, geography, philosophy, politics, literature, and popular culture.

Folk performance and narrative is also an important and embedded part of the curriculum. This, of course, is not surprising, as folklore often plays a large role in the curriculum of schools with a multicultural emphasis. Through folklore—meaning the daily expressive culture or traditional activities of a particular group of people—students learn new ways to understand the practices, performances, and material art forms they encounter in their community and homes, but often are seemingly invisible to them in their everyday lives. For instance, in some classes students read folk stories to complement their study of historical events in India. In others, students wrote plays about current social issues in the United States drawing upon Indian narratives, characters, and motifs. During my time at SILC, I was often asked to help facilitate classroom activities, from guiding the creation of folk art projects to teaching longer "special sessions" on traditional Indian folklore and storytelling practices.

For extracurricular events, like the Festival of Nations, students and teachers often mix genres, combining mythology, fables, and classical texts to create dynamic displays for mainstream audiences. As Rama Padamnashan has recalled, at one Festival of Nations, "we depicted three different scenes from three different time frames of Indian mythology. We chose the *Ramayana*, a scene from the *Ramayana*. We chose a scene from the animal fables, the *Panchatantra*, and we also chose a scene from the Sanskrit classical play, *Shakuntala*. These three depicted three different types, three different styles of legends and myths that India is quite well known for."[8]

Such cultural performances were an important part of school life.[9] These performances, along with the relationships they fostered, were meaningful to many of the students I spoke with each week. As Shruti Mathur wrote in the twentieth anniversary yearbook, "Attending SILC helped me know that there are other kids "like me." I'm not the only kid whose parents won't let them date, or who come down hard on the issue of school or other such things. My house isn't the only house that smells like curry, pipe smoke, and incense. I'm not the only one who is 'American' at school and 'Indian' at home. Lastly, it has made me realize the fact that I don't mind being 'Indian at home.' I feel like I have more than some others. I can speak and understand (to a point) two languages, I've tried many more foods, and seen many more places, and I can say why August 15th is an important date in Indian history. I've been involved at the Festival of Nations and other events since I was little, dancing or being at the exhibit booth, something most people are only experiencing now for the first time. Sure, American may be the melting pot of the world, but I still managed to come out with a little bit more spice than others do" (86).

Indeed, organizing and participating in the Indian performances at this festival takes up a significant amount of SILC teachers' and students' time each year; though most viewed participating in the Festival of Nations as an important opportunity, as it provides a public forum for the grassroots organization to showcase the multicultural Indian activities that the students learn each year. Moreover, it offers an opportunity to gain positive recognition not only from mainstream Americans, but also from fellow members of the Indian American community with whom they may want to coalition-build. Appreciation for these opportunities is often tempered by caution, as the process of creating these emblematic performances and texts is fraught with potentially problematic issues of representation about the histories of India and Indian American communities, as well as rhetorical constraints and exigencies of festival events.

During my fieldwork at SILC, I was asked to serve on the Festival of Nations committee and help to design a booth around the theme on "Indian Temple Art," and this opportunity gave me unique insight into the process, from beginning to end. To be sure, this was no small task. The process began with meetings to discuss the festival theme, design architectural plans, and buy building supplies. In addition, people gathered props for the booth. Neena Gada has remembered, "this was my chance to educate people . . . half of my things in my house were used in all these kinds of Festival of Nations exhibitions and things. We didn't spend money in those days, you know, because we couldn't afford it, so we used what we had or borrowed from someone we knew."[10] In this process, many different, and sometimes opposing, concerns are weighed. How should "India" be represented? What is "Indian folklore?" What will be aesthetically pleasing and intellectually interesting to a diverse group of audience members? What performances and practices will best showcase Indian folk culture? In the next phase of the process, I was sent along with another SILC teacher to a meeting the Festival of Nations sponsored for participants. Here, they outlined the policies and procedures of the festival. Finally, as the days before the event unfolded, a group assembled to physically build the booth, decorate it, and set up whatever was necessary for the cultural performance.

1998 SILC Festival of Nations booth on "Temple Art." Author photo.

Festival of Nations

This experience of helping to plan a cultural booth for the Festival of Nations was such an interesting one for me during my fieldwork that I made a decision to return to this site each year. In 2000, I moved from St. Paul to Madison, but came back regularly to visit friends. That same year I decided to make a trip to attend the SILC Festival of Nations, an event that took place from Thursday, May 4, to Sunday, May 7. That weekend, as I entered the Saint Paul River Center amid throngs of other visitors the mood was festive. Folk music played by a small Scandinavian band wafted through the air and crowds of people consulted their guidebooks to decide what they wanted to experience first. Some wanted to visit the Hall of Flags, while others chose to participate in folk art demonstrations or buy items at the folk bazaar. Newly immigrated families seemed interested in the flag ceremony or naturalization ceremony for new citizens. Still others wanted to attend free mini-language classes offered by the International Institute Education Department.

In the liminal space and time of the Festival of Nations, visitors encountered cultural displays that playfully mimicked the experience of tourism. "Learning guides" led hundreds of tour groups through halls of cultural exhibits, explained ethnic performances, and facilitated "treasure hunts" for the adventurous. Many of the visitors who attended the event also carried an "interactive passport" to be stamped at the cultural booths. In keeping

Ethnic booths. Author photo.

with this theme, the festival brochure replicated the form of a travel destination pamphlet, promising that on their "trip" participants would enjoy folk art demonstrations where "ethnic artisans demonstrate unique skills passed down from generation to generation," cafes with "a whole world of tantalizing ethnic foods available for purchase," and an ethnic bazaar in which "unique items for your home, yourself, or someone special" can be found.

As I slowly made my through the crowds, I was immediately struck by the enormous red, white, and blue banner in the main hall. On it, Lady Liberty—wrapped in a "Festival of Nations" scroll—looked down at the throngs of people. This piece of visual rhetoric served multiple purposes that included reminding visitors about America's history as "a country of immigrants" to constructing contemporary civic attitudes about immigration and democracy. The banner also enacted a constitutive function—evoking positive feelings of "oneness" before visitors were challenged by the "diversity" the ethnic groups represented. That is, the artwork interpolated the audience—a body of strangers—into citizens who together constitute a nation.

While the other visitors mulled over their festival choices, some gave in to the smells of the cafe and feasted on Native American fry bread, Armenian

Cafe. Author photo.

baklava, and Filipino lumpia or Indian chicken curry, tandoori chicken, rice pilaf, chole, salad, samosa, papad, and mango shakes.

Meanwhile, on the cafe stage, audiences were entertained by a continuous stream of vocal performers, from French Canadian singers, a Mexican Mariachi band, and a Polish choir. Not far away, dancers, storytellers, and musicians in the huge village square held the attention of hundreds of visitors.

According to International Institute of Minnesota records, the first "East Indian" group to perform at the Festival of Nations was in 1961 (Festival archival material). By 1964, records reveal the presence of an Indian food booth in the International Cafe. Over time, the "East Indians" expanded their involvement to include performances and a cultural booth. Later, in the mid-1970s, the Bharat School (renamed the School for Indian Languages and Cultures) began their work at the festival at the behest of local Indian Association of Minnesota leaders. In past years, SILC booths had featured "Cuisine of India," "Indian Weddings," "The Festival of Lights," "Textiles of India," and "Storytelling in India—Myths and Legends," to name but a few. These booths tend to be one of the most popular attractions perhaps because, as Kirshenblatt-Gimblett (1991) explains: "Public and spectacular, festivals have the potential advantage of offering in a concentrated form and at a designated time and place what the tourist would otherwise search out in the diffuseness of everyday life, with no guarantee of ever finding it" (418). While visitors appear to appreciate this immediacy, many critics of festivals have rightly cautioned people to remember that these performances of everyday experience, in stories, dance, music, art, and food, are just that—performances. Here, the mundane is reimagined so that everyday use is sacrificed for a choreographed audience aesthetic; one that has dramatic form and emotional attraction. In this process, these performances often make implicit reference to social assumptions, values, and culturally appropriate behaviors. Moreover, as many cultural critics have noted, the cultural performances and exhibitions also perform problematic claims of authenticity related to gender, national, or ethnic identity (Prashad 2001).

SILC's "India" Culture Booth at the Festival of Nations

The 2012 SILC booth was positioned near other national booths featuring folk art demonstrations such as Hmong needlework, Iranian rug weaving, Scandinavian folk carving, or African American doll making. The festival theme was "Seasons of Childhood" and in accordance, SILC's booth centered around recreating an idealized "family moment" within the red-brick courtyard of an Indian village home. Volunteers, performing as family members, appeared to be sitting underneath a grass roof or in doorways outlined with green, red, yellow, and white triangular shapes. With the use of various puja items, from a *kalash*, to *dharapatras*, to *devos*, the performers enacted or explained aspects of traditional folk and Vedic "childhood" rituals drawn from the Vedas.

Not surprisingly, these performances, by and large, upheld traditional gender roles evoking a history of gendered Indian nationalist rhetoric regarding the family home as the site of India's authentic identity. At the same time, it attempted to also point toward how "home" transcends place and time; how it is understood as a potential site of care and hospitality for humanity. For example, the performers played out aspects of the Grihya Sutras that celebrate significant milestones in a man's life. Out of forty sacraments, SILC chose to highlight only five related to childhood: *Jata Karman* (Birth ceremony), *Nama Karanam* (Naming the baby), *Anna Prasham* (First feeding of solid food), *Moondan/Chuda Karanam* (Tonsure of hair ceremony), and *Vidyarambham* (Commencement of education). These performances often made appeals to "tradition" or an idealized sense of the past. This was, to my mind, an odd choice for SILC, which emphasized a secular, Gandhian approach in representing India in the classroom. To select such a decidedly

The SILC booth for the
2000 Festival of Nations.
Author photo.

Hindu set of sacraments, and to focus on formal religious practices, seemed both potentially exclusionary and overly prescribed.

In contrast, it was the smaller, more intimate performances that typified the principles and precepts of SILC. These everyday folk performances made the "home" come alive for audiences, and were traditionally performed by women. Sheela, who gave a demonstration of how to create a rangoli—a powered floor painting—provides an excellent example of this type of women's folk performance. Her performance, embedded within her personal narrative of creating rangoli in both India and U.S. contexts, presented her audience with more than one set of critical discourses regarding gender norms in India and the diaspora. In addition, through conversations with audience members that were interwoven throughout her rangoli performance, Sheela contested the potentially atemporal or homogenizing discourses of the festival by engaging people in a playful exchange that sought acknowledgment within a context of difference.

A finished rangoli. Author photo.

Rangoli: A Design of Colors

So, what is rangoli and why is it typically a women's folk art form? Rangoli, a type of ground rice or stone sand painting, is a popular women's folk practice in India. Performed by women during festivals, auspicious occasions, or as an everyday ceremonial activity, rangoli is a means by which to beautify and welcome guests and deities into the home (Huyler 1994). In a culture where guests and visitors hold a special place, rangoli is an expression of hospitality and understood as an invitation, a gift, and a traditional form of greeting that brings good luck to the house. To say that rangoli is a hereditary folk art means that it is learned without any formal training. Rather, rangoli designs are often passed down through generations of women, with some designs hundreds of years old. While these are sometimes drawn with attention to traditionalism, other times they are the basis of innovative contemporary patterns. For example, today in India one can even find "rangoli groups" who engage in grassroots activism by creating designs that call attention to social and political issues and displaying them in public exhibitions.

In some ways bearing a resemblance to hex signs on Pennsylvania Dutch barns, rangolis are a means of protecting the home from ill will and caring for those who dwell within it; this includes the union of man and wife, their fertility, the nurturing of children, and family relationships. Households, it is understood, do not always remain in balance. There are many dangers to guard against, including natural disasters, accidents, violence, disease, and the malice of others. Through rangolis and pujas, women are in charge of acknowledging, invoking, and honoring the manifestation of the goddess and, in the process, caring for those they love (Huyler 1994, 15). In doing so, the designs do more than beautify; they pay tribute and perform visual prayers to secure blessings. In addition, as I learned during my fieldwork in Gujarat, women often use rangoli in celebrations of important occasions. This could include holy festivals for particular gods and goddesses, astrological phases, or seasonal rituals that accompany the first rain or planting of crops. It also is done to pay special attention to notable events in families, such as birth, puberty, marriage, pregnancy, death, or the arrival of a special guest (Huyler 1994, 15).

As Huyler notes, "Until recently in India, folk art was considered inferior, hardly worthy of mention when compared to classical urban or royal art. Because these wall and floor decorations were created in the domestic sphere by women rather than professional craftsmen, they were, for the most part, ignored. However, it is clear that they serve an important purpose in the social and cultural contexts in which they are found" (Huyler 1994, 15). Rangolis not only link mother and daughters, they link together women of past generations in every kind of family, community, and class. They also connect women from diverse religions and castes, for "although it originated as a Hindu custom, the practice . . . is now popular among Christians and Muslims" (Huyler 1994, 164). If rangoli is performed as a daily activity, as it often is in eastern and southern India, women begin early in the morning, typically taking about thirty minutes in the process. In contrast, during important festivals, rangoli can take about an hour. Each rangoli painting is unique. Each region and group of communities has its own artistic style and each household creates its own innovations. Using finely ground powder, women create floor and wall designs that feature geometric figures with lines, dots, squares, circles, triangles, or swastikas. Within these patterns no line should be broken, as it may allow evil to enter. Sometimes these designs take on a three-dimensional form by shading the traditional two-dimensional designs. Often motifs featured are taken from nature, such as mangos, peacocks, elephants, sun, moon, trees, the sea, or flowers.

Traditionally, the colors for the designs are made from natural dyes, barks of trees, or vegetables. Today, however, bright synthetic colored powders are the norm. This colored powder is usually applied freehand by letting it run from the gap formed by pinching the thumb and forefinger. If the rice powder is used to craft the images, it is considered particularly auspicious because the substance sustains the lives of birds and insects. In addition, powder can be made from sand, crushed bricks, or marble dust that is dyed naturally using leaves or bark. Similar to Buddhist and Hindu mandalas, using powder or sand as a medium for creating *rangoli* is sometimes thought to symbolize the fragility or transient nature of life in that they do not last. "The designs are smudged as the sun rises and people move in and out of the house. Within an hour or two no trace of them remains. It is the moment of creation, the intent of the heart, that is important. Art, like life, is considered transitory. Swept away each day, the paintings are newly created before the following dawn . . . as they have been for centuries" (Huyler 1994, 14–15).

The Performance

Sheela entered the "stage" for her rangoli performance dressed in a royal blue and gold-trimmed sari. Her gold bangles and earrings shimmered in the stark lighting as she sat on the floor of the "village home." Her elegant and traditional dress stood in contrast to other Indian Americans gathering around the performance space in casual clothes like jeans and T-shirts. Indeed, her appearance had much more in common with the girls from SILC who had come to folk dance in the arena and were waiting with their parents near the culture booth.

Sheela, glancing at the crowds, the idealized culture booth, and the other ethnic exhibits, paused for a moment and then smiled while shaking her head. Her bemusement at the festival context seemed to have much to do with her hesitation about representing herself as some sort of ideal, "traditional" Indian woman. It raised difficult questions about what "being Indian" in an "authentic" sense even means. Consequently, in this gap between the ideal and the real, she began to construct a space of contestation by articulating cultural difference in a more complicated way.

On the floor of the "village home," she began by carefully laying out the materials for her design, brightly colored finely ground powder in zippered baggies. Using her fingers to pinch the powder, she began to sketch the outline of a star. With a delicate touch, she placed a single dot in the middle and then drew lotus petals around the points of the star. Slowly, curling vines were drawn from the lotus flower petals. This woman, on the floor of an imaginary home, enacted an artistic practice that she had done a hundred times before. Her performance called attention to echoes of the past, while also addressing the specific context of the festival.

As the design emerged, three older Indian American women and one Indian woman standing to the side of the booth began to comment on the quality of the powder and the choice of design, while sharing some of their own life experiences with *rangoli* in the process. One of the women spoke extensively about how hard it is to get good materials here and what you might have to substitute. I turned to speak with them about how my aunties had brought me a rangoli-making set from Vadodara a few years prior.

Meanwhile, the circle around Sheela was now growing larger and tighter. A group of young local schoolgirls made their way to the front and sat on the ground next to her. Next to me, an Indian American woman began to describe to her daughter the artful and complex designs her mother used to make during Diwali festivals in their village. Overhearing this conversation, one SILC teacher turned to her and described a few of the intricate rangoli designs she had seen her cousin create at weddings that featured flower petals and devos. I chimed in that I knew a woman who had immigrated to Kenya from India two generations before and she often used these embellishments as well.

Two African American women joined in and began to compare their experiences of designing quilting squares within their own communities to Indian rangoli patterns, remembering family designs and the women's culture that surrounded this folk practice. The other audience members outside of the main circle (both men and women) seemed interested in listening to these various conversations unfolding around the performance. It was a moment, out of many fieldwork moments, that I will never forget. Slowly, and without conscious intent, a women's space had been created. These personal narratives drew lines of connection back through generations and across the globe—connecting the diverse group of women in ways that had not been visible moments before. Moreover, through this sense of presence, this group of women had become more than mere spectators. In lingering with one another and engaging in these small interpersonal acts, they enacted an ethic of care within this public space. And it is just these types of small acts that Sickels, Sevenhuijsen, and Noddings all believe are at the center of love for our neighbor.

Throughout the performance, Sheela glanced up to share information with various audience members, reflecting upon her own experiences of doing *rangoli* in the United States as opposed to India, as well as regional, local, and ethnic variations in *rangoli* art from Gujarat to Kerala. In response, another Indian American woman began to tell the story of a relative who had made a *rangoli* design on her front doorstep in America that featured the religious image of a Hindu swastika, only to be told later that a neighbor thought she was invoking Nazi symbolism. Sheela agreed that cultural awareness about such issues was always an important issue in public spaces and self-reflexively called the audience's attention to the context in which she was performing and the constraints of her performance.

In doing so, she began breaking down the boundaries between herself and her audience, as their questions and stories played off one another, creating a more dynamic sense of the women's practices being represented in the booth. It became clear that rangoli was an important part of everyday women's history, a craft that required artistic expertise, cultural competence, and local sensitivity. The narratives that these women offered showed the ways women's folk practice are integral to daily life—one that honored women, their relationships, their labor, and their communities. These narratives put this gendered perspective at the center of this booth's performance and took into account the ways gender and kinship identities are implicated in these practices.

As Sheela spoke, she filled in the petals of her design with purple, pink, gold, blue, and green powder. Children and adults alike began to suggest that more colors to be used, Sheela laughed and asked the audience members which materials they would like for her to use next. In the midst of this play, Sheela was intent upon drawing her audience close and creating interpersonal relationships within this festival context. In the process, she made it clear that she wasn't performing a generic Mother, Wife, Sister, or Daughter-in law in this imaginary "Indian house." In doing so, she sounded a call of conscience and asked for others to listen as she spoke about her life and the reasons none of these roles defined the limits of her self-understanding in this context. Rather, she used her personal narrative to encourage subtle but subversive conversations that demonstrated her subjectivity.

For example, one part of the encounter unfolded as follows:

JAN (Mother of child adopted from India): "What is your name?"

SHEELA: "I'm Sheela." (Looking up and then continuing to draw.)

JAN (turning to her child): "That looks like mendhi done on the floor, doesn't it?" (to Sheela) "Are the colors natural colors? That looks like turmeric."

SHEELA: "Yes, it is turmeric." (Looking up and happily surprised.)

JAN: "Do you usually do this outside of the door for special occasions (in India)?" (Looking at the posters hanging in the booth that explain the childhood rituals for Hindu males.)

SHEELA: (Sheela looks at the posters, too, and hesitates before replying.) "No. In my home every day we used to do. Every morning, early morning, we clean our floor outside of the front door and then we put this. Because it is a tradition for us . . . a family tradition. *Not everyone.* You know? Some in India do it and some don't. Even some Hindus don't." (Long silence, looking at audience members.)

JAN: "Now, at festival time, would men and wome work on the same one?"

SHEELA: "No, at each house the women do it."

JAN: "Do they still teach the young girls now how to do this?"

SHEELA: "Sure."

JAN: "Do they do this in India in the big cities and not just the villages?

SHEELA: "Yes, they do it there. I do it here, too, in the U.S. You know, I do it here in the U.S. It is different but I do it here, too. I do it but most people don't know why." (Big burst of laughter.)

JAN: "Are there books that show you how to do this?"

SHEELA: "Oh, yes, so many books. So many designs there are. But you know . . ."

JAN: "Oh, so *you* have it in your head. "(Laughter between the two.)

SHEELA: "Yes. We don't need books or to follow those designs (looking at the posters) . . . we have imagination. We can draw any designs. (Pause.) *It is different.*" (She begins to expand upon her drawing.)

JAN: "Sure. I know what you mean." (Garlough 2011)

Analyzing such dialogue as "performance" has a long and prominent history in cultural studies and performance theory. Dwight Conquergood, in particular, has been influential in this area, lending insight into how conversational performances bring "self and Other" together to question, debate, and challenge one another. He felt these performances are significant because they emphasize a "living communion of felt-sensing, embodied interplay, engagement between human beings." Within these moments, there is the potential for reciprocal giving and taking. Moreover, as Thomas Farrell astutely notes, conversations, such as this one, hold valuable rhetorical dimensions, particularly due to their situatedness within a larger public performance event (Farrell 1993). I would add that conversational performances, like the one that took place within SILC's booth, go beyond simple acts of recognition or celebration of difference and identity politics. Rather, many functioned as rhetorical acts of acknowledgment.

In doing so, these conversations performed an ethic of care through which audience members and performers addressed the issues of others, showed mutual concern, and demonstrated attentiveness. Within the festival context, these conversations were a way of being-with-others. They were not only characterized by talk but by a deliberate listening, such that the audience created a sense of presence that was palpable. Indeed, for many scholars—including Charles Bingham, Emmanuel Levinas, John D. Caputo, and Sharon Todd—such listening is a practice that occurs before recognition (Todd in Bingham 2003, 336). Bingham argues that "listening has the potential to happen before recognition if the listener, in receiving the speech of the speaker, honors the aspects of the speech that go beyond comprehension, the aspects of speech that need not be understood completely in order to be heard . . . listening to another person should not be understood solely in terms of the meaning of that other person's words . . . there are many times when listening is about making a communicative connection rather than understanding the other's words themselves" (Bingham 2006, 336). In this way, listening is a form of care that manifests rhetorically as acknowledgment.

Notice, of course, that these conversations are often brief. The potential for engrossed attention may last only a few moments and may not be repeated in future encounters. Consequently, we may ask how can we have a "relation" with people who will forever be strangers. To be sure, strangers may stay strangers. Yet, they can have this lived experience together, facilitated by the performances. In listening attentively and responding, the encounter is a form of care. Although it is not a mature relationship like those that develop over time, it is a caring relation nonetheless (Noddings 2000).

There is an important part for visitors to play at the festival. Strangers offer opportunities to respect those different from ourselves. Moreover, they help us to define ourselves in the process. And in a nation that is characterized by diversity, they call upon us to defend our differences. When scholars like Nel Noddings and Paolo Friere discuss the importance of such conversation in educational contexts, they are quick to point out that dialogue involves respect. It is not one person acting on another, but people working *with* one another. Rather than a monologic argument, dialogue is open-ended. "Neither party knows at the outset what the outcome will be" (Noddings 2000, 253). In the search for understanding, empathy, or appreciation, conversations can be serious or playful, imaginative or goal oriented. In the process of connecting us to others, there is always the risk of being misunderstood, misinterpreted, or even interrupted. Yet, the potential also exists for conversation to be a means by which acknowledgment and mutual appreciation may flourish.

Interestingly, due to the fact that they are simultaneously pervasive and typically taken to be inconsequential, such conversations often go unnoticed. They are the "small change" of everyday life (Hawes 2006, 25). Indeed, through their imperceptibility their ideological power is brought into play. While conversations can work as a medium of hegemonic control, they also may function as a powerful means of agency and subversion (Schechner 1985, 117). That is, while conversations often appear to be effortless or improvisational, rituals and customs—such as traditional greetings, terms of address, politenesses, and so forth—are a means of negotiating potential situations of risk for strangers, acquaintances, and friends (Bourdieu 1991; Turner 1987). These conversations, as acts of acknowledgment, bring people together in moments that create caring contexts of testimony and witnessing that take notice and honor others.

Moreover, Sheela's performance offered an opportunity for performers and audience members to exist *in relation to one another*, making them coeval. That is, her critical play made time for both her and audience members to consider what it means to dwell in a deeply multicultural context like India or America. As Sheela's performance continued, her stories provoked inquiries from the audience. In return, she asked questions. The play between these various actors created, in this moment, a sense of presence that was obvious. Visitors to the festival were able to come together, in a sense, and cultivate a feeling of acknowledgment that held the potential for an ethical set of relations, not only as Americans, but also as human beings. These exchanges reflected the type of acknowledgment that Alice Sickels had imagined.

Americanization

As I indicated earlier, it seems to me that the acknowledgment that occurred through the conversations within the SILC booth were not chance.

This is not to suggest that every interaction at the Festival of Nations culture booths would have such an outcome. Such moments are only a possibility. It is easy to imagine the ways that everyday realities inherent to any public performance (overwhelming crowds, fatigue, boredom, or power dynamics to name but a few) might preclude such possibilities. Yet, Alice's unique design, growing out of a critique of the "Americanization" movement, hoped otherwise. Responding to the influx of immigrants in the first two decades of the last century—more than 15 million people—Americanization's primary goal was to speed up the assimilation process. State-sponsored organizations and local community groups promoting Americanization pushed immigrants to speak only English or wear American attire. During this time many immigrant children were taught to be ashamed of their parents' background. Parents hid their cultural history from their children, leaving a generation with questions about their family's heritage. Documents in the Minnesota International Institute archives suggest that the Minnesota Festival of Nations' beginnings were closely related to the "immigration work" started in 1919 by the local board of the Young Women's Christian Association (YWCA). Without the benefit of significant financial resources, this group offered citizenship classes, casework, services, and activities for immigrant women in an abandoned saloon called Jake's Place in the city of St. Paul. By the 1930s, the International Institute broke off from the YWCA and began to define itself as a nonpolitical, interfaith, interracial social agency. In addition to group work services, it also began offering community members opportunities like foreign film features, foreign food lunches, the Street Party, the Pan-American Fiesta, folk dance classes, and, the most important, the Festival of Nations. As she wrote in her book, titled *Around the World in St. Paul*, "Although there had been programs of folk songs, dances and exhibits on a small scale all through the years since the International Institute was founded in 1919, the 1932 Folk Festival was the first attempt at a complete three-day festival" (75).

Of course, in some senses, the Festival of Nations has always been comparable to many other large-scale festival events supported by city, state, or federal organizations during the beginning of the last century. These festivals have often been credited with creating a way in which ethnic cultures can be preserved, revitalized, and valued in community life. Within these festival contexts, individuals often bond more strongly with their ethnic culture, allowing for them to satisfy a basic need for group belonging (Stoeltje 1992, 262). Consequently, ethnic groups are often pushed to feature the most "traditional" pieces of their heritage through means that reveal both cultural and rhetorical competence. In this process, the folk arts—be it dance, art, food, or song—provide a "sought-for common ground" where people can join together around "the interest that everyone felt in his own background" (Sickels 1945).

Certainly, this may have positive effects. For example, disenfranchised individuals may come to feel as though they are viewed and accepted as publicly committed members of the participating group. Experiences such as this one may have long-term effects for the individual, strengthening loyalty to their ethnic group and raising self-esteem. Moreover, ethnic festivals have been successfully used to bring back to life struggling ethnic communities by highlighting ethnic distinctions in the face of acculturation.

However, there are also serious concerns to take into account. Scholars responding to critical theory have, in recent years, considered the ways that festivals promote particular nationalist ideologies and histories, as well as facilitate the objectification of minority participants, despite the good intentions of organizers.[11] Kirshenblatt-Gimblett (1990, 432) argues that "the danger here is what Stuart Hall calls self-enclosed approaches, which 'valuing tradition' for its own sake and treating it in an ahistorical manner, analyze cultural forms as if they contained within themselves from their moment of origin some fixed and unchanging meaning or value. The pressure is there to do just this." Scholars, such as Elizabeth A. Povinelli (2002), also charge that in festival situations ethnic groups may feel forced to identify with liberal multiculturalism in order to gain access to public sympathy and recognition, thus pressuring subaltern and minority subjects to identify with the impossible object of an authentic self-identity—one that is traditional, domesticated, and nonconflicting. As argued by Povinelli (2002), this call inspires impossible desires to be an impossible object forcing diasporic subjects to attempt to perform an authentic "Other"—an essentialized presentation of self—in exchange for the "good feelings" of the nation.

In this scenario, it becomes the responsibility of minority subjects to make themselves recognizable. In many festival contexts, cultural exhibits exacerbate this problem by featuring stage appearances that convert everyday practices into "artifacts" that are alien to the ways in which they are encountered and produced when embedded in the flow of life (Kirshenblatt-Gimblett 1991). Separated from the complexity of the everyday, these cultural performances are often reduced to simplistic claims of authenticity and treated in an ahistorical manner. Therefore, while festivals do make visible traditions that would otherwise not have a public venue, it is also the case that those who perform those traditions tend to be represented in fixed terms. That is, despite organizers' intentions of "making good" through the festival context, it is also clear that there are ways in which acknowledgment could potentially be compromised by the tourist discourses and practices that frame this event.

Alice hoped to overcome these constraints by designing a festival that "put a value on difference and encouraged people to be themselves" (Sickels 1945, 186). However, what, more specifically, distinguishes the Festival of Nations from other similar festivals is the great commitment and attention devoted to the *relational process* of inventing each year's festival event. Alice contended, "All of them, old and new Americans alike, need first of all an opportunity to know one another, and in order to get acquainted, people must do something together. The Festival gives them a chance to work and play together" (Sickels 1945, 182–83). What was needed was a festival—founded on an ethic of care—that built in opportunities for acknowledgment. For Alice, such acknowledgment was a type of advocacy that potentially contributed to ideals of democracy and integrated attentiveness, responsiveness, and responsibility into a concept of citizenship. In this way, she envisioned the Festival of Nations as a "people's festival." As she stated: "The initiating and sustaining force behind the Festival is a clear conviction that firsthand experience in the democratic method and the feeling of actually being accepted as copartners in a democratic undertaking are more useful methods of helping people to become effective citizens of a democracy than formal instructions, preachments . . . Every person needs the experience of belonging—of the *we* feeling" (Sickels 1945). Sheela's performance within the context of the India culture booth typified this "we feeling" by both inviting audience members into her artistic production and seeking acknowledgment for her complex position of being Indian in America. In this way, her performance, and the festival that hosted it, supported liberal multiculturalism and democratic discourse, but did so by presenting grassroots advocacy work as art. This innovative approach to a festival event piqued the curiosity of many leading social activists and politicians of the time. As the success of the festival grew, Alice was asked to advise government committees on immigration issues and act as a mentor for other folklorists and festival organizers. In particular, Alice's focus upon the potential of acknowledgment within the festival context did not go unnoticed, and, as a result, many public figures visited the festival. One important example is Louis Adamic, who wrote *Native's Return, Thirty Million New Americans, From Many Lands, What's Your Name?* and hundreds of articles and speeches on the topic of immigration and assimilation.

Over the years, the Minnesota Festival of Nations has continued to grow, with Alice's philosophy of acknowledgment continuing to inform the event. As one of the largest and oldest international festivals in the country, it has often been used as a model by other cites. Selected by the American Bus Association as one of the "Top 100 Events in North America," and chosen by Discover America as one of the top two hundred events in America, it generally attracts over eighty thousand people to St. Paul's River Center annually, including many organized tour groups from surrounding states. On specially designed student days, more than thirty thousand youth from a five-state area come to visit the Festival of Nations with their teachers. As the festival Web site notes, "Since 1932, the Festival of Nations has been committed to providing a hands-on learning opportunity for students to share the ties with our past and take pride in the riches of diverse cultures in our community."

This festival performance context also provides such audiences time and space for reflecting upon important political questions: Who is welcomed in this national imagination that the Festival of Nations represents? What is the relation between the citizen and foreigner in the eyes of the nation, and how is that relation performed? As these questions and counternarratives emerge, the illusions of cultural and political transparency fade and complexities related to immigration and identity become more apparent. In cultural booths and their attending performances, these questions grow from conversations—some of which begin as idle chatter and evolve into friendly exchange. As Hans Georg Gadamer has shown, the success of such friendly dialogue is directly related to the enthusiasm participants show toward lingering and "giving in" to the conversation to gain mutual understanding and form relations. This "giving" between the self and the other grow from a shared desire to hear and acknowledge each other. In the festival context, such acknowledgment manifests as attention—attention that has at its center the notion of care. This acknowledgment may point toward a beginning. It seems there is promise in the ways that acknowledgment and its attending relations, like care and hospitality, may extend beyond institutional discourse and law. As Alice Sickels, Nel Noddings, and Selma Sevenhuijsen have all noted, these are political as well as moral concepts that help us to conceptualize humans as interdependent beings. They offer an enhanced sense of citizenship that foregrounds the values of attentiveness, responsibility, responsiveness, and an attitude of solicitousness toward others. In this process, acknowledgment is a gift performed in the name of potential relationality.

Chapter Four

❖   ❖   ❖

A Future in Relation to the Other

❖   ❖   ❖

Since the horrifying terrorist attacks, things have been different . . . I've seen people whisper-
ing to each other as they eye my *salwar kameez*, and I know that to some of them the loose
pants and long tunic seem just like the clothes of the Palestinian women we all saw on T.V.
rejoicing after the attacks. Well-meaning friends have emailed warnings that I should wear
only western attire, not go anywhere alone, and even buy a gun. I want to laugh off these sug-
gestions, but I can't. Since the attacks, too many people have faced verbal or physical abuse,
been ordered off airplanes, been beaten—or even been shot to death. The other day, as I was
walking into the local grocery with my sons, a man shouted, "F***ing Ay-rabs, why don't you
go home?" I hurried my children into the store, my face burning. "Mommy," asked my younger
son, "Why was that man so angry? Was he talking to us?" "What did he mean 'go home'?" asked
my older one. "We are from right here." I had no words with which to answer them.
—**Chitra Divakaruni** (2002, 89)

As I write this, the tenth anniversary of 9/11 is upon us. In the decade following the terrorist attacks on the World Trade Center and the Pentagon,
much has changed in the United States, particularly for South Asian Americans. As Divakaruni's quote suggests, while South Asian American community members mourned the terrible events, for many their horror was mixed
with fear. In this crisis, an unfortunate number of South Asian Americans
became the target of verbal insults and physical threats from both strangers and neighbors, sometimes despite lifetimes spent participating in civic
activities, building local relationships, or creating community connections.
Indeed, while it is certainly true that many people tried to forestall retaliatory attacks by publicly making calls for peace and community building, it
is also the case that there were more than one thousand incidents of hate

violence reported in the United States after September 11 that range from murder and mosque bombings to everyday harassment in public venues (Volpp 2009, 78). Most recently, on August 5, 2012, in Oak Creek, Wisconsin, a gunman with ties to white supremacist groups murdered six women and men worshiping at a Sikh temple. Clearly, the aftermath of 9/11 still resonates today, from small midwestern towns to large urban landscapes. In all these spaces, relations require repair as people struggle, among other things, to feel safe in their communities, navigate the political discourse of "home" and "foreigner," and acknowledge one another as fellow human beings.

Here at home, South Asian Americans have responded in a variety of ways to the xenophobic rhetoric and hate crimes following 9/11. Some have taken to the streets, protesting through mass demonstrations that demand media attention. For example, in Illinois the Chicago Coalition Against War and Racism organized South Asian American activists from the Devon Avenue community to launch a multiracial peace march that drew thousands of participants. Others have protested by producing public texts that carefully document hate crimes, xenophobic rhetoric, and government programs that promote ethnic profiling.

In Washington, D.C., for instance, the South Asian Americans Leading Together has composed several documents recording hate crimes following 9/11. They then used these documents as the basis for their testimony to groups like the House Subcommittee on Constitution, Civil Rights, and Civil Liberties who met to discuss the rise in racial profiling of South Asian community members. In addition, they also produced a documentary called *Raising Our Voices* that focuses on anti-immigration rhetoric and hate crimes pre- and post-9/11 and promoted its use on college campuses and in community groups across the country (Garlough 2011). On a more individual level, some South Asian American activists have protested on the Internet by writing blogs that reflect their personal experiences of discrimination, such as the popular New York City site *politicalpoet(ry)*. Still other South Asian Americans have addressed the exigencies facing their communities by using theater performances, though less attention has been paid to this mode in both public media forums and academic discourse.

It also is important to remember that 9/11 was an event that resonated globally. This is evident, for example, in Frank J. Korom's fieldwork in West Bengal, India. Here, Korom (2006) vividly describes how a popular theater group (*jantra*) staged a five-hour show about the 9/11 tragedy titled "America is Burning." This performance, culminating in pyrotechnics and "a sensationalistic crashing of two cardboard airplanes . . . into cardboard and wood replicas of the Twin Towers" brought together Hindus and Muslims in a small town to engage with the disaster from local, transnational, and global perspectives (17). Even more interesting are the ways that this performance generated further deliberation and artistic commentary in this small community, inspiring, for instance, a local group of scroll painters (*Patuas*) to produce scrolls and songs about 9/11 using a traditional repertoire that reaches back centuries.

Rise

What the map cuts up, the story cuts across.
—**Michel de Certeau** (1984, 129)

In this chapter I consider this mode of political protest, providing an ethnographic analysis of a semiautobiographical performance called *Rise*. This event took place at the Overture Center in Madison, Wisconsin, on a cold October night in 2005. Wielding a plunger and dancing on top of a porcelain toilet seat, Shyamala Moorty invoked the figure of the goddess in this narrated dance performance to address issues of racial profiling, xenophobic rhetoric, and hate crimes post-9/11. The theater—filled to the point of people sitting in the aisles—hosted a diverse audience from the local community that included South Asian Americans, American war veterans, UW

Shyamala performing *Rise*. Photo credited to David Flores.

Post Natyam Dance Collective, Shyamala Moorty, Anjali Tata-Hudson, Sangita Shresthova, and Sandra Chatterjee. Photo credited to Lilian Wu.

students and faculty, as well as participants in an annual conference on South Asia.

The performance, told from Shyamala's situated perspective as a biracial South Asian American, combined ballet and contemporary dance with a variety of dance forms important within South Asian American communities encompassing traditional folk dance, *Bharatanatyam*, and Bollywood styles. Shyamala's inventive approach grows out of her membership in Post Natyam, a Web-based grassroots performance collective of South Asian American women. So, this chapter begins with a background about Shyamala's involvement with this group and what they hope to accomplish. Together, these young women use multiple dance forms to create sites of progressive political activism through performances that simultaneously address local, national, transnational, and global contexts and concerns.

Next, I consider the political and cultural backdrop for Shyamala's calls for acknowledgment regarding the American public sphere post-9/11. Particularly, I am interested in how and why she chooses to draw parallels between racism against South Asian Americans in the days following September 11 and a second set of violent events much less known to mainstream American audiences—the 2002 riots between Hindus and Muslims in Gujarat, India. These violent riots between Hindus and Muslims were closely followed in the international media by many South Asian Americans who watched their TVs in horror as thousands of Indian individuals were massacred or displaced from their homes. Read together and through Shyamala's situated perspective as a second-generation, biracial South Asian American woman, the events of 9/11 and the Gujarati 2002 riots are explored in a performance that raises calls for acknowledgment as it plays with and effectively blurs the lines between "here and there," "home and exile," "self and Other," as well as folk, popular, and classical culture from diverse cultural contexts.

To consider this, I reflect upon how Shyamala's acknowledgment of her own positioning as a diasporic, biracial woman enables her to explore her lived relation to the racial, class, sexual, and national scripts embedded in both U.S. and South Asian culture. In the process, I argue that Shyamala's performance seems to engage in an exploration of what Chandra Mohanty calls "feminism without borders." As Mohanty (2003) notes,

> Feminism without borders is not the same as border-less feminism. It acknowledges the fault lines, conflicts, differences, fears, and containment that borders represent. It acknowledges that there is no one sense of a border and that the lines between and through nations, races, classes, sexualities, religions and disabilities, are real—and that a feminism without borders must envision change and social justice work across these lines of demarcation and division. (2)

The fact that these borders both invite and prohibit potential relations is reflected in Shyamala's artistic choices. Her performance engages her experiences of living in a world where people and art forms constantly challenge national lines.

In this process, her diasporic performance negotiates exigencies in ways that are marked by hybridity, polysemy, or incommensurability. Consequently, in my reading, I pay close attention to the ways Shyamala presents both her narrative and her body eclectically, as a transcultural site of exploration. Appropriating and transfiguring Indian and American cultural forms—from folk dances to religious narratives—Shyamala simultaneously recognizes and refuses borders in order to enact a feminist critique of violence and an ethic of care. As I reflect upon Shyamala's work, I draw upon the feminist concept of "intersectional praxis" in order to understand how the rhetorical potential for acknowledgment is expressed through critical performances of difference (Townsend-Bell 2009).

With this in mind, my analysis of this performance then turns toward questions about the viability of "representations of suffering" in political performances. What potential lies in Shyamala's representations beyond voyeurism? What is the relationship between truth and invention in her semiautobiographical performance testimony? In reflecting upon these questions, I consider how representations of suffering may move us to action and renew our sense of collective responsibility for the lives of others, especially those whom we view as foreigners. I also contend that the viability of representation may lead to a concern about the limits of acknowledgment. That is, if I cannot know the pain of the Other, what is it to relate to such suffering? Does our personal experience of traumatic images and stories encourage acts of identification or illuminate encounters with ourselves? What would it mean to endure the suffering of others—to hold them in our minds and remain open to the suffering—to let them haunt us and move us toward compassion toward the Other? How might *Rise* enact calls for acknowledgment that simultaneously awaken awareness, communicate care, and make claims for justice? To ask for such acknowledgment is to solicit a future in relation to the Other in a way that affirms the viability of difference—accounting for the fault lines that run through nations, races, religions, classes, and sexualities.

Finally, I pay particular attention to the Madison audience for this performance. To do so, I draw upon discourse from the discussion session that took place at the conclusion of the performance where audience members were given the opportunity to ask Shyamala questions about the performance and engage in a discussion about the issues at stake. Here, I am particularly interested in the ways in which Shyamala explicitly asks the audience to take upon the role of witness and participate in the political work of ethical listening and dialogue.

This request for audience participation is enacted throughout the performance, through a series of scripted inquiries and interactive dance choreography. However, it is the most apparent at the conclusion of her performance when Shyamala engages the audience in a question-and-answer session about the issues at hand, the ways that her performance addressed them, and the potential of social change and compassion. This is a critical performance technique quite similar to those used by feminist groups in South Asia at the conclusion of political street plays (Garlough 2007). Taking all of these aspects into account, I contend that the piece invites the audience into a space characterized by acknowledgment that remains open to new understandings of justice and care.

Shyamala and Post Natyam

As the preface to this book describes, Shyamala and I met for the first time in San Francisco at a feminist event called "Day of Dialogue" that was organized

Shyamala as Artesia
Strong. Photo credited
to by Jen Cleary.

by the San Francisco feminist group, South Asian Sisters. At this function, Shyamala performed a piece that explored the challenges facing women of color who seek to negotiate biracial diasporic identities in contemporary mainstream American society. I was deeply moved by her narrative, as were many others in the audience. I was also intrigued by her eagerness to engage the audience in a dialogue about these social issues at the conclusion of the performance, her openness to different perspectives, and the potential for compassion this seemed to create.

Over the years, Shyamala and I remained in contact, over the phone, by e-mail, and meetings at performance events, due to our mutual interest in performance and grassroots activism by women in Indian and the United States. I watched with great interest as she developed performances like *Balance*, *Sensitize*, *Emblem*, *Potty Talk*, and *Carrie's Web* that challenged audiences to think carefully about feminist politics from a diasporic perspective that emphasized South Asian traditional movements, narratives, and figures. In recent years, we have read and cited each other's academic work and visited each other's performance rehearsals and classrooms.

Through our conversations, I learned more about her biracial background, and how she engaged with her Indian heritage through cultural forms like dance:

> I grew up in the Monterey Peninsula in CA. My father was one of the few South Asians around and there were only two other families in the area that spoke Telugu (his native language from Andhra Pradesh, India). My father didn't speak Telugu at home because my mom, and later my step-mother, were American. The few things that marked our Indianness were being vegetarian, eating South Indian food, having Indian decorations, listening to Indian music, reading Indian comic books, and visiting India a couple of times. We were not religious (my father is a philosopher), nor did we have any strong cultural practices. So, I had culture shock when I met many other South Asians in college and I learned what many other South Asian families were like. For example, I thought that arranged marriages had ended in the 1800s, and yet, I was suddenly surrounded by friends who were expected to have them.
>
> Also in college, I started studying Bharata Natyam as a way to find a connection to my heritage. It took quite some time (many years) to appreciate the dance form and understand its beauty, which is so different from ballet (my first training and love in dance). My piece "Balance," made in graduate school, was the first time I creatively looked at the two dance forms, their aesthetic differences, and their historic power imbalances as metaphors for both my personal identity and post-colonial politics. (S. Moorty, personal communication, January 13, 2012)

Indeed, along with a growing group of second- and third-generation South Asian American performers, Shyamala has cultivated a diverse expertise in both traditional and contemporary movement as an embodied way to understand herself from gendered, multicultural, global, and transnational perspectives. While earning an MFA in dance from UCLA's Department of World Arts and Cultures, she trained in Indian folk dance, ballet, Bharatanatyam (where she was a disciple of Malathi Iyengar and Medha Yodh), contemporary Western dance, theater, visual art, and yoga. As such, her work situates her within a movement of women exploring the "choreography of women of color."

Shyamala has performed as a soloist and principle dancer with the Aman International Music and Dance Ensemble (1997–2004) and the Malathi Iyengar Rangoli Dance Company (since 1994). In addition, she and Sandra Chatterjee produced a commissioned dance performance by the Brigham Young's

Folk Ensemble. As a dance instructor, she teaches courses like "Intercultural and Interdisciplinary Performance" and "Culture Jam: Theoretical and Artistic Explorations of Mixed Heritage." Her advocacy work, which is extensive, includes being the first executive director of Women and Youth Supporting Each Other (WYSE)—a national mentorship program for young women of color to be matched with university women (www.Wyse.Org)—and serving as a volunteer with a domestic abuse NGO called SAN, the South Asian Network. Shaymala shared that her life experiences inform almost all aspects of her dance activism:

> Many life experiences become a part of my work: "Balance" tells the story of my parents meeting, falling in love, separating, and in the process creating me—a hybrid. "Potty Talk" is a satirical piece where my teenage self carries her Western expectations of hygiene to India and is shocked to find that people often use water instead of toilet paper. This point of view is counter-acted by a Dalit woman character, that I researched to create, who complains about Westerners and all their paper waste that she has to clean up. Often in my work, my life events or someone else's story lays a foundation of detail and experience, while research shapes those experiences, adding social-political context and purpose.
>
> Much of the community work I have done is with South Asian American communities, where I simultaneously feel like an outsider and yet strangely at home. These communities include South Asian survivors of domestic violence, a Muslim American youth group and the diverse artistic community Artwallah and their arts mentorship program Youthwallah.

As all of this suggests, Shyamala's dance performances blend traditional aesthetics with contemporary political concerns.[1] That is, while the question of "authenticity" speaks in particular ways to issues of "cultural authenticity," it also engages deeply with issues related to an "authenticity of self" (Foucault 1986). Regarding her choice to mix these elements, she offered the following in one of our interviews:

> I'm not sure if I have a choice, partially because just dancing or just doing those things isn't enough. I don't feel interested in them, like I just used to. I felt like I was faking it. Sort of like a clown. Here I was doing these Hindu, religious dances and I wasn't a Hindu. It didn't feel genuine. I love dancing and it feels good. But I guess I just feel driven internally somehow, that for me as a performer, I have a sense of purpose. And for me as a performer, that purpose is driven by the things I care about. In the

case of *Rise*, 9/11 and the riots in Gujarat hit me so hard. I thought about it for so long. I mean, I thought about for so long. I think I thought about it for a year before I did anything. It just lived in me and kind of tore me apart inside. It was my way of coming to terms with it. Or to figuring it out. Or having a dialogue with myself by performing. Or by creating work around it that was my way of figuring out what my relationship was to it. Other people might write, or journal, or paint or whatever it is. For me, this is what is going to come out now. (S. Moorty, personal communication, January 13, 2012)

Of course, Shyamala has been met with some resistance from South Asian American community members over her performance activism. Yet, there has been a great deal of support to sustain her as well. Her most significant support system in recent years has been Post Natyam—a grassroots arts collective that she helped to found in 2005. The members of this group met at the Department of World Arts and Cultures at UCLA, where they bonded through their shared experience of delving into contemporary Indian dance, theater, and video/multimedia.[2] The members' decision to form a collective grew out of many concerns. Certainly, there are always the practical ones, such as sharing administrative responsibilities that making the organization more sustainable. However, there are philosophical reasons as well.

For example, the group has a strong desire to oppose "a single orthodox approach to South Asian contemporary dance" (http://www.postnatyam .net/). Rather, the Post Natyam Collective "strives to acknowledge the complex diversity of South Asian movement forms and their migrations to multiple performance contexts, geographical locations, and bodies." Post Natyam's core concern involves developing a transnational choreographic process that critically and creatively engages with South Asian dance forms and aesthetic concepts. In doing so, they aspire to have "their interdisciplinary cutting edge explorations break through gender stereotypes, refuse exotification, disrupt strict dichotomies between East and West" and engage with folk and traditional arts. As Shyamala put it:

Post Natyam is a home for my hybridity. In Post Natyam I can combine post modern ideas with South Asian aesthetics and social issue topics and share them with a community that understands them all and thus can push me to make stronger work. When we first started working together (Sandra and I in 2001, and with Anjali in 2004) there were so few contemporary Indian choreographers that we had access to. We often felt pulled in opposite directions by the Western postmodern perspectives of some of our professors at UCLA vs. the more traditional stances of our classical South Asian dance teachers. Post Natyam gave us a safe laboratory to make work together that addressed our unique hyphenated realities. (S. Moorty, personal communication, January 13, 2012)

In terms of their scholarly interests, they believe, like many others, that performance and dance studies are uniquely poised to contribute to migration and global studies, as well as related topics like citizenship, territory wars, labor refugees, religions, and political occupation. Their work is related closely with that of other immigrant choreographers like Jose Limon, Pearl Primos, Hanya Holm, and Geoffrey Holder, who transform folk forms in the service of art and politics.

The mission of Shyamala and her colleagues is complex. The Post Natyam Collective seeks a transnational presence for contemporary South Asian aesthetics. The goals of the group as outlined on their Web site (http://www .postnatyam.net/) include:

1. Developing creative works, including dance, scholarship, and interdisciplinary works, that challenge aesthetic, geographic and cultural boundaries.

2. Creating and documenting new approaches to dance education.

3. Fostering an international community of artists, scholars and supporters of the arts to encourage exchange and dialogue about contemporary South Asian arts and aesthetics.

The collective's ability to fulfill this mission grows from their diverse life experiences within the South Asian diasporic communities. It also is facilitated by the informal and formal training these women received in diverse folk and classical South Asian dance styles. Certainly cultural performances, like dance, are often an important part of everyday life as ethnic groups develop and grow. In this process, traditional culture works as a community builder—bringing people together for important events or holidays, and sometimes helping to form relationships across regional or class divides. Early in the immigration process, when local groups are small, these functions are typically organized by women and take place in home settings. Here, folk dances, rituals, and food preparation for the event are taught informally by family and friends. As the community expands, festival celebrations are often held in larger venues like community halls, school facilities, or temples and can draw up to several hundred people.

In contrast, learning traditional classical dance seems to play a different role, much more closely tied to markers of identity status or "authentic" cultural belonging. As Katu Katrak (2008) observes, "For immigrants, especially first-generation parents, the dance is a repository of cultural knowledge to be imparted to their children growing up in the United States where there exist many assimilative imperatives enticing for youth" (221). These Indian dance academies offer training not only in classical Bharatanatyam, but also diverse regional folk dances and choreography from popular Hindi movies. Depending upon the diversity of the community, participants can range from South Asian Hindus, Christians, Jains, and Muslims to girls whose families come from locations like South Africa, Pakistan, the Caribbean, Sri Lanka, or South Asia, to mainstream Americans (Leonard 1997, 135). As Karen Leonard remarks, women also play a crucial role in this context by training and costuming young women, as well as in sponsoring these performances. Typically "the performances inculcate proper South Asian female behavior, but they also express the sexuality of daughter and expand the parameters for permitted behavior in public for young women" (Leonard 1997, 136). For some families, dance is just another extracurricular activity; for others, it provides an opportunity for an extravagant, culturally appropriate public display of "eligible" daughters.

However, these early training spaces develop more than skills; they can be generative sites for artistic invention and self-discovery. Moreover, these early experiences with body movement and cultural exploration open up an understanding of dance, in general, as medium for personal development, as well as cultural discovery and creativity. As Cynthia noted,

> I was born in Framingham, Massachusetts, and grew up in Houston and Southern California. Many of my childhood summers were spent with my grandparents and extended family in Taiwan. Being the child of immigrants, I constantly straddled different languages and cultures while growing up. Often I felt that I was unable to belong fully to either culture, though I have made more peace with my status as border-crosser as an adult. In fact, I often feel most at home in communities of people who have multiple, diverse belongings . . . .
>
> More than anything, the "double-consciousness" of being bicultural fed an interest in dance as a way to engage with cultural difference. Nearly every piece of choreography that I have created lives in between dance forms, disciplines, cultures, or collaborators. I have also created works that draw explicitly on my cultural background: *fish hook tongue* investigates Taiwan's history of linguistic colonization, while *Meet me*

here, now—I'll bring my then and there draws on the personal stories and cultural histories of my collaborator, Jose Reynoso, and myself. Autobiographical biographical material often finds its way into my work . . .

When I started to learn kathak, my discomfort with the form's representation of gender—particularly what I perceived to be a hyper-feminine, coy, submissive representation of women—sent my radical American feminism into crisis. I found myself torn between my feminist beliefs and wanting to challenge myself to understand another worldview from the inside out. I draw on this conflict in my solo, "Learning to Walk Like Radha," which you saw as part of *SUNOH! Tell Me, Sister.*

This conflict was the first step in a long, complex road of grappling with gender in Indian dance, which usefully challenged several tenets of my largely Western feminism. First, I came to understand that I had excised the performance of femininity from both my choreography and my daily life in favor of a more gender-neutral embodiment. Kathak revealed that embodying femininity can be pleasurable. I realized that not being able to perform femininity is, in fact, as oppressive as being forced to perform femininity. I learned that the technique of abhinaya enables a performer to switch between different gendered characters, allowing for a certain range of gendered performance. It also gives the performer the freedom to inflect poetic lines with multiple emotional interpretations, allowing for a degree of agency in her or his interpretation of a given script or character. Initially, my gateway to performing femininity was through the lens of bhakti, which is rooted in a spiritual movement that historically overturned caste hierarchies in favor of direct engagement with the divine. How does the submission of the female to the male resonate differently when it is understood as the surrender of the human soul to the divine? How does the performance of gender shift when the gaze between performer and spectator is reciprocal and mutually transformative, as in darshan, rather than a Mulveyian male objectifying gaze? Later, I realized that my turn to bhakti was complicit with an erasure of the secular Muslim history of the tawaif, or courtesan, causing me to question the ways I had, as a Western feminist, developed resistance to performing the erotic out of a fear of sexual objectification. This sparked curiosity about how I could perform eroticism from a position of power and agency. (Personal Correspondence)

These many worlds, however, are sometimes challenging to manage. For example, as Anjali Tata, a member of Post Natyam, noted, "When I began training in modern dance and other dance forms in college, it expanded my experience of what dance could be and prompted my initial explorations into contemporary ventures. Also, at the college level here in the U.S., my experience was that I was not considered a true 'dancer' because I was an 'ethnic' dancer and not trained in the mainstream concert forms of Modern or Ballet."[3]

Sandra Chatterjee, another member of the collective, takes this desire for fusion and invention a step further. She states, "I think it was primarily audience reactions to Kuchipudi performances outside India, where I felt exotified, that encouraged me to respond to the audience reactions through dance itself. I began studying Western contemporary dance, but I soon realized that simply fusing Western contemporary dance with classical Indian dance did not solve my dilemma. Studying Polynesian dance while at the University of Hawaii, I fundamentally changed the way I perceived my own body. That experience in addition to intellectual engagements prompted my first ventures into contemporary choreography."[4]

Sangita Shresthova, a fourth of the five members of Post Natyam, concurs when reflecting, "While I value and cherish my classical training (in Bharatanatyam and Charya Nritya), I have always felt a disjuncture between my own fractured cultural experiences as a Czech/Nepali, my life defined by a state of permanent in-betweenness, and the world of completeness perpetuated in my dance training. My 'contemporary' work grew out of a necessity to reconcile these schisms."[5] Similarly, Shyamala's approach to diasporic dance performance is significantly informed and also complicated by her biracial identity. In an interview she commented, "The fact that I have both South Asian and European heritages generally gives me fairly comfortable inclusion into both groups on the surface, until I am called out and made unwelcome for not being enough of one or the other." Such demands for "authenticity" in performance or displays of "cultural competence" are not uncommon, and this is what makes Post Natyam a particularly important space.

Certainly, Post Natyam is a unique organization in many ways. Most striking, however, given their transnational focus, may be their "location" in the virtual. As members of the group are currently living across the globe, from Los Angeles to Munich, getting together to collaborate is difficult. To find a solution, the members decided to attempt working together via the Internet. As Cynthia notes, "Because we are physically scattered across continents and are not often able to gather in a studio, the Post Natyam Collective decided to experiment with using the Internet to collaborate artistically towards the end of 2008." This online collaborative process, which has included giving assignments to one another, posting videos, and providing feedback, is centralized on this blog in the hopes of "inviting a larger public

Post Natyam on Skype, *left to right, from top,* is Anjali Tata-Hudson, Cynthia Ling Lee, Sandra Chatterjee, and Shyamala Moorty. Photo courtesy of the Post Natyam Collective.

dialogue into our process" (personal interview, January 2012). Throughout the year, these performance pieces are staged in diverse international locations. In this way, local, global, and transnational concerns are "launched into dialogue" as different audiences respond to the situated events.[6] In addition, the group presents their work in other forms that "travel" such as dance-for-camera-videos, scholarly articles, art books, and installations.

This inventive arrangement has been the type of work that sometimes escapes the notice of folklore scholars, particularly those who are not as interested in exploring the ways that folklore intersects with fields like cultural studies or communications studies. As Trevor J. Blank (2009) notes, "When the World Wide Web took off in the 1990s, the allied disciples of anthropology, sociology, and communication studies began paying careful attention to various sociocultural dimensions of the Internet, but amid this dialogue only a small handful of thoughtful folkloristic articles on the burgeoning Internet culture appeared (Baym 1993; Dorst 1990; Howard 1997; Kirshenblatt-Gimblett 1995, 1996; Rouch 1997)" (3). While the Internet is often considered from the perspective of mass culture, it also is an important storehouse and a vital system for the transmission and creation of folklore in small groups (Bronner 2002; Dundes 1980). In my opinion, I believe it is crucial that this work continue to deepen as it provides new ways to understand folklore's disciplinary givens, contemporary subjects, and increasingly transcultural texture. It opens up new ways to understand performances like Shyamala's that are collaboratively produced, are global in nature, and can be productively approached from several disciplinary standpoints.

Post Natyam's collective structure and communication over the Internet also allows members to share teaching methodologies and offers an inventive South Asian contemporary dance curriculum. Within their lectures, master classes, workshops, and residencies, members focus on a diverse set of traditional and contemporary South Asian technique, including *Bharatanatyam*, *Abhinaya*, *Navarasas*, *Kathak*, and *Kuchipudi*, as well as Contemporary Indian Dance, Dance-Theater, Music-Dance Collaboration, and Text-Movement Improvisation. In addition, the collective offers theme-based courses that are linked to current Post Natyam projects such as "The Politics of Femininity," "Meet the Goddess," "Erotics Rerouted," "Indian Dance in Transnational Contexts," or "Hybridity as a Creative and Theoretical Perspective."[7] For example, in terms of "Meet the Goddess," Shyamala notes:

> To me the idea of the goddess is an iconic image that needs to be questioned even as it is invoked. In our show "Meet the Goddess" the Post Natyam Collective members each examined our relationship as real women to iconic femininity in Hindu mythology. Powerful figures like Durga, Parvathi, Kali, and Saraswati are given a power and reverence that contrasts hugely with how real women are treated under the patriarchal values of mainstream Hindu society.
>
> The section of Meet the Goddess that I created, "Sensitize," was about female desire, acknowledging it and giving it a space to flourish. I was making woman the subject rather then the object of the male's gaze as Laura Mulvey has theorized in her ground-breaking article "Visual Pleasure and Narrative Cinema." For this piece, I was drawn to the image of ardhanarishvara, the half male, half female god/dess. But even as it reaches toward equality, it isn't always the ideal—what if the couple is same sex, or if there is more than one partner? In "Sensitize," the issue remains unresolved and the woman's desiren is left unsatisfied when the temporary union is over too soon. (S. Moorty, personal communication, January 13, 2012)

Most recently, their online work has focused upon a central project that contains three major threads: (1) the use of Internet-age technologies; (2)

Shyamala in *SUNOH! Tell Me, Sister*. Photo credited to Michael Burr.

the figure of the courtesan in the Indian subcontinent; and (3) community work with survivors of domestic violence. As Shyamala notes,

> While we're interested in the courtesans of the past, we're also interested in the stories of real women today, especially stories of resistance and healing. Cynthia and I have been honored to be a part of such women's experiences through the South Asian Network (SAN). I have been facilitating workshops for their support group for women who have faced emotional and physical violence or sexual abuse. In these workshops, I have concentrated on stress relief through yoga and self-expression through writing. (S. Moorty, personal communication, January 13, 2012)

In the process, she has worked with individual survivors of physical and sexual violence to create performances using dance as a therapeutic or creative rite to witness the abuse they have undergone.

Shyamala in *SUNOH! Tell Me, Sister.* Photo credited to Michael Burr.

Along these lines, in the spring of 2011, Shyamala and Cynthia did a national tour to perform material from *SUNOH! Tell Me, Sister* that features new multimedia collaborations. The performance uses multimedia and contemporary Indian dance theater to bring to life "women's stories of being silenced, finding voice, and the importance of sisterly community. The work draws on the stories of contemporary South Asian survivors of domestic violence, the performers' own experiences as contemporary women artists struggling with tradition, and images surrounding the courtesan/dancing girl of the Indian subcontinent" (http://www.narthaki.com). The show reflects Post Natyam's long-term community work with AWAZ, the South Asian Network's support group for women survivors of domestic violence, sexual assault, or harassment. Using dance "on a continuum of tradition and innovation, theory and aesthetics, art and activism," this latest performance showcases the potential of performance as powerful politics (http://www.narthaki.com).

Diasporic Performance and Intersectionality

Without question, Shyamala understands her artistic performances as practices of political intervention that create public forums, inviting discussion
and encouraging deliberation. This is the case both when her performances
contain overtly political content and when the political material is more
covertly delivered and simply engenders a critical stance from the audience.
To her, cultural performance is understood as a critical practice and agenda-
setting tool that provides an opportunity to recognize silenced voices.
Of course, all this political work does not necessarily lead to progressive
change, regardless of intent. Each event only holds potential. Nevertheless,
like other performance activists, she believes the stage serves as a powerful
site for political action, even if the changes are small.

Performing *Rise*

Shyamala has performed *Rise* in a variety of settings, both in the United
States and abroad. And in each new context, she strategically varies the form
and content to meet the demands of the cultural, social, and political backdrop, as well as the audience composition. *Rise* is a one-woman show that
tells the story of an Indian American woman, Shakti. While her husband is
visiting Gujarat, India, riots between the Hindus and Muslims erupt and
Shakti becomes increasingly anxious about his well-being. The situation also
has deeper resonance because Shakti is Hindu and her husband is Muslim
and their families have had disagreements in the past regarding religious
issues. To compound her upset, Shakti turns on the TV and is bombarded
by news stories about 9/11. Overwhelmed, she sits on her toilet, only to find
it is plugged. In the rest of the performance, a series of characters "rise" out
of Shakti's toilet to tell their stories of violence and comment upon the pollution of humanity due to political and religious divisions. To answer these
exigencies, a secular goddess emerges—symbolized by the River Ganga—to
mourn the dead and cleanse the world of this violence.

Not surprisingly, *Rise* was a successful endeavor from the first performance and acclaimed a "Tour du force" by the *Los Angeles Times*. Consequently, in 2005, as the chairperson for the thirty-fourth "Annual Conference
on South Asia" I was pleased to have an opportunity to bring *Rise* to the
UW Madison campus. Typically, the conference's evening entertainment is
comprised of folk and classical performances by internationally renowned

Shyamala. Photo credited to David Flores.

musicians. However, this year I was interested in providing a performance with a focus on social justice. One that took into account human rights concerns related to gender, generation, religious affinity, economic class, and immigration—one that would offer our community, and conference members interested in South Asia performance and politics, a chance to explore together the issue of 9/11 and the Gujarati riots.

Certainly, the horror of September 11 and the subsequent U.S. bombings in Afghanistan have led to difficulties for South Asian and Middle-Eastern people.[8] Indeed, even model-minority South Asians have been subject to "racial profiling."[9] Consequently, many post-9/11 South Asians have found themselves in a difficult position—wanting to mourn the terrorists' victims, while simultaneously denouncing the violence against South Asians.[10] In the midst of national crisis, public mourning often provides the grounds for nation building. By mourning the dead together, we affirm our civic connectedness—constituting our "we." As Derrida (2001) argues, mourning is not only related to the political, but arises out of the political because through its rites and rituals it opens up the possibility of a political space and relationality (19). However, while many Americans were able to publicly mourn the losses of 9/11, many South Asian Americans felt they were denied civic participation, because they were figured as "the Other." Thus, for many South Asian Americans, the loss of 9/11 became a double loss. Moreover, in the years following the attacks, many South Asians—particularly Muslims—reported feeling "unsafe and insecure" in the United States because they feared incarceration en masse in internment camps (like those that held the Japanese after Pearl Harbor) or expulsion from the country. As Cainkar aptly notes, "These fears did not seem unfounded as communities watched thousands of Muslim noncitizens deported for visa violations, nearly a thousand jailed for long periods of time without charge and tens of thousands interviewed by the FBI and hundreds of thousands watched" (3).[11]

Sadly, not long after 9/11, another set of violent events rocked the South Asian American community. In 2002, between February 28 and March 2, the Sabarmati Express train was stopped at Godhra, a town in the Panchmahal district of Gujarat (Dugger 2002). This town has suffered from a long history of communal (i.e., religious) tensions. During the stop, a fire broke out in Coach S-6 of the train. This resulted in the death of fifty-nine people. Gujarat chief minister Narendra Modi, and others belonging to conservative Hindu nationalist organizations, alleged that the Godhra tragedy had been a preplanned Muslim conspiracy to attack Hindus, weaken the economy, and undermine the state (Coalition against Genocide 2005).

In response, Hindu nationalists called for a *bandh* (a general strike), to take place on the following day. This act was condemned by human rights organizations because *bandhs* are frequently associated with violence, and consequently have been made illegal. However, the Government of Gujarat, led by Modi, endorsed the strike. The attacks that followed prompted retaliatory massacres against Muslims on a large scale. Between February 28 and March 2, thousands of people, mostly Muslims, were killed in Gujarat. Following this, thousands more were internally displaced. According to independent human rights observers, the events in Gujarat "meet the legal definition of genocide" and a climate of uncertainty permeates civil society in Gujarat even today (Coalition against Genocide 2005).

The response from South Asian communities around the United States was complicated. Many "anti-communal" NRI organizations from New York to San Francisco rallied to decry the violence and the government's response in terms of the murder and displacement of thousands of Indian Muslims and Hindus. Other NRIs supported the Hindu nationalistic government of Gujarat. As Gayatri Gopinath notes, this situation provided "a stark illustration of the double-sided character of the diaspora" (2005, 196).

For Shyamala and I, these two events, taking place oceans apart, were connected by religious fundamentalism, acts of terror, and community disintegration. The script and choreography of *Rise* were meant to address these exigencies and invite the audience to consider these events from alternative vantage points.

A Moment of Introduction

That night the Madison performance of *Rise* took place on the Rotunda Stage at the Overture Center on Saturday, October 8, 2005. The performance space was overflowing and audience for the event was diverse, as advertisements had been sent to many different South Asian organizations, posted in Indian grocery stores, and advertised with student organizations, as well as publicized in the South Asian Conference literature. More interesting was the unexpected inclusion of American war veterans who, by chance, became a part of the audience after attending an event at the Wisconsin Veteran's Museum located near to the Overture Center.

Before the performance began, Shyamala walked around the auditorium talking to audience members distributing flyers that described her background as a public intellectual, educator, and performance artist. The flyer also included notes and references for the audience regarding the material that inspired that show. For example, Shyamala explains that her character of a Dalit cleaning woman was partially inspired by the article "The Stink of Untouchability and How Those Most Affected Are Trying to Remove It" by Mari Marcel Thekaekara (2005) in the *New Internationalist Magazine*. In addition, a portion of the Hindu politician's discourse is partially quoted from the former chief of the R.S.S. (Rashtriya Swayamsevek Sangh, a Hindu nationalist organization) and the Muslim politician's text is partially inspired from the poem *"Waa Ahl Gujarataah"* by Ha Moslimat Hodi. Shyamala also reveals that the sound bites of the American politician are from George W. Bush, taken from CNN broadcasts. Providing this context to the audience is part of her "critical approach" to performance advocacy.

A Media Montage of Terror

The performance begins with a blank stage. A single spotlight appears, illuminating Shyamala sitting on a toilet while reading a newspaper. Her hands shake as an audio montage blares out political and religious rhetoric from American and Indian media sources. Media that serves to fuel divisiveness and terror. The rhetorical force of this montage lies in the eclecticism of its parts. Through it, Shyamala directs the audience's attention to the work of managing public meaning and memory as they focus on her choice, assembly, and unexpected juxtapositions of media fragments. In doing so, she foregrounds complicated relationships between peace and war, friend and enemy, citizen and stranger, or victim and attacker. The force of this eclectic play with images lies precisely in its incongruity, its deviance, and the tensions integral to the relationships it proposes. In this process, political discourses and representations are brought into conflict, so that contradictory relationships (or incommensurabilities) are foregrounded and made visible.

In this way, the play of this montage can be understood through the notion of "hermeneutical rhetoric" (Jost and Hyde 1997). Put simply, by this I mean "hermeneutical rhetoric" involves the ways idioms, styles, and premises from the past are made meaningful in cultural practices, offering up emotional values that function as rhetorical capacities and constraints. As Eric King Watts (2002) argues, "The emotions attune us to the character of communal relations and to the significance of others and of their pursuits. Practical wisdom requires more than calculative thinking; it demands a sort of reflexive openness to the possibility of placing oneself in a productive relation to the other . . . it works through an aesthetic praxis that moves people to the places in which to find the right words to touch others" (22). It is the site where the ideas and aesthetics of past discourse are interpreted for contemporary rhetorical situations (Garlough 2007). Through this media compilation, Shyamala signals to the audience that her performance is entering into a dialogue with popular discourses in the public sphere (Bakhtin 1990; Garlough 1997). In doing so, she makes us hear the words differently.

The Significance of Flags and Toilets

In the next scene, Shyamala gracefully dances with the American flag, simultaneously honoring it, evoking predatory eagles, and wrapping it around herself to suggest a loving caress. It also suggests the ways that many South Asian Americans in towns all across the country, like Madison, struggled against racism by performing signs of allegiance to the nation, such as displaying the American flag. This served both as a protective device and also, for some, as an "affirmation of their future in the United States" (Grewal 2005, 212). As Robert Hariman and John Lucaites (2002) point out, abstract forms of civic life—citizenship or patriotism—have to be filled in with vernacular signs of social membership to provide some basis for identification (365). It is not surprising then that during the aftermath of 9/11 many South

Asian Americans chose to display the flag as a sign of their civic engagement and love for their country.

Yet for others, such a display felt disconcerting. As Chitra Divakaruni, a popular South Asian American journalist, writes: "I've been advised to display the American flag prominently on my house and car. This upsets me in a strange way. I love the flag, just as I love America and its commitment to liberty, equality and justice. But it bothers me that my patriotism is suspect unless I put up a flag to demonstrate it. And why? Because I don't fit the public's notion of what a 'good American' looks like" (2002, 89). Divakaruni's ambivalence about publicly performing "good" citizenship and displaying the symbols of American patriotism calls attention to the violence of having one's home made foreign to us (Das 2007).

This sentiment seems to resonate in the closing moments of the dance as Shyamala rips the flag off her body and plunges it down the toilet—the singular prop placed center stage. This leaves many audience members shocked, particularly the American war veterans who are watching from the balcony above. At the very least, most audience members seem to struggle as they attempt to interpret these acts. On the one hand, they seem to function as a rhetorical means of addressing a diasporic experience of alienation and disacknowledgment. How can one express the experience of being made to feel a stranger in one's home or a foreigner even when one has American citizenship papers?

On the other hand, Shyamala also seems to propose that the toilet and the waste inside symbolizes the waste of fundamentalist rhetoric—both religious and political. The flag becomes part of the abject horror of death infecting life (Kristeva 1982, 3). Her performative act challenges audiences and draws attention to the deep rules of citizenship that prescribe specific interactions among citizens in public spaces. It is a moment in the performance that resonates with both potential and threat. It provokes. For many, seeing the American flag in a toilet is an incommensurable image. Thus, through this dance, she raises a radical set of questions. They are questions that maintain a disruptive force and embrace uncertainty. And, in allowing the question to remain there, she accepts a certain amount of risk—the risk of being wrongly understood, wrongly interpreted, demonized, or interpreted too soon. In an interview, I asked her to comment on this choice:

CG: When you envisioned the plunger and the flag for your performance, what did you want those images to evoke for your audience?

s: I did realize when I made it that it was a pretty intense statement. Originally, I had everything coming out of the toilet only and my director asked why does the toilet overflow in the first place? What is all the garbage and the mental waste and the rhetoric that causes it in the first place? And that's how the flag came to be pushed into the toilet. It was about rhetoric. It was about these huge statements that are being made and the way the nationalism and patriotism, in the case of Iraq and in particular 9/11, are a part of that. The moment (the flag) gets tossed in the toilet, the main character asks what is that nationalism used for? For her, she just can't deal with it. So what does she do? She flushes it down the toilet.

The whole dance with the flag is about an eagle, a predator. But also there is a moment where I hide in the flag or take refuge in it and evolve to other things. And the Katrina image is what I had in mind.

cg: That's what is really useful about images. They can be recycled. Different people use them for different reasons. That particular image has been used over and over again.

(S. Moorty, personal communication, August 16, 2007)

Shyamala's 9/11 Testimony

Next, as described in the introduction of this book, Shyamala engages the audience with a personal testimony—the story of a hate crime that happened to her after 9/11. She was walking down a local street when she encountered a man watering his lawn. Although she smiled at him warmly, he gestured and angrily aimed his gardening hose at her, attempted to douse her with water. Humiliated and afraid, she left feeling like a stranger in her own community. As Hartman (2006, 254) writes, personal testimonies like these provide "histories from below," filling in the gaps of mainstream discourse in the public sphere. Not only does testimony provide accounts of violence, but it attempts to put us in the individual's place, or at least in their presence, drawing the listener in to the experience of suffering and fear. In this way, these testimonies remain personal and subjective, even while they are shared.

Shyamala uses this narrative to point toward a question. Why did hate crimes against South Asian Americans soar by 1,600 percent immediately following the disaster—as a barrage of media images and stories directed our gaze toward a devastated lower Manhattan, the bodies of victims, the testimony of witnesses, and the grief of those who lost loved ones? Across the United States, South Asian Americans, misrecognized as "terrorists," were beaten with baseball bats studded with nails, attacked in their places of work and worship, violated verbally with racial epithets, and frightened by death threats (http://www.saalt.org/). Moreover, given the "rally around the flag" phenomena that characterized most mainstream discourse, reports of this violence were not prevalent in the public sphere, and were generally unacknowledged by the wider American population, even by many South Asian Americans.

The deeply personal character of these life stories allows them to "touch heart as well as mind [appealing] to a human commonality that does not imply uniformity" (Hartman 2006, 254). Further, the testimony Shyamala offers is deeply relational. As she speaks to audiences about the ways in which she has been wounded, the wound itself bears witness. Consequently, this testimony is addressed to a double recipient. That is, this testimony is addressed not only the audience of listeners but also to Shyamala—the survivor/narrator who is providing testimony, whose sense of identity has been shaken, and who must relive her victimization through her performance of the initial experience of violence. As audience members see Shyamala slip into "back there," the emphasis shifts from the perpetrator's behavior to the humanity of the victim (Hartman 2006, 257), thereby encouraging us to acknowledge the victimization they have experienced.

Of course, not everyone wants to hear this story or feel her pain. She is performing as a *parrhesiastes*—speaking at great risk, in front of an audience where power relations are unbalanced, freely confessing the truth of her experience, although the threat of retribution is quite real. In doing so, she discloses something of herself and the truth of what she believes (Foucault 2001). The everydayness of such personal stories makes apparent the relation between violence and the humanity of the Other (Levinas 1981). It communicates what is precious and injurable and enacts calls for acknowledgment. To ask for such acknowledgment is to solicit a future in relation to the Other. That is, Shyamala's testimony evokes a pathos of pain, calling attention to the ways that performances of suffering may inform acknowledgment (Das 2007).

Eclectic Dance as Cultural Critique

Next, in Shyamala's performance, she explodes into a dance that combines both ballet and Bharatanatyam simultaneously, demanding from the

Shyamala, Half Ballet,
Half Bharatanatyam. Photo
credited to David Flores.

audience recognition for multiple ways of realizing a South Asian American identity.

Split down the middle, her right side presents a graceful ballet form, her left side artfully displays traditional Bharatanatyam dance movements. Here, gestures have complex and layered uses, expressing the *ntta* vocabulary (and movements that also traditionally convey stories and legends from the Indian epics and folktales). In addition, gestures render the emotional states of the characters being represented (Katrak 2004). As Katrak (2008) observes, "A solo female dancer (in the traditional form) communicates stories and emotions via a wide range of gestures: expressive, representative, and emblematic" (218).[12] Shyamala combines these styles to explore her own biracial identity and create an awareness of diversity within the South Asian American community. As the dance grows to a fevered pitch, Shyamala begins to eclectically mix these movements and deliberately falls off balance. Shyamala's combination of disparate traditions requires a multifaceted fluency—a cultural competence that combines "East" and "West" in complicated ways and widens the category of South Asian diaspora from within. It is both a personal and political commentary on strategic identity presentation.

In each of these scenes, Shyamala's performance engages in intersectional praxis. Intersectionality—first coined by Kimberle Crenshaw (1989)—is a feminist approach to political discourse and research that at its most basic level suggests the ways that race oppression and gender oppression interact in women of color's lives (Knudsen 2005, 61). Scholars employing this approach focus upon analyzing how social and cultural categories of discrimination—based on gender, race, ethnicity, age, disability, sexuality, class, religious orientation, immigration status, and nationality—interact on multiple and simultaneous levels. The outcome of this interaction is systemic inequality.[13] By evoking the image of streets cutting through one another, intersectionality calls attention to the ways individuals live with multilayered identities and may be members of many communities simultaneously. These identities, derived from social relations, history, and the operations of power, may sometimes be at odds. Consequently, people may simultaneously experience oppression and privilege.

While intersectionality was originally guided by liberalism and Marxism, more recently it has been influenced by postmodern theoretical approaches that range from discourse theory, deconstruction, queer theory, and postcolonialism (Feree 2009). Consequently, intersectionality has been adopted by a range of disciplines from anthropology to sociology. Feminist scholars interested in folklore, for example, have found this approach useful when studying the everyday practices and performances of women through the intersections of social and political forces, as well as personal, psychological, emotional, and physical characteristics that undergird the relationships and values they communicate through folklore (Garlough 2007, 2008; Mills 1991; Sawin 2002). As Martha C. Sims and Martine Stephens (2005) point out, "Scholars who are interested in intersectionality frequently focus on oppressed or under-represented individuals or groups, those who have been excluded, ignored, or discriminated against by mainstream groups—in other words, those who have been pushed to the margins" (199). This perspective provides a framework for folklorists to discuss the dialogic interplay between performance contexts, as well as the ways power within social contexts operates to influence those texts and performances.[14]

However, scholars are not the only ones who have used the concept of intersectionalty in their work. Activist efforts by women, like Shyamala, who are interested in social justice issues also often display an "intersectional praxis" (Townsend-Bell 2009). These grassroots activists use intersectionality to provide a critical lens for bringing awareness to social justice endeavors and interventions on the ground. For instance, this might occur when grassroots activists are involved in a case where ethnicity, gender, and class work together to limit access to social goods such as employment or fair immigration.

Erica E. Townsend-Bell (2009), drawing from a political science perspective, argues that intersectional praxis, like Shyamala's has two requirements. The first is a commitment to a politics of accountability that would assist in the elimination of oppressive relations (2–3). The second requirement is that activists should pay attention to the impact and role of difference in their political work. She labels this "intersectional recognition." Intersectional recognition, she believes, should grow from the group's own experiences. It also should provide the grounding for continuing education on what differences are relevant to the problem at hand and an acknowledgment of the ways these differences relate to each other.

When applying this framework to Shyamala's performance, we see something interesting about the form this recognition takes. That is, certain acts of recognition perpetuate beliefs that a collective identity is fixed. These identities, often based upon notions of "authenticity," emphasize *differences between* groups and the *homogeneity within* them. They are identities that reference their own stereotypes and classify people in reductive ways (Phillips 2007, 31). These representations often are not emancipatory, even when used by in-group members, because they work, sometimes inadvertently, to constrain individuals and keep them on the margins of society (Hall 1997).

In contrast, Shyamala's dance resonates well with something Greta Snyder (2011)—drawing from cultural studies literature—has called a politics of "multivalent recognition." Here, participants demand recognition for multiple ways of realizing a collective identity. Put differently, actors engaged in the politics of multivalent recognition use demands for recognition to create an awareness of the diversity *within* a category (Schiappa 2008, 114). This type of recognition does the critical work of calling attention to the ways that recognized identities can sometimes reinforce reductive visions of collective identity. Snyder (2011) argues that four features of this type of recognition are (1) it works to highlight the visibility of marginalized groups; (2) it tries to widen the category from within; (3) it is a strategic identity presentation developed with the awareness that this representation is political and with a sense of the historical backdrop against which the representations are interpreted; and (4) calls for the cultivation of different and contradictory visions of this identity (15–16).

Critical play with recognition is an important part of the intersectional praxis that occurs in activist performances, like Shyamala's, particularly when interrogating the complicated and sometimes contradictory representations advanced by diasporic activists in political contexts. However, I believe simply focusing upon the impact, role, relevance, and relationships between identity differences does not do justice to the sort of activist performances that Shyamala works to invent and facilitate. Rather, her approach takes into account more than recognition of identities and their complex interrelationships. It goes beyond focusing simply on claims for individual or abstract rights and the consistent application of the latter to the former. Her choice of medium is based on a desire to develop a context that also places a premium on valuing attentiveness and responsiveness, as well as the building of trust and an ethic of care.

For this reason, I believe that Townsend-Bell's second requirement—intersectional recognition—would benefit from being reconceptualized, so that recognition and acknowledgment are not used interchangeably. Instead, I would like to deepen the ways that acknowledgment is conceptualized in order to understand the ways it may work to generate the potential for an ethic of justice and care in activist performance contexts. That is, chapter 1 provided readers with a sense of *what* acknowledgment is. In this chapter, I am most concerned with illustrating *how* acknowledgment operates rhetorically in performances. Most specifically, how the performers' intersecting "ways of being" argue for caring relations within communities, as well as with distant others. How might performances encourage self-care? How might performances persuade audience to more ethically acknowledge those who are strangers or very different from themselves? How might an audience be encouraged to acknowledge their own need for moral responsiveness in their communities and the world at large? How might these performances serve the goals of citizenship in ways that exceed the goals of recognition and inspire careful judgment?

For example, reflecting further on intersectionality in an interview with me, Shyamala stated,

> S: I put together this dance piece in *Rise* out of my own physical confusion and that physical confusion being a metaphor of course for who I am.

> CG: How are you feeling when you do it?

> S: When I did it in the beginning when I first created it, it was very difficult for my body to do and I was really trying to figure out the

energy. There is a real energetic difference between the two. With the downward energy versus the upward energy and in the beginning I really felt the confusion and the difficulty and it was more of a stressful piece to do in the beginning and now it's easy.

CG: So when you do it, does one sort of take over the other or is it balanced?

S: I work to keep them at a pretty good balance; it's interesting because I feel that ballet is more in my past than in my present. So there is definitely more of a sense of ease, or a sense that it's okay for me to be doing this movement, and that's what my body does now. Versus when I do ballet, there is a little more insecurity there.
(S. Moorty, personal communication, August 16, 2007)

This multivalent representation works through eclecticism, rather than synthesis, cultural syncretism, or pastiche (Delgado, 1998; McGee 1990) in order to juxtapose apparently unrelated fragments. At its core, the notion of eclecticism directs our attention to the work of managing meaning. As a method of creating discourse, eclecticism addresses such epistemological concerns by directing the choice, assembly, and rearrangement of elements into texts, such that they manifest unexpected juxtapositions and disjunctions. In this process, culturally accessible forms and logics are carefully organized so that a contradictory relationship is foregrounded. Indeed, the force of the eclecticism lies precisely in its incongruity, its deviance, and the tensions integral to the relationships proposed. As such, eclecticism, I argue here, should be understood as a deeply rooted type of hermeneutic and rhetorical strategy and practice where the ideas and aesthetics of past discourse are interpreted for contemporary uses in rhetorical situations.[15] Eclecticism provides diasporic individuals in these complex social conditions a means for flexible transformation that has facilitated the coexistence of rich and historically diverse cultural traditions.

Shyamala's performance is extremely reflexive—drawing attention to itself as art, deferring meaning, and challenging assumptions of an easily consumable "multiculturalism." Her body in this performance presents a diasporic way of being through a refusal to speak or communicate within a single cultural or rhetorical competence. Through eclecticism, this performance calls attention to the ways that hybridity—though fashionable in cultural theory—is not always easy to live. As Sunaina Maira (2009) suggests, "social institutions and networks continue to demand loyalty to sometimes competing cultural ideals that second generation youth may find difficult to manage. For many, liminality is an ongoing daily condition of being betwixt and between cultural categories." She goes on to argue, "The performance of a visibly hybrid ethnicity occurs in specific contexts and is not always optional; it belongs to a range of performances and cultural scripts in every-day life" (Maira 2009, 301). Shyamala echoed these concerns in an interview with me, stating:

> CG: The question of responsibility and representation . . . How do you negotiate that?

> S: It's interesting because in the making of this piece, at some points I was tempted to make it more simple, and just represent a Hindu. My director, who is also of a mixed background, was like, "no way." It's so important that that existed and, and was part of the equation and dialogue. That's what was so difficult.

> CG: Why was it so difficult?

> S: It felt like her identity was so confusing in the first place and I didn't want that to take over the piece because it was about all these other things.

> CG: What helped you to negotiate the sticky spots?

> S: I guess I do identify with the words like hybridity, multiplicity, and multiple heritage. I don't like to think of it as biracial so much because I feel like there aren't just two things in there anyway . . . I feel like if you're thinking about hybridity or multiple heritages, it really expands into a whole other group of people, nearly everyone in one sense or another. Because I'm living in a society where you can get Italian food on one block and the hybrid version on another. And we're all affected so much by each other, whether we know it not, that I think I like a more open term like that.
> (S. Moorty, personal communication, August 16, 2007)

Clearly, Shyamala's performance transgresses expectations by not conforming to traditional categories. Moreover, the fusion represents for the audience how she is kept off balance by her identity. In the process, Shyamala's critical play with dance calls into question the constitutive power of stereotypes and makes visible how these stereotypes work to exclude South Asian Americans. It strategically performs the uniqueness of a diasporic identity and uses that distinctiveness to make claims for an intersectional recognition that embraces diversity within the broader group constituted as South Asian American. Again, as I mentioned previously, these acts of testimony shift the focus of attention from "what" people are (i.e., immigrant, citizen, American, South Asian) to "who" they are. When humanized, each person's story is understood as unique, thus contesting simplistic representations.

In refusing to make essentialized claims about recognition, the dance works not by telling people *what to think*, but by asking them *to think*. It accepts the risk of being wrongly interpreted and addresses the questions of recognition in a way that suggests South Asian American identity is not a puzzle that can be resolved definitively one way or another. South Asian American identity, like all diasporic identity, is more or less permanent aporia—an undecidable within diasporic and national discourse. Her dance performance suggests to audiences that we must live within the uncertainty that these questions pose. We must learn to develop a heightened sensitivity to the complexity and undecidability that haunt and disturb reflections upon South Asian American identity, while maintaining our vigilance about the particular ways this aporiatic identity may threaten the groups' ability to act collectively. This dance also raises the question of who may be included in the category of a 9/11 victim, opening the limits of a publicly acknowledged field of appearance.

Peace and the Goddess

I am an ocean of sorrow,
a cool stream to rinse away the hate,
a drop of hope,
I am a watery grave . . .
where all will, and must
find peace.
—Line in *Rise* spoken by the Goddess

So, given these critiques, what can be done in the name of care and social justice? Throughout this performance, Shyamala makes claims for the potential of the figure of "the goddess" to heal our communities and work toward peace. Indeed, one of the first dance pieces in *Rise* gestures toward folkloric aspects of a daily puja—one dedicated to a universal manifestation of the goddess. In an offering of welcome, Shyamala scatters red flower petals on the stage. It is a public form of devotion and dedication that can be read as a traditional "womanly" manifestation of care.

Interestingly, this call to the goddess is later evoked by Shyamala as she plays the part of a little Muslim girl whose mother has died violently in the Gujarati riots. The goddess takes the form of the child's favorite doll. And the girl explains to the audience, "My doll's name is Ganga. I call her that after the river Ganges. Isn't she perfect for a river goddess, all dressed in blue? I read about her in a comic book. She heals and purifies." Certainly, this turn in the plot is not intuitive, given what the performance has just revealed about the complexities of communal violence. However, as Shyamala demonstrates, the meaning of "goddess" is not fixed. Rather, the goddess is a multivalent symbol associated with a rich set of meanings that might be strategically employed for rhetorical purposes. Through this surplus of meaning, Shyamala advocates peace and a women's centered spirituality. Here Ganga is refigured as a universal force of nature—a purifying force that cleanses the pollution of humanity. As Shyamala puts it, "The innocence of a young girl has allowed her to embrace the goddess anyway. It is her determination and hope that can help to create a transformative force beyond our human tendencies for revenge. The goddess is merely a symbol of higher consciousness or a natural force beyond humanity or a revolutionary state of mind. It is not that I think a Hindu goddess is the universe." At the conclusion of the performance, Shyamala transforms into this "fierce goddess." This entity seeks to help the audience mourn the nonsensical violence, embrace social justice, and begin the work of repairing the communities and lives that have been torn apart.

Many South Asian feminist scholars, like Elizabeth Gross, have argued that the Hindu pantheon may offer powerful resources to reimagine and connect with a female power for women in religious traditions that do not have goddess figures (Gross 1983, 217). Conversely, others, such as Rachel McDermott and Cynthia Eller contend that it is not only difficult but sometimes culturally insensitive to appropriate goddess traditions. Shaymala, aware of these concerns, disclosed in an interview:

In making *Rise*, when the idea for using the goddess arose, I was interested in what Ganga/the Ganges can represent: cleansing, or literally plunging, away the filth of human prejudice and intolerance. Of course, using a Hindu goddess is tricky when dealing with religious conflict, and yet developing tolerance and justice doesn't mean erasing religion or religious differences. So, in *Rise* I call on the goddess but bring up her contradictions and adapt her to allow space for other interpretations. She rises out of the toilet, so the intrinsic idea of purity is questioned right away. Her weapon is a plunger, which is slightly humorous as it brings her heroism to the mundane realm of literally cleaning up the shit that clogs our brains in the form of rhetoric, pride, and the painful never-ending cycle of retaliation. The way she wears the sari pullu, or end, over her head references a Muslim style instead of a Hindu one, thus she stands in solidarity with her Muslim sisters. The goddess is invoked, but not as an icon of Hindu nationalism—which has happened with other Hindu deities, especially Lord Rama. Rather, I hope that she creates an alternative space for empathy, humanity, dialogue, and clarity. She is the energy of transformation amidst tragedy. (S. Moorty, personal communication, January 13, 2012)

In this performance, the goddess for Shyamala is a rhetorical and hermeneutic endeavor that does not draw on an authoritative sacred text or primary revelation. Rather, it is a representation that refuses the identitarian—instead choosing a middle space. In this figure, a feminist ethos is invoked—one that conceives of a sacred deity through the metaphor of "nature," where nature is understood as all that exists. This figure has a political focus and is used to provide a simultaneously new and old space from which to speak about violence. The eclecticism within this representation helps the audience put into play an alternative notion of religion or spirituality and consequently suggests a different way of thinking about being with an "other."

As Shyamala observes, the idea is to "honor the divine spark within us all, whatever superstructure you want to invoke. This entity names the life that flows in and through others, us, earth, and lets all of us be the being that we are. It strives to release us from manipulation and controversy and encourage us to treat all with respect. Ultimately, it is an attempt to find spirituality beyond the diatribes of any given religion" (Pamphlet from *Rise*). In doing so, the goddess is a rhetorical figure that speaks to our ability to learn to inhabit the world again in a "gesture of mourning" (Das 2007, 206). Her universalist interpretation of Hindu religious tradition becomes a source of invention. And the goddess metaphor becomes a potentially powerful way to evoke care and critique the divisiveness of religious fundamentalism.

> CG: When you talk about fundamentalism, what do you hope audience members will think about? What do you hope some of the potential might be for that performance?

s: I would hope, one, that it's just making people aware of this major thing . . . so the conversation is still continuing. And just to bring aware- ness to somebody who is really interested in the topic. Trying to create awareness around it and in our communities . . . Of course, it's hor- rible but it's especially horrible when nobody listens. There are always all sorts of theories about whether something is true or not. But to me, part of it is awareness and dialogue. I hope people would continue talking about it and questioning themselves and others around them. Maybe just creating a curiosity. Like, wouldn't it be interesting to find out more about Islam?

(S. Moorty, personal communication, August 16, 2007)

In the focus groups that I conducted following the performance, while some audience members agreed, others felt Shyamala faced insurmountable constraints in using the metaphor of the goddess. That is, the goddess calls up too many associations with Hindu religion and consequently the repre- sentation is too fraught with rhetorical constraints to function effectively as a tool for social justice. Indeed, in focus groups that I conducted following the performance, both Hindu and Muslim students expressed concern about using fraught religious figures and discourse to make calls for peace. As one audience member observed, "In my opinion, negotiating the ways these mine fields of religious belief connect up with politics is tricky. People get edgy when someone else's religious belief seems to get privileged, no mat- ter what the intention." In addition, many focus group members noted that there is a second risk in trying to appeal to audience members who identify as feminists of color or third-wave feminists through the figure of the god- dess because in the 1970s and 1980s this metaphor was so frequently—and some argued loosely—evoked in second-wave feminist discourse.

Question and Answer: The Potential of Audience Participation

At the close of *Rise*, the audience is asked to "perform" as well by participat- ing in a question-and-answer session very much like those one might find in street plays in India (Garlough 2008). In the process, their interpretation and inquiry becomes part of the acknowledgment that occurs through the performance; that is, included in their roles as witnesses is an invitation to be part of "an active process of spectatorship, rather than a passive con- sumption of a pre-narrated spectacle" (Patraka 1999, 92).

In an interview about this process, I asked:

CG: How do you approach the audience?

S: Well, I normally think of that idea of rasa and rassika. I'm just thinking of the audience as a collaborator in the performance, so that partially it's me dropping hints of ideas and partially it's them making their own connections. I'm just hoping that they're bringing open minds to it. Obviously, not everyone is going to have an open mind to start with. I try to open people up with humor toward the beginning. And then, ideally, with them being in a more relaxed and open place, they can meet me with an open mind and be very active in making connections and asking questions later on.

CG: So, in part, you want to get them to a place where they are no longer sure about what they think?

S: Yeah, I want to get them to an engaged place where they are caring about the issues. And if that means being not completely sure, then that's fine.

CG: The concept of the rassika gets at that in a way. Where did you first learn about that idea?

S: Mostly through UCLA. It's interesting that that term was thrown around a lot through all my classically Indian dance trainings. But in my training I don't think anybody ever really clearly defined it. I think I learned about in my theoretical studies at UCLA and in my own readings . . . there was a natural interest there. My friend Sandra has done a little bit more on it. So through her interest, I keep hearing things too.
(S. Moorty, personal communication, August 16, 2007)

As Katrak notes, "In Indian dance, the performer-audience relationship has historically been considered crucial in determining the quality of performances. If a performance is to be deemed successful, there must be rasa" (Katrak 2005, 227). The *Natyasastra* tells readers that rasa comes through the expression of the nine primary emotions (disgust, grief, heroism, sorrow, wonder, fear, peace, laughter, and love) on the stage. Rasa—translated as "juice" or "essence"—is a meaning that "touches the heart" and is rhetorical in the ways that it functions to move audiences and enhances the chance that the audience will hear what the speaker has to say. In looking at the interactive aspect of ancient Indian aesthetic theory of rasa, Uttara Asha

Coorlawala (2003) notes that rasa occurs as "audiences draw closer, become restive, still, discussing the event as it occurs, giving love and support, draining energy, bearing witness to an inner journey and adding their intensity to the mix . . . or even withdrawing in resistance" (Coorawala 2003, 38).

This can occur in a performance setting, even when one is just beginning to understand another's needs. As Held (2006) argues, even at this beginning point when we are thinking about how to respond to calls for acknowledgment and care, practices of empathy and involvement are called for (34). In fact, just actively listening and observing can be a form of relational labor, producing an intimate and shared experience that promotes civic engagement and virtue. Communicating and struggling for each other in this way may enable performances to function as public forums with disruptive potential. This potential is illustrated in the following example, when a student asked Shyamala to offer a solution for the violence she addresses in *Rise*.

> AUDIENCE MEMBER: Because of the fundamental differences between the Hindu and Muslim viewpoints, what would you think would be one possible way that this might be solved? Because, it is a problem. But it is really a complicated problem. So what do you think would be some way to solve it?

> SHYMALA: Yes, it is really, really complicated, and I definitely don't have the answer. But I felt that I could address it by juxtaposing my own life experience . . . being someone who is mixed, between cultures. I know that so many people who are, because either their parents came from two different places or because they immigrated to a new place and they have to deal with new cultures. It involves a kind of figuring out, you know? How do you react to someone who is so different from you?
> And I think that there is something there. There's something about that. That, in one individual . . . that in so many of us . . . we are more than one thing. We're not just an essential identity that's pure and perfect. I don't know what pure is anymore. So, you know, it's wrong putting people . . . pitting them against each other in extremes, rather than realizing that those kind of opposites are really just mirroring each other. And I know it's really hard because there's so many cultural differences. But that is what so many people and institutions, like our government, do every day of our lives. So, I don't know what the answer is, but that's what I'm thinking about when I'm trying to put all of these things together in one piece.

AUDIENCE MEMBER: As far as your art goes, I found it fascinating that you can take all of those experiences and make them very graphic.

SHYMALA: Thank you very much. I think that, one of the many things that I've been dealing with, or I've been trying to figure out in chore-ography, is how to make dance real to people who don't know what my experience is. And this is one of the many experiments . . . mixing it up . . . combining different contexts. I hope that it always communicates feelings.

In discussing these issues, as part of the performance, theater holds the potential to go beyond entertainment evoking acknowledgment through both an ethic of justice (questions of fairness, equality, and individual rights) and an ethic of care (attentiveness, responsiveness to need, and presence). And yet, what happens if the audience is not ready to hear what the performer has to say? What if they came to the performance to hear a different message? What if they refuse a response? This concern arose in the question-and-answer session when a student posed the following inquiry:

AUDIENCE MEMBER: The performance is a very charged political event . . . I mean with the imagery towards 9/11, and the burka, and the American flag, and all sorts of things. What sort of responses are you getting from the community? And what sort of responses do you expect from the community? I mean, I know there's people here, too, but?

SHYMALA: This is really sad, but I always expect the worst, because it's scary to put these things out there. I'm doing some stuff that people could get really angry about. But I'm hoping that, as I put it out there and take those risks to say it, people will stop and listen and not just judge quickly. And, amazingly, I've always had very good responses from every community that I've done it for so far. And, you're actually the first audience to see the sixty-minute, full-length piece. I've been tour-ing a twenty-five-minute version of this for about three years. It didn't have the multiracial stuff, and it didn't have the U.S. stuff. It only had the religious stuff, and, so I did it for a lot of different audiences. The American audiences were mostly amazed and interested to hear about the situation, which doesn't normally get highlighted in the media. And most Indians, from both camps, and from other camps, have really respected it . . .

I don't know, is there anybody mad here? I'd like to hear your responses to what happened.

Gadamer suggests that the success of dialogue like this depends on the continuing willingness of its participants to give in to language—to be carried along by conversation for the purpose of letting meaning emerge in an event of mutual understanding. The success of this venture, Derrida would argue, turns on the question of risk. That is putting one's own meanings and self at risk is the only way to let one come toward an Other. Shyamala encourages just this type of emergent understanding, as can be seen in the following excerpt:

AUDIENCE MEMBER: Hi, I wondered if you could talk about the ending. As we were commenting, we were in the midst of violence . . . Hindu and Muslim and America's President Bush. And then the river Ganges came, and I was unclear about the ending.

SHYAMALA: I will definitely answer your question from my point of view, but before I do, I just am very curious how different people interpreted it. I mean, I think that art is all about the artists meeting with the audiences, and so, if people have different ideas, I don't want to squelch them and make you think that they are wrong, just because I had a certain idea when I made it. So I am curious . . . what did you guys think about this coming out at the end?

AUDIENCE MEMBER 1: The Ganges may represent something that all Indians have in common.

SHYAMALA: Ah, maybe, yeah. So this river of life, basically, that offers water to everyone. Could it be anything else?
Audience Member 2: I kind of got the impression that you were saying that this method of division was going to lead in the downfall of everyone.

AUDIENCE MEMBER 3: Well, I first thought of the doll and the connection with water. You dressed up as the doll, so, maybe, it's how children have a lot easier time getting along with friends than adults do. That's what I thought.

STUDENT: Well, I thought about the doll also. But I also was thinking about purification. So, after all that violence, I kind of got the impression, the Ganges was a form of purification.

AUDIENCE MEMBER 4: I am going to interrupt and just ask that people speak loudly so that people all the way back can hear because we have a vortex right in the middle.

SHYAMALA: And why don't you guys come up? There's plenty of room up here, come up! Don't be shy.

So, for me, I also was feeling some hope or an idea that there is some sort of humanity or something greater that can unite us. Maybe that's where that idea of the river connecting everybody comes. I think that's really beautiful and I hadn't really thought necessarily of the river in particular. But yeah, she is. She is the river. And she is nature. And she is a goddess. And I particularly tried to mark her as both a Muslim and Hindu, on purpose. Other questions?

Performance, Citizenship, and Social Justice

I have sought to show that performances, like Shyamala's, work to engage audiences in moments of political potential. They are sites of struggle where the social and cultural are articulated. Through performances, audiences engage democracy; the theater is "a participatory forum in which ideas and possibilities for social equity and justice are shared" (Dolan 2006, 519). As Dolan notes, the potential of these performances stems, in part, from people's attraction to live theater for emotional, spiritual, or communitarian reasons. That is, "sharing liveness promotes a necessary and moving confrontation with mortality" and "trains our imaginations and fuels desires that could create incremental social change." Ultimately, it is the "actor's willing vulnerability that perhaps enables our own and prompts us toward compassion and greater understanding" because "being moved emotionally is the precursor to any political movement" (Dolan 2006, 521).

Shyamala's performance of *Rise* is committed to an engagement with speculation, experimentation, and curiosity. It asks audiences to participate actively, make connections, and sometimes disagree. It is performance that provokes and moves audiences beyond voyeurism. I have argued that representations of suffering may help facilitate the work of acknowledgment, and that *Rise*—through the critical play of testimony, commentary, and images of suffering—is an example of such a performance. This performance invites audience members to become present and to become a "we" while honoring the intersectional differences that characterize our lives. This is an aporiatic "we." As Derrida notes, this indeterminate "we" does not necessarily presuppose any sympathy, community, or consensus (Derrida 2000). What such a "we" does do, however, is open time and space for the potential of ethical relations and social protest—for understanding and action. As Shyamala eloquently stated:

> I'm not interested in making art "unless it relates to the world I live in, the things I care about, the people I work with." I care a lot about social justice and there are certainly endless issues to engage with, open up a conversation around, or provide a new point of view into. Lately I've been more interested in the transformative possibilities of art and involving community in the art making process. (S. Moorty, personal communication, January 13, 2012)

This performance, which continues to be presented to audiences across the globe, shows the humanity of the "Other" in a way that issues a call for a safe home that recognizes and welcomes diversity. It responds to a call of conscience that acknowledges the suffering of the self and others. Therefore, this performance manifests a commitment to radical hermeneutics—engaging with the difficulty of knowing an Other (Caputo 1987). This richer understanding, this acknowledgment of the Other, cannot take place unless someone makes the time and space for such acknowledgment to "be." As Hyde argues: "Acknowledgment is a moral act, it functions to transform space and time, to *create* openings wherein people can dwell, deliberate, and know together what is right, good, just, and truthful. Acknowledgment thereby grants people *hope*, the opportunity for a new beginning, a second chance, whereby they might improve their lot in life" (Hyde 2006, 7). *Rise* offers such a call for respect, for acknowledgment. It remains to be seen whether or not we will accept such invitations.

Chapter Five

❖   ❖   ❖

Cultural Activism and
Sexuality in Feminist Performance

❖   ❖   ❖

Growing up in a dominant society where the appropriation of my culture has become a sort of fad, having the raw and honest reality of our diasporic experiences performed is invaluable. *Yoni Ki Baat* is a medium in which we can begin to address our problems, and value the struggles of our womyn.

—Swati (personal correspondence, 2011)

In the United States today, consumer culture often fuels the multicultural attraction to everyday "ethnic" performances. Nose rings, mendhi tattoos, belly chains, and bindis—these traditional fashions associated with South Asian American women can now be found in most mainstream shopping centers as stylish accessories. Over the years, traditional styles from Asia have become popular in international fashion. Most recently, in large public venues, celebrities like Madonna or Katy Perry showcase these appropriated ethnic markers of identity to position themselves as "citizens of the world."

Consequently, it is understandable that during my fieldwork, I interviewed many young South Asian American women, like Swati, who found that having their cultural traditions co-opted was more than simply disconcerting.[1] Rather, these cultural appropriations complicated for them what it means to be affiliated with an ethnic community. Interestingly, many women felt that the process of co-opting these everyday cultural performances and turning them into commercial fads is historically informed by the West's sexual objectification of women from the East. They argued it is a consumptive appetite that has grown, in part, out of mainstream media and popular

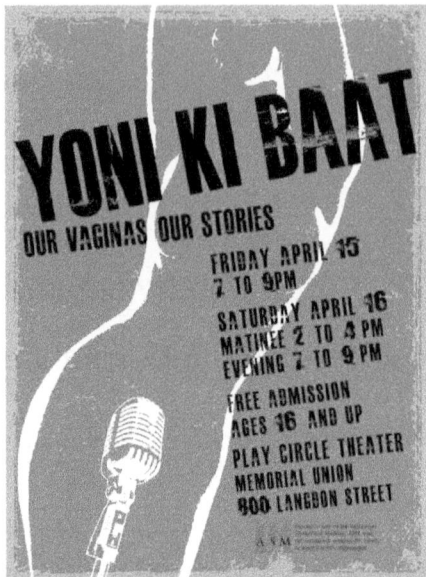

Madison Yoni Ki Baat poster. Photo
credited to Madison Yoni ki Baat directors,
poster by James Ahoy.

culture's fascination with harem girls or the Kama Sutra. Scholars have also
criticized "Asian chic" for "perpetuating Oriental structures of knowledge
and power" that reinforce stereotypes of Asians as timeless and traditional
(Leshkowich and Jones 2003, 281).

In contrast to such mainstream appropriations, across the United States,
there is a growing number of young South Asian American women who have
found other, more progressive and politically resistive ways to engage with
South Asian cultural traditions. Playing critically with folk dress, narratives, songs, poetic forms, dance, and material culture, these women engage
in debates about sexuality and gender in their communities. This chapter
offers an ethnographic account of one such emerging movement—a feminist performance movement called *Yoni Ki Baat (Our Vaginas Speak)*.

Characterized as a South Asian American version of *The Vagina Monologues*, these performances offer young women an opportunity to embed
personal testimonies within traditional cultural forms in order to address
controversial issues connected to ethnic essentialism, sex positivity, and
sexual violence, to name but a few. *Yoni Ki Baat* began as a single performance event by the South Asian Sisters. Recently, it has grown into a movement that has spread from coast to coast, involving women's collectives with
diverse agendas and compositions.

In the process, *Yoni Ki Baat* performances have become an important
part of broader efforts for South Asian American feminist activism. Since

Director of South Asian Sisters,
Vandana. Photo courtesy of
Vandana Maaker.

the early 1980s, a diverse range of South Asian women's organizations have been founded in the United States (Gupta 2006). Forging inroads into the public sphere, these groups confronted stereotypes of Asian women and proposed new models of advocacy and community service (Khandelwal 1995). As Mohanty (2003) notes, these women found strength not only in their commonality but in their diversity and differences as well. This appreciation for the complex relationality and intersectionality that shapes South Asian women's lives certainly is apparent in the ways these women have sought to understand notions of "feminism," "gender," or "sexuality" in diasporic contexts. This awareness also can be observed in the issues and exigencies South Asian women's organizations chose to focus upon; for most, domestic abuse, wage discrimination, or immigrant law reform have been areas of deep concern.

In this sense, growing out of a third-wave feminist orientation, South Asian Sisters offers a unique agenda. Unlike many South Asian women's organizations, they focus their attention upon issues related to both sexual violence and sex positivity and do so by drawing upon situated and personal sets of experiences. Their activism manifests in many ways, from sponsoring community discussion forums to designing a feminist Web log. One of their most distinctive contributions is their annual performance of *Yoni Ki Baat*, which they first conceived and staged in 2003. As Vandana Makker observes, "The yoni (Sanskrit word for 'vagina') has long been held sacred in Hindu mythology, but, through years of patriarchy and colonialism, it has rarely been allowed to speak its mind. In 2003, South Asian Sisters, a collective of progressive desi (of Indian origin) women, decided that the yoni needed a chance to get on stage and tell its side of the story. Thus, 'Yoni ki Baat' was born" (Bhargqva 2012) This event, I argue, meets several important objectives, that extend from providing a distinctly South Asian perspective upon "women's issues," to exploring diverse experiences of sexuality, to reflecting upon different ways of relating compassionately to those in the community who need support.

That is, though Eve Ensler's piece—*The Vagina Monologues*—"has been performed around the world, including Pakistan and India, South Asian Sisters felt that putting on a production of the original show simply wasn't enough" (Makker 2004, 1). They needed to create a space in which South Asian women could express their own views on sexuality and their bodies— "topics that are traditionally kept 'hush-hush' in desi culture" (Makker 2004, 1). In the process, *Yoni Ki Baat* bridges divisions between religion, class, and immigrant status to create a forum that gathers women for political reasons—creating spaces for women that are women friendly to name what is often culturally unspeakable.[2]

However, an intertwining objective is for South Asian women to explore and express their diverse experiences of sexuality, in their own terms, as diasporic community members. In some cases, their discourses revolve around issues of sexual identity. In other performances, women speak about different dimensions of their sexuality, openly exploring sex-positive attitudes and sharing their personal experiences with fantasy, orgasm, masturbation, and other forms of sexual desire and the erotic. Through autobiographical testimonies, these women delve into a variety of issues important to their lives and communities. I believe these narratives call for attention for a variety of reasons, not the least of which is that "research examining how desire is actually conveyed through language in social life is rare" (Cameron and Kulick 2003, 108).

Yet, it seems important to grant that some of the same concerns second-wave feminists have expressed regarding *The Vagina Monologues* would seemingly apply to *Yoni Ki Baat*. One might ask, does such a focus on sex positivity too easily equate sex with power? Do performances like these inadvertently promote the sexualization of women or do they open the parameters for feminist activism? Do they address the politics of sex, sexuality, and sexual violence at a systemic or institutional level? Or do they value personal empowerment over collective social activism? These certainly are interesting points to consider.

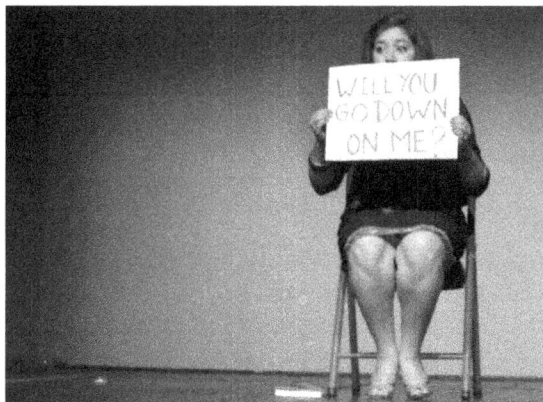

Madison Yoni ki Baat
performance. Photo
credited to Madison
Yoni ki Baat directors.

However, I will argue that such claims become problematic when they are considered with an understanding of South Asian and South Asian diasporic cultural contexts. As Gupta (2001, 3–4) points out, in South Asia, there has been more than a "conspiracy of silence" regarding sexuality. For example, the discourse management of female bodies was crucial to several political projects, from British colonialism to Indian nationalism. These discourses continue to find purchase in conservative communities in the diaspora. Given these historical legacies for South Asian American women, developing a space to discuss sexuality in positive and personal ways may be crucial to a feminist agenda.

In addressing needs of local communities, I believe South Asian Sisters' work also suggests that performance offers us important ways to be-with-others. These are ways that create time and space for talk and deliberation about the problems we face in public and domestic spheres. Theater provides opportunities to envision new ways that justice, equality, peace, and democracy might take root and flourish in our everyday lives. It holds the potential to create moments in which people, as part of an audience, can connect emotionally with those around them. As Dolan (2005) aptly notes, "performance creates ever-new publics, groups of spectators who come together for a moment and then disperse out across a wide social field, sometimes (hopefully) sharing the knowledge they gained, the emotions and insights they experienced at the theater" (90).

My exploration of these concerns begins with a spotlight upon the origins of the *Yoni Ki Baat* movement, focusing on South Asian Sisters' advocacy work and its connection to other South Asian American feminist projects. To reflect upon the potential of *Yoni Ki Baat*, I then offer an ethnographic account of a specific performance by a South Asian American feminist activist and scholar named Roopa Singh.[3] Taking place in 2006 at Club Ambrosia in San Francisco, her spoken-word poem addresses the topic of sexual violence in the family and makes visible in the public sphere what has often been considered unspeakable, even in the private sphere, in South Asian communities (Dasgupta 2007).

Roopa makes calls for acknowledgment through a riveting spoken-word poem that features an eclectic style blending Hindi and English languages, hip-hop and Sanskrit form, as well as events and figures from the *Mahabarata* and her personal life. Her calls for acknowledgment extend to her relationship with the audience—drawing them closer, in a call-and-response exchange after revealing particularly difficult details about her experiences of sexual violence. "Are you with me?" she asks. Then audience members are called upon to respond, "Yes, I am." It seems to me that within this dynamic movement a reluctance to publicly address and support survivors of sexual violence is challenged by a public experience of what I call "passionate acknowledgment." That is, passionate acknowledgment within this performance supports both a relational space and a space in which to explore questions of relationality. Working within this framework, I ask how performances, like Roopa's, may constitute affective networks of social relations and contribute to "intimate citizenship" (Pollock 2005). Finally, I conclude by focusing on the proliferation of *Yoni Ki Baat* performances, especially in the Midwest. In particular, I look at attempts to balance creating a strictly South Asian American event, as opposed to women who are interested in creating more of a multiracial forum.

South Asian Sisters

As I mentioned in chapter 1, in 1995, I began working with two small autonomous women's organizations in Gujarat, India—Sahiyar and Olakh—who use street performances to address issues like domestic abuse, dowry death, or sex-selection abortion (Garlough 2007, 2008). I wondered if similar performance practices were used by South Asian feminist groups in the United States as ways of advancing progressive political agendas. My investigations led me to San Francisco and the South Asian Sisters. Founded by Mauli Daas in 1999, the South Asian Sisters is a grassroots collective, comprised of a diverse group of politically progressive South Asian American women and dedicated to empowering the South Asian American community "to resist all forms of oppression through art, dialogue, conscious alliances, and grassroots political action" (http://sasisters.blogspot.com/).

In several respects, they share commonalities with many of the South Asian women's organizations that arose in the 1980s and 1990s in the United States like New York's Asian Indian Women in America, founded in 1980 or New Jersey's *Manavi*, founded in 1985. These early activists often had high levels of education, professional accomplishment, and economic resources. Frequently their mission began with a rejection of dichotomized notions of tradition and modernity and a challenge to mainstream feminism (Das Gupta 2006). Moreover, these groups understood the importance of political partnerships. As a result, they were open to male participation and alliances with other progressive groups across ethnic and racial lines. For most groups, their areas of interest revolve around advocacy work that approached women's issues (domestic abuse, age inequity, civil rights struggles, immigration law reform, etc.) from a gendered perspective.

These leaders were often skilled orators, and used literature, art, and scholarship as their medium of expression. Focusing on local community issues, with an eye toward the global, these women's groups sponsored film nights, concerts, dances, and community forums. In this effort to build their own feminist agenda, they showed the ways gender intersects with colonialism and social and economic hierarchies, and aligned themselves theoretically with Third World women's movements and women of color in the United States (Maira 2002). Consequently, the coming together of South Asian feminism and progressive South Asian communities in the United States was not chance. Rather, these organizations consciously drew attention to the ways South Asian women's feminist agendas grew from and moved among cultures. As Madhulika S. Khandelwal (1995) notes,

> For a long time, Asian American women have been depicted like other American immigrant and minority women, as having linear stories of empowerment after arriving in the United States. According to this perspective, women in Asia are uniformly subservient and powerless persons who learn to struggle for women's rights because of their being in a Western society. Such an approach not only treats gender in Asia in an ahistorical fashion, decontextualizing it from socioeconomic and political changes over several millennia, but also ignores the complex realities of immigration, racism, sexism, class, and cultural issues faced by minorities in the United States. (351)

These general features of South Asian women's organizations are certainly apparent in the South Asian Sisters' work. As their name suggests, the group works toward constituting a feminist identity that reflects a productive tension between feminist notions of "sisterhood" and multiple sites of South Asian American identity. "Rather than assuming an enforced commonality of oppression, the practice of solidarity foregrounds communities of people who have chosen to work and fight together. Diversity and difference are central values here—to be acknowledged and respected, not erased in the building of alliances" (Mohanty 2003, 7). Indeed, the name itself is meant to produce certain rhetorical effects, calling attention to its own use. As Vandana Makker, a founding member of South Asian Sisters, told me, their choice of the word "sister" is meant to evoke a figure of friendship, as opposed to references to an androcentric ethnic, religious, or national group. Yet, the name also works rhetorically to gesture toward their positionality as South Asian.

Moreover, as another South Asian Sister named Anjali commented, this choice also emphasizes the ways that women are always divided by issues related to race, class, and cultural norms. It provokes inquiry into second-wave feminist contentions that "sisterhood is global"—a perspective that has been critiqued as a form of essentialism that assumes homogeneity among a diverse group of women. Instead, South Asian Sisters grounds its work in a commitment to embracing multiple ways of being "a woman" or "sister" that refuse containment within a fixed category—a sense of community and political activism that advocates for a future based upon respect through care. This works to keep the question of "sisterhood" or "South Asian" provocatively open in ways that contribute to a politics of reflection.

South Asian Sisters is about providing a safe space for Desi women to express their desires, frustrations, and whatever else makes them who they are as individuals. We have a book club, we have performances, we have lunchtime discussions and workshops, we have political and social campaigns, and we are open to having much more. Perhaps most controversially, we have rage. Certainly not all of us get worked up about the same things, as was probably best reflected in this year's production of *Yoni ki Baat*. Many of the pieces seemed to conflict with each other: what some women found deeply offensive, others embraced and reclaimed, and yet others thought to be relatively trivial. That diversity is what makes us whole, human, and multi-dimensional. There is no singular identity for a "South Asian Sister." But what does unite us is a common struggle to find empowerment as South Asians and as women. We, along with our Desi brothers, stand up against atrocities committed against our community—whether they be political repression, racism in general, or stereotyping in the media. But we, as Desi sisters, also stand up against atrocities committed against women—whether they are committed by the government, by the media, or, or more tragically in my opinion, by our own brothers. (http://www.southasiansisters.org/)

South Asian Sisters' political outreach work also involves occasional public-speaking engagements, discussion and reading groups, as well as an active Web site and blog where interested audiences can chat about everyday issues important to the South Asian community and network with other politically oriented groups. For example, in their political work, South Asian Sisters has collaborated with local groups such as Trikone (an LBGTQ organization for people of South Asian descent), or Narika and Maitri (groups that support victims of domestic violence in the South Asian community). They also join forces with national groups that engage in social justice and human rights campaigns. In the spring of 2006, South Asian Sisters joined with SAALT to campaign for immigration law reform. On their Web site, South Asian Sisters issued public statements detailing their belief that immigration reform is absolutely necessary to protect against civil rights violations (April 6, 2006). Through this statement, they publicly aligned themselves with other South Asian progressive groups like Adhikaar (New York), Desist (San Francisco), Desis Rising Up and Moving (New York City), Manavi (New Jersey), Raksha (Atlanta), South Asian Progressive Action Collective (Chicago), and South Asian Network (Los Angeles) to engage in what Monisha Gupta characterizes as *unruly behavior*. In this way, each year South Asian Sisters has grown to meet the emerging needs of community. Together, these organizations "simultaneously address the inadequacies of the state, their communities, and the larger social movements of which they are a part" (Gupta 2006, 9).

Yoni Ki Baat

Yoni Ki Baat is a central piece of South Asian Sisters' activism. It features an original and ever-evolving script that is written and performed by South Asian women from diverse social and cultural backgrounds. Inspired by the first South Asia performance of *The Vagina Monologues*, which took place in Bangalore, India, in 2002, it has sought to provide "groundbreaking, moving, and passionate" performances from diasporic perspectives. Certainly the ability of feminist performance to create social change in local communities and the broader public sphere has been the subject of academic debate. In her book *Presence and Desire: Essays on Gender, Sexuality, and Performance*,

Dolan (1993) wonders about the efficacy of collective, grassroots feminist theater. Many would argue that few movements in contemporary theater have been as significant as feminist theater (Case 2008). However, Dolan expresses concern that perhaps grassroots feminism and the theater it inspired in the 1960s "can no longer communicate in a postmodern era that deprecates the local while appealing to some superficial imperialist sense of the global through communication technologies" (14). In this historical moment, she rightly questions whether local or grassroots theater performances provide an alternative sense of the global in a way that contests the often essentialistic representations found in mass media environments. She also worries that "too often political theater work either seems hopelessly nostalgic or naïve, or it can't adequately address the multiple sites of oppression at which any radical politics has to work" (14).

For those interested in alternative forms of local political activism, these are certainly legitimate concerns. Indeed, they are the very concerns that have stimulated South Asian Sisters' production of *Yoni ki Baat* for the past nine years. Through their annual performance, this grassroots feminist organization seeks to confront social issues at a local level, reaching across multiple sites of oppression related to gender, sexual orientation, race, class, and national affiliation. It has done so while providing alternative representations of South Asians in America that are unavailable through mass media, and by offering perspectives from the margins of the margins. In so doing, they have gained a sizable following, drawing audiences in the hundreds.

Yoni ki Baat and Eve Ensler's Gift

It seems to me that one of *Yoni ki Baat's* important contributions is the way that it implicitly addresses postcolonial feminist critiques of Eve Ensler's *The Vagina Monologues*. With the permission and support of Ensler, the South Asian Sisters "took the underlying messages of that show: women's rights, female sexuality, voicing the taboo in a quest to end domestic violence, and made it personal to our South Asian community" (Assisi 2007, 1). To understand why this critical appropriation is significant, one must grasp the mission and scope of Ensler's project. At its core, *The Vagina Monologues* is a series of first-person narratives in which women reflect upon their relationship to their vaginas, often connecting it to sexual experience and gender identity. The scripts are a mix of fictional narratives that often rely heavily upon extended verbatim quotes from Ensler's interviews with more than two hundred women about their sexuality, sexual practices, and experiences with sexual violence (Ensler 1998). In these performances, audiences encounter a range of voices, distinguished by age, race, ethnicity, region, class, and sexual orientation. The monologues seem to be grounded in the consciousness-raising practices found in the second wave of feminism in the 1960s.[4]

The power of *The Vagina Monologues* also stems from its explicitly political stance on violence against women. Across the globe, the script is performed annually near Valentine's Day to raise awareness about various forms of violence and generate funds for domestic abuse hotlines, women's shelters, and feminist organizations. For example, proceeds from V-Day in India are used by women's organizations to confront, "domestic violence, female infanticide, acid attacks, and dowry related deaths" (http://www.vday.org).

These performances also facilitate outreach and seek to build bridges *between* Western and Third World feminists. For instance, in March 2004, Eve Ensler, Jane Fonda, and Marisa Tomei joined a cast of Indian and Pakistani actresses for eight sold-out shows of *The Vagina Monologues* and *Necessary Targets* in Himachal Pradesh, Mumbai, and Delhi.[5] Still, despite all the popular acclaim attributed to *The Vagina Monologues* and the political work in which it engages, serious critiques have been raised regarding both the performances' form and content (Frueh 2003).

Critiques of *The Vagina Monologues*

In terms of form, some feminist scholars express concern about the monologue as a rhetorical option. For example, Christine M. Cooper (2007) argues that through monologues audiences are offered what appears to be "direct access" to voices and experiences, while this certainly is not the case. Moreover, she expresses concern that, "in both their form and their content, the monologues reduce their speakers to versions of the same, whatever the patina of diversity adorning their surface" (729) This critique relates not only to essentialism in terms of sexual orientation and practices, but to race and ethnicity as well (Bell and Reverby 2005). For instance, some have argued that within *The Vagina Monologues*, alternative forms of sexuality are excluded or treated superficially. Rather than explore these alternatives, the philosophy of sex positivity is used for its commercial value and made generic in its orientation. In this process, consciousness-raising becomes a rite of passage that ends when the curtain closes, rather than being a prelude to talk. Others also contend that there is not enough diversity in terms of voices from the Third World. As Meiling Cheng (2002) notes, "It is intriguing to consider how the 'vagina experiences' of 200 mostly American women might speak to women as diverse in origins as a Masai village in Kenya, Paris, Beijing, as the V-Day Web site proclaims. In TMV and V-Day, the anatomical female body—encapsulated in the vagina—is proclaimed as the universal site for women's solidarity regardless of class, ethnicity, and religion. As such, the diverse experiences of women become essentialized" (327). As Ayeshah from the Madison, Wisconsin, *Yoni ki Baat* observes,

> I had the opportunity to participate in the UW Madison production of Eve Ensler's *Vagina Monologues* in 2006. I was given the role of an Iraqi woman who had her face destroyed in the U.S. bombings. I accepted the role because I wanted to make a statement about the U.S. invasion of Iraq and how detrimental it was to the daily lives of the Iraqi civilians, especially women and children. I realized however, that my monologue did not feature the voice of the Iraqi woman herself, but that of her father. I don't remember the exact lines, but I remember that the monologue was written in third person. Eve Ensler was observing the father who hated his daughter because he could not marry her off now that her face was destroyed. The line went something like, "he hated the planes, which dropped fire from the sky, he hated the soldiers . . . but right now, he hated his needy, helpless daughter more." There were two other cast members who were women of color. They performed monologues featuring a Pakistani woman whose husband burns her face with acid and a Mexican maquiladora. Both these monologues did not foreground the voices of these women. Instead, the Pakistani woman's monologue is in her husband's voice. It shows how he hates his wife and in a fit of anger, beats her mercilessly with his belt and throws acid on her face. In the maquiladora's monologue, Ensler imagines where these women have disappeared. There is another optional monologue about an Afghani woman . . . titled "Under the Veil." I was actually angry after reading that piece because it further exoticizes these women, giving them no agency. Again, Ensler imagines how it must feel like being hidden and oppressed behind the veil. I read Ensler's monologues through the lens of South Asian postcolonial literature, especially Gayatri Spivak's writings, except in this case, Ensler was the Western woman trying to save third world women from their men. It is not that patriarchy does not exist. It does and I am a staunch defender of women's human rights. But Ensler's focus on oppression alone makes the monologues a little too one-sided. Where were the voices of third world women, of women of color, of minorities? It wasn't that they . . . or rather . . . we (I count myself in the category) didn't have a voice, it

Madison Yoni ki Baat performance. Photo credited to Marisa Sarto. Courtesy of Madison Yoni ki Baat directors.

was just that we didn't have an organized platform from which we could express ourselves.

The Emergence of *Yoni ki Baat*

Yoni ki Baat was conceptualized by South Asian Sisters as a reaction to such critiques. Staged annually in university auditoriums or intimate local venues, the performance creates an atmosphere of grassroots community activism, rather than just a theatrical performance. That is, it provides a forum for South Asian American women who are interested in sharing narratives that offer audiences a sense of the diverse ways of being and becoming a South Asian woman. Unlike *The Vagina Monologues*, each year scripts for the performance are solicited anew through a national call. In addition, scripts from previous years are compiled and kept on file for future performers to access.

The audiences, from the first year onward, have been an integral part of the performance, helping to create the message and the meaning of the event. Typically, one evening is open to the public and at this event spectators tend to be quite differentiated across lines of class, religion, sexual orientation, age, and gender, although most would identify with some form of South Asian heritage. Another evening is often set aside exclusively for women to attend, in the hopes of creating a women-centered space for political and personal exploration. In each case, the dynamic between performers and audience members helps to create the understanding of sexuality that emerges. For example, as Vandana said, "The performances, which were held at the UC-Berkeley campus in July 2003 were extremely powerful in that they brought together the dynamism of the pieces, the performers, *and* the audience. Nineteen women took turns performing before a five-hundred-plus audience, in a show that broke the barriers our culture often unwittingly creates for us" (South Asian Sisters 2004, 1). The excitement of both the performers and the audience was palpable, observes South Asian Sisters' member Maulie: "I thought it was overwhelming. It was like we all came out of the closet at the same time—the writers, performers, and the audience. We all were standing up for the yoni, whether it was just by our presence or our serious involvement. I have never, ever been in a more supportive environment on that grand of a scale in my entire life" (South Asian Sisters 2004, 1).

Within *Yoni ki Baat*, there exists a wide range of poetic forms that vary from straightforward autobiographical narratives to songs to spoken-word poetry. The performances reflect the diversity of experiences for South Asian American women, in terms of immigration/citizenship status, ethnicity, or LGBTQ affiliation. Some pieces are intensely personal and signal a sense of anger or suffering, while others are more celebratory or comedic. These performances tend to revolve around important sites of inquiry to the South Asian Sisters. For example, how does conceptualizing the notion of "woman" necessarily involve an appreciation of the intersectionalities that shape women's social and political lives? Other sets of questions revolve around traditional South Asian views on gender roles, sexuality, kinship traditions, and arranged marriages and intergenerational conflicts. Consequently, a common concern for exploration involves the ways South Asian American women are perceived as being "at risk" sexually, until they are married. In addition, the topic of sexual violence continues to be at the core of many performances, with concerns ranging from rape to incest. Moreover, there is significant attention to the often-unspoken problem of domestic abuse in diasporic households.

Attending these performances invokes thought-provoking critiques of Western feminist discourse and their theorizing about women from the Global South. For example, while exploring the question, "What is the color of my yoni?" a number of performers simultaneously ask, "Are we really all the same on the inside?" How might we balance the political necessity of forming strategic coalitions across lines of race, class, and nation and a serious consideration of "difference" as we work toward sisterhood? Moreover, what are the effects of discursively creating a singular or monolithic figure of the "Third World woman" that elides the cultural heterogeneity of women here and abroad?

In a related vein, some performances pose questions about diasporic understandings of South Asian sexuality or eroticism and focus upon problems related to the discursive creations of "the exotic Other" and Kama Sutra stereotypes. Other performances are related to inquiries regarding sex positivity and desire—a perspective upon sexuality that embraces consensual activities and experimentation as healthy and pleasurable. In all cases, sexuality is not simply accepted without thoughtful examination; instead, performers explore it based upon their situated cultural perspective. For example, one might ask, "Do you have to love your yoni to be a feminist?"

Indeed, is loving one's yoni a feminist act? This critically engaging question was posed by Vandana Makker in her 2006 *Yoni Ki Baat* performance. Her monologue truly explores, rather than simply celebrates, one of the central questions underpinning this event. She begins her performance by stating,

> So, anyone that knows me knows that my favorite television show is . . . (Audience yells "Sex in the City"). Thank you. Yes, that is correct. I watch this show endlessly . . . So, I was watching the episode where Charlotte, who if you are not familiar with this show, is the prissy, optimistic, romantic one of the bunch. She admits to her friends that she has never looked closely at her vagina. That, in fact, she thinks it is ugly. The other girls are horrified and insist that she take a look at her nether regions immediately. Eventually Charlotte does take a look and she finds herself transfixed. Now even though I think I'm more Carrie than Charlotte, I could definitely relate. I have never looked closely at my vagina. I don't really find it worth looking at. I too find it upsetting and vaginas in general ugly. And then I couldn't help but wonder. Do you have to love vaginas to be a feminist? . . . We have brains, we have livers, we have stomachs. But you wouldn't find it unusual or unfeminist if a woman found those parts of her body unattractive . . . Anyway my point is that just because I think vaginas are ugly doesn't mean that I don't value them. I do. I'm extremely proud to have one. But you will not find me aiming my pussy in a mirror any time soon . . .

This is just one example of the critical discourse on sexuality that appears in *Yoni Ki Baat*.

Without a doubt, the range of discourses is diverse. Some women offer emotional autobiographical testimony that describes their experience of being chastised or physically abused by parents when it is discovered they are sexually active before marriage. Still others celebrate their first orgasm, experience masturbating, or journey to an S&M club. Some explore aspects of their queer racialized body or experiences of giving birth. And others delve into questions that relate directly to women's experiences in South Asia, such as the connection between sexual violence and nationalism.

Roopa: Critical Scholar, Spoken-Word Poet, and Grassroots Activist

Here, I wish to explore, in particular, the role of "passionate acknowledgment" in diasporic life narratives that ask us to bear witness to testimonies of personal trauma. To do so, the next portion of this chapter is devoted to an analysis of Roopa's performance of "Surviving Childhood Sexual Abuse in the Family" at the 2006 *Yoni ki Baat*. This event was held at Amnesia, a trendy bar in the Mission District of San Francisco. Long before the show was scheduled to begin, the dimly lit performance venue was packed to capacity with a young progressive—primarily South Asian—audience comprised of community members, family, friends, colleagues, allies from Trikone, and strangers. Not surprisingly, the crowd was also, for the most part, women. The performers mingled among the audience, identifiable only by their various red and black outfits that ranged from Indian churidars to slinky red cocktail dresses to black trousers, tank top, and tie. I arrived with my video camera and notebook and took in the scene. Young hipsters with drinks in hand mingled, while the organizers of the event checked the sound equipment and stage set up. Absent any seating, I decided to stand to the side of the stage next to Vandana's partner who was serving as the event's photographer. I had heard rave reviews of Roopa's performance abilities from other South Asian Sisters, so I was looking forward to the show.

Like many South Asian feminists, Roopa describes herself as a performer, scholar, and social activist, making no distinction among these roles. She is connected intellectually to a long line of notable South Asian feminists, like Malini Bhattacharya, who see the "necessary and integral connection between feminist scholarship, political practice, and organizing" (Mohanty 1988, 61). Her contribution to contemporary debates within critical cultural media studies, political science, and feminist theory grows from her grassroots activism on the behalf of marginalized and diasporic communities, as well as her interest in forming strategic coalitions across race, class, and national boundaries. She has been an outspoken advocate—from courtrooms to comedy clubs—not only for immigrant rights but also for survivors of sexual abuse, often employing eclectic performances as a means to draw attention to her cause. As she noted in one correspondence, this eclecticism grows from her experiences in the diaspora. She wrote, "at home and through the funnel of my parents, my life was Indian, Indian parties, bhajans, temples, Indian food, Indian music. At school, with friends, through music and books, and in particular hip-hop, my childhood experiences were influenced by an array of cultures. This duality, broken into so many parts, made for a powerful mosaic. My cultural backgrounds, with an s, all played a role in my childhood experiences."

In an interview in Chicago, several months after this performance, Roopa told me that she began working as a grassroots advocate with an AIDS foundation at an early age, focusing on harm reduction for sex workers and drug addicts in her local California community. Her developing interest in human rights and social justice issues led her to pursue a law degree at the University of California, Berkeley, specializing in First Amendment violations, as well as sexual violence against women. This expertise led her to an internship at National Public Radio in which she was engaged at the Supreme Court. Not satisfied with confining justice work to a courtroom, she created a blog called political poet(ry) where she posts poetry, social commentary, and short essays to respond to current news events from a South Asian feminist perspective. On the weekends, her performances of slam poetry and stand-up comedy draw audiences interested in issues of race, ethnicity, sexuality, and gender. During the week, her classrooms at universities are filled with students studying politics and culture, and her hip-hop yoga courses draw people interested in self-development and cultural connection.

In this conversation, she commented that this work and its connection to performance is somewhat of a natural choice, as she comes from a long line of conscientious objectors and community advocates:

How I came to do what I do is build bridges and mine for questions . . . What I do is I share (a.k.a. perform) aliveness to audiences. There is a way that the justice figurehead has functioned as a storyteller and as orator from ancient times to now. My grandfather in India was a lawyer and was also consulted for spiritual guidance, and his ability to fight landowners on behalf of the people. So, how I came to do as I do, well, I've always [performed]—even as a child I pretended to teach—and now what I do is teach . . . as one arm of an overall strategy of building bridges and mining for questions. I feel like in this era it's crucial that we focus on the creation of questions, more so even than revealing answers. I try to insert the questioning ability or critical eye. (Personal interview, 2007)

While she sometimes regards what she is doing as "performing a lifeline," she also points out the ways that performance is a fraught word for her. "I don't like the word 'perform'; I just think it's over used . . . So lately I have been using the word *sharing*. I think *invitation* is a beautiful word too, to be able to invite, hosting an experience." This is difficult work, she maintains, "It's no wonder it's hard to be an artist, it requires people to feel, you're watching a human being practicing being alive in different ways than you are and there are reasons people are alive in all those ways and it's hard to be one of them" (personal interview, 2007). In order to honor the difficulty of her work, the sensitive nature of the issues at hand, and the depth of the feelings at stake, Roopa and I spent a good deal of time talking about the process we were engaging in together. During visits, over the phone, and in e-mails, we discussed our approaches to activism and art, our families and our future research plans. We talked about my positionality vis-à-vis this research. Did my commitment to feminist pedagogy extend beyond the classroom? Yes. Had I worked in community center contexts? Yes. Was I a survivor of sexual violence? No. What might that mean for our ability to understand one another? Sometimes we disagreed about issues at stake but we seemed to agree upon the importance of speaking one's truth and actively working to maintain a level of trust and transparency. For example, we explicitly discussed the options for how she wished to be represented—a pseudonym? her first name? or her first and last name? In the end, she chose to use her first and last name.

Often central to the challenges confronting Roopa when she shares her experiences with others from the stage is the very nature of the phenomenon she is sharing—the difficulties of being a survivor of sexual violence. It is a sensitive topic not often addressed in the South Asian community at large but consistently present in *Yoni Ki Baat* performances throughout the years. The struggle of living with a history of sexual abuse stems not simply from the weight silence or emotional toll takes upon the individual or family. In addition, women often feel that their stories of sexual violence do not merit public notice. As Cvetkovich points out, "Sometimes the impact of sexual trauma doesn't seem to measure up to that of collectively experienced historical events, such as war or genocide. Sometimes it seems invisible because it is confined to the domestic or private sphere. Sometimes it doesn't appear sufficiently catastrophic because it doesn't produce dead bodies or even, necessarily, damaged ones" (Cvetkovich 2003, 3).

By no means is Roopa the only performer to explore these issues. Indeed, the topic has been addressed in almost every *Yoni ki Baat* performance I have attended. All of these concerns are explored, for example, in Anjali's 2003 *Yoni Ki Baat* performance of "Get Your Hands Out of My Vagina"—a personal account that describes a relative who preys sexually upon young women in his family's household. Everyone knew, she relates, but nobody ever said, "Get your hand out of my vagina." This silence emboldens him and it was years before anyone was able to name his abuse. So, as Anjali's eloquent performance concludes, the volume of her voice begins to rise and she shouts into the microphone, "Today I have the courage to say . . . get your fucking hands out of my vagina." The audience—filled to capacity with a diverse set of South Asian Americans, as well as other community members and friends—was visibly moved to shock or tears and clapped vigorously as she held their gaze before leaving the stage.

The Toronto-based psychotherapist Smita Vir Tyagi (2007) highlights some of the cultural challenges facing discussion of childhood sexual violence in this diasporic context. "When people talk about sexual molestation by family, they don't talk about *zabardasti*, which is 'force'—a person forced you to do this or that. Sometimes they use a kind of minimizing language like *chherchhaar*, which means 'a little bit here and there,' 'pushing and shoving,' playful kinds of things. This language doesn't allow you to get the sense of how serious and how intrusive it is, and what a deep violation this is" (Poore 2007, 111). With no name for this type of sexual abuse, women and girls are faced with the difficulty of trying to describe a violent event in language that misrepresents the experience as noncoercive sexual play. Those who perpetrate this violence, choosing to gratify themselves at the expense of someone with very little or no power to give or withdraw consent, often take advantage of family connections. This sense of family connection is somewhat different from that in the West, so that in South Asian households, the notion of "family" includes "current and past family friends, frequent visitors to the house, distant cousins, and houseguests who may or may not be biologically related or even closely connected to the family." Consequently, "children experience ICSA [intrafamilial childhood sexual abuse] in these settings because perpetrators' access to them is made possible by their access to familiar and familial spheres" (Poore 2007, 107). Equally important, during abuse and in its aftermath, silences prevail because survivors recognize perpetrators as belonging to the very context in which they have experienced violence.

For many South Asian American women, divulging their experience becomes even more complicated due to the cultural stigma associated with inappropriate sexuality, sexual desire, and sexual pleasure. "To talk about sexual abuse without conjuring up images of pain and injury opens the door for all kinds of insidious accusations, including, 'You liked it, that's why you didn't try to stop it' or 'don't pretend you didn't enjoy it,' which re-victimizes victims. In many cases, only years after the abuse has stopped, survivors are finally able to articulate why they felt forced into the situation" (Poore 2007, 110). Moreover, protecting the family through bearing suffering in silence is a culturally valorized practice (Das 2007). This silence only further perpetuates the sense within the South Asian American community that incest is not a serious community issue. Indeed, most South Asians react with skepticism when the problem of sexual violence in the family is associated with the community. It runs counter to myths of sexual abusers as strangers, or the mentally ill, rather than the "well-known" perpetrators that are often involved in these types of crimes. "The South Asian immigration story makes no room for images of South Asians as perpetrators of domestic violence or child abuse. Instead, members of the community strive to project a model minority status, which for survivors . . . conflicts with daily lived reality" (Poore 2007, 117). Indeed, it seems to me this daily disconnect between lived reality and social appearances was, in part, what led Roopa to engage in such activist performance.

Roopa's Performance

At the 2006 performance of *Yoni Ki Baat*, Roopa not only performed "Surviving Childhood Sexual Abuse in the Family" but also took on the role of *Yoni ki Baat* MC. Taking the stage in a traditional South Asian churidar and sneakers, her presence elicited an immediate and positive response from the audience who cheered wildly and shouted words of encouragement.

Roopa began the program by framing it in terms of testimony and witnessing practices, enjoining the audience members to listen carefully and compassionately to the stories they were about to encounter and know that this respect was going to be returned in kind.

> *Yoni Ki Baat* is important for a lot of different reasons and I want to encourage everyone here to know that we honor you. And that we feel the way that you are honoring us by bearing witness. Anajli used the word diversity. Diversity is kind of a played out word in the Bay Area. Am I right? Am I right? Am I right? (Audience applauds and some shout "Yes!") But what we are talking about actually is a type of diversity. It's the many

different faces a South Asian woman can have. It's the many different ways of being creative that a South Asian woman can hold. So thank you for bearing witness to something that we don't see in mainstream American media. So this in a way is alternative media. So thank you for bearing witness. Get ready for a great show.

The audience clapped loudly in response to Roopa's opening—both an invitation and a welcome—that laid the groundwork for the potential of resonance between performers and audience members (Wikan 1992). What struck me was the way her words and presence on the stage made a compelling call for the compassion and critical reflection that sought to foster passionate acknowledgment. In this moment, she quite explicitly exhibited care for audience members and illustrated ways that they might acknowledge her as well. This opening was designed to hold the potential for building trust, mutual concern, and connectedness.

In the section that follows, I want to offer the reader a long excerpt from Roopa's performance of her poem, "Surviving Childhood Sexual Abuse in the Family." As I mentioned in the introduction, such a strategy on my part is meant to keep her voice present and highly visible in this chapter. As I do so, I pay close attention to three central issues: (1) her self-positioning as a diasporic feminist activist and scholar; (2) the ways her diasporic identity contributes to her sense of sexual violence and self-care; and (3) how she reconceptualizes the traditional notion of dharma into a feminist response to violence in the family.

"Surviving Childhood Sexual Abuse in the Family"

So my name is Roopa. I grew up in San Diego. I was one of three Indians, and I mean Indians, no other South Asians, in a graduating high school class of a thousand. So figuring out my cultural identity has always been a process. Now, right about this moment, many desis in the audience are wanting to ask me, so where were you born? For some reason this question gets asked of me like all the time. Strangers come up to me . . . like where were you born? . . . Because it seems to matter. But I don't really think it does. I think that we all form our cultural identity as we go. So this is one version of one of the stories that I have in my life . . .

So, as the diasporic daughter currently on stage will you engage in some call and response with me for this piece? Is that okay? (audience responds enthusiastically). So when I say "I am," will you say "with you," so that I know that you're there with me. So let's give it a try . . . "I am" (audience responds and replies, "With you," and Roopa smiles and hugs herself. Audience members laugh and murmur amongst themselves).

This piece goes out to Birjinder Anant RIP. (Audience applauds.) And I am doing this in the name of not keeping silent. *Surviving Childhood Sexual Abuse in the Family.* A nice light topic. (The audience laughs.)

How the reasons birthed, learned to fly in to fill in the blanks, and how it could happen. Or why it could happen. How the reasons flew in to tell me how it never happened. Land mine memories glint in the sand. At twenty-eight years old, about to be twenty-nine, I still uncover clues of what was going on in their mind when they did it. Did me. Undid me with a most unfortunate torture.

Reasons. She's American. She was born here, so it's different for her. American girls don't have honor to begin with. Right? They always want sex. It's not rape. They like it. American girls may look Indian sometimes but they're always American on the inside. And American girls don't feel. Reasons. Reasons fly in to fill in the blanks. And even now I find my father pausing when I speak to him in Hindi, and I myself pause before I speak to him in Hindi. I pause because wrapping my tongue and my lips around Hindi feels different, sensual in a different way, and I am aware of my mouth, I am aware of my language. And I am always really aware of not wanting to do anything that could turn him on. He pauses every time I speak Hindi . . . He pauses every time I utter more than a Ram Ram or a Gita ji . . . . He pauses in utter surprise because it makes me more human to him. He forgets every day that I speak and understand his mother tongue. His mother tongue.

My mother tongue. Was forked. It split in two ways. I call her ma. My mom wasn't told much about her culture either. Maybe it was only the men in her Brahmin family that really got to love learning. Maybe caste like class varies within families. Maybe she was treated like a Dalit girl by her Brahmin family and had to pick over her brothers' leftovers. Like I did. Leftover stories, leftover instruments, leftover cultural cues. Even though my mom was born and raised in India, she gets on Google just like me to find the specific meaning of Holi. (Audience laughs.) But she does know every bhajan in the whole fucking world. (Audience laughs.) And as long as you're not her daughter, she'd be willing to teach you some bhajans too. But she won't hardly teach me. "I am." (Audience responds, "With you.") "I am." (Audience responds, "With you.") . . .

My mom has been jealous of me in an unnatural way. Palpable sometimes so thick in the air it makes me nauseous, cut myself gross. My dad loves it when she sings. So singing, that's her turf. So I still don't. And at least in that way, I know I'm being a good daughter.

(Lesson from the *Mahabarath*): White horses thunder a steady gallop. Wind whips time through the tendrils of their manes. The great beasts shoulder a golden chariot running it across the epic tale of a land planted with rows and rows of soldiers. Two sides. Impending battle. Arjun turns to Krishna. Chin trembling, eyes bouncing in time to the beat of the horses racing underneath them. Hey Krishna. Do you understand? Either way, I face unbearable loss. Either way. There's no way out. No matter who wins, we all lose.

Krishna was beatific in his compassionate state, eyes lay low, lashes curled out to meet the blue sky. Lips turned dark with truth's passion. Hey Arjun. Understand? Do I understand? Yes, I understand. And no there is no understanding. All you can do is do what you must. Do. Proceed in battle and don't give up on life . . .

"Reasons Fly In to Fill in the Blanks"

My impression was that in her performance, Roopa is careful to situate this sexual violence within the diaspora. She argues that the "reasons" offered for being sexually assaulted have much to do with immigrant identity and the way one appears within their own community. These reasons, she notes, are about how she is perceived to occupy an "either/or" identity. "Inauthentic" or "tainted" cultural identity becomes an excuse for making sexually violent behavior acceptable. In this process, she is "Othered" beyond recognition. Until, of course, she speaks in Hindi and is seen as "more human" because she can speak and understand this mother tongue.

What struck me was that Roopa not only addresses these "reasons" in terms of her use of Hindi. She acknowledges that her understanding of Indian culture is, to a certain extent, limited. Although she enjoys singing, she does not know many bhajans. Although she likes to participate in Indian festivals, she does not know the meaning of Holi. Yet, she stresses that even her mother does not possess a perfect knowledge of Indian cultural traditions (even though she was born there), and offers a critique by suggesting that such knowing may have more to do with family culture and gender roles.

What interests me most are the ways that Roopa critically plays with the Hindu epic the *Mahabharata* to address "women's issues" in ways not unlike what women have done and still do with folk tales, legends, and epics in India to this day (Garlough 1997; Mills 1985; Narayan 1986; Richman 1991). The *Mahabharata* is one of the longest epic poems, at over 100,000 verses and eighteen books. It explores basic human concerns with personal motives, sensual gratification, sexual fulfillment, righteous duty, virtuous behavior, and the path to liberation and salvation. Roopa references the part of the *Mahabharata* called the *Bhagavad Gita*, which comprises just a few hundred verses, but is viewed by many as a distillation of Hindu philosophy. Translated as *Song of the Divine*, it is told from the perspective of Lord Krishna as he advises Arjun on the battlefield of *Kurukshetra*, just prior to the start of an eighteen-day war. Looking at a battlefield where both sides are lined with family, friends, and teachers, Arjun begins to weep and feels a deep sense of moral confusion. He is loath to fight the people with whom he has close relations—despite their tyranny—for a kingdom he does not particularly want to rule. He feels it might be better to simply give up his weapons and allow himself to be killed because to destroy his family would be the greatest sin of all.

Eventually, Arjun throws down his weapon and refuses to fight. At this point, Krishna and Arjun begin a dialogue in which Krishna advised him to follow the path of right action, knowledge, as well as devotion. The Gita ends with Krishna telling Arjun that as a leader it is his duty to fight for his kingdom absent any personal desire that would lead him to worry about the end result or future consequences. In doing that, the balance of good and evil will be restored, Arjun's dharma will be complete, and by providing selfless service. Arjun understands this and proceeds into battle. For many Hindus, this narrative offers a seminal lesson regarding how to face the struggles of life, live within complicated relationships, do our duty, show leadership, and offer selfless service.

I was struck by the way that Roopa masterfully used the *Bhagavad Gita* as a vital rhetorical and hermeneutic resource and through it figured herself in ways that provides important insight into how she understands the difficulties of being a survivor of sexual abuse. Specifically, what intrigued me was her skill in appropriating key figures and elements of the *Bhagavad Gita's* plot. Just like Arjun, who finds himself in the impossible situation of having to battle his own family, Roopa acknowledges and asks the audience to acknowledge the "unbearable loss" she is facing. There exists simultaneously a deep love for family and a sense of duty to herself and other survivors—a need to battle what is "right." In the end, "no matter who wins, we all lose." Her answer—like Krishna's—is that all that one can do is what one *must* do, engage in battle and strive to live a just and good life. In this way, it seems to me Roopa's performance attempts to deliver a difficult message without covering or explaining away what remains baffling about it. Such play within performance helps sustain the encounter with the Other and provides a pathway to passionate acknowledgment. It opens the time and space for disclosure, as Roopa's words and body force us to reexamine our assumptions about her, reconsider the categories in which we can easily place her when we do not risk acknowledgment, and recognize her struggles and suffering. That is, such performances offer care through gestures that invite recognition to be compromised a bit in the name of both acknowledgment and inquiry.

Body and Voice

In addition, Roopa's performance addresses silence on two levels: through the visibility of her body, and through poetic discourse that not only identifies a problem and testifies to violence, but offers an account of "a most unfortunate torture." Her body—eclectic and critically playful in a traditional *bindi* and *churidar* paired with a pair of canvas sneakers—helps her to shift and destabilize ethnic identity positioning.

Her presentation speaks to the ease of misrecognition and the fact that visibility is always a negotiated relation between self and Other. This negotiation has two levels: incomplete knowledge the self has of the other and the incomplete knowledge that one has of oneself (Phelan 1993). Roopa draws attention to the fact that she often is misrecognized as someone untouched by sexual abuse just as she can be misrecognized as traditionally Indian in her *bindi* and *churidar* until attention is drawn to her "checked sneaks."

My sense was that Roopa, speaking as a feminist activist, hopes not only to testify to the existence of childhood sexual abuse but also survival. As Ken Plummer (1995) observes, "From many different persuasions, the argument has been made that the stories we tell of our lives are deeply implicated in moral and political change" (144). Members of collective movements use personal narrating to witness forms of terror and trauma, including sexual violence, domestic abuse, political degradation, racism, terrorism, and genocide. Within tribunals and national investigations of human rights offenses, personal witnessing may play a key role in the creation of new rights protections (Schaffer and Smith 2004, 16). Moreover, in Linda Martin Alcoff and Laura A. Gray-Rosendale's (1996) work on sexual violence, they suggest, "A principle tactic adopted by the survivor's movement has been to encourage and make possible survivor's disclosures of our traumas, whether in relatively private or public contexts . . . This strategic metaphor of 'breaking the silence' is virtually ubiquitous throughout the movement . . . speaking out serves to educate the society at large about the dimensions of sexual violence and misogyny; to reposition the problem from the individual psyche to the social sphere, where it rightfully belongs, and to empower victims to act constructively on our own behalf and thus make the transition from passive victim to active survivor" (199–200).

These acts of bearing witness, like Roopa's spoken-word poem, have been understood in a variety of ways. First, some see them as a sacred responsibility, related both etymologically and historically to martyrdom (Sommer 1995, 197). To tell a story of suffering and to be heard by others can be gratifying because it allows one to address the significance of their experience. Yet, often it is also painful. As Felman (1992) claims, these memories awakened for a public purpose can also be a "radically unique burden that is characterized by the solitude of responsibility" (3). She points toward the words of Elie Wiesel, who said, "If someone else could have written my stories I would not have written them. I have written them in order to testify. And this is the origin of the loneliness that can be glimpsed in each of my sentences, in each of my silences" (Wiesel 1984, 23). In these moments, the burden of the witness is his or her own, despite any alignment with others.

Second, many scholars argue that these stories, as Roopa does, has some therapeutic value in helping individuals to work through "horror, gain support from their community, and re-affirm their sense of well-being" (Schneider 2002, 42). In many cases, witnessing is thought to provide a means of giving cognitive and emotional coherence to traumatic experience, as well as aiding in the construction and negotiation of personal and social identity.

Indeed, some argue that this witnessing is more of an obligation than an option. For example, Pollock (2005, 4) contends that performance "enacts what Kelly Oliver calls 'the response-ability in subjectivity' (139): the sense that the ability to respond (response-ability) that inheres in the obligation (responsibility) to do so defines what it means to be a human self . . . Beyond storytellers, we are witnesses. We see each other and we (must) see to each other through the performance of witnessing. Any one self is thus ontologically and ethically inextricable from 'others.'" Moreover, she argues that it is the very dialogic structure of witnessing—grounded in the potential of address and response—that connects witnessing to the performative. That is, to conceive of oneself as a subject is to have the ability to address oneself to another, real or imaginary, actual or potential. Of course, these benefits are tempered by limitations as well. For instance, Alcoff and Gray-Rosen-dale (1996) have written persuasively about the ways the speech of sexual violence survivors has been sensationalized and exploited. Most often, this occurs in the mass media, in journalistic formats, reality TV shows or fic-tionalized dramatic accounts. These outlets tend to employ a confessional structure that, as Foucault argued, disempowers the "confessor" and privi-leges the discourses of the institutional context.

I Am . . . With You . . .

Roopa desires to make clear that survival depends upon social support (an interaction that she hopes will carry forward into the future). Thus, in the initial segments of her performance, Roopa seeks to establish a connection with audience members. Through her gaze and her call for acknowledg-ment—("I Am") and response ("With You")—she establishes an aesthetic and ethic of 'being-together-with' (Pollock 1999) and a sense of relation-ality. The audience in this tightly packed performance venue played along with enthusiasm with call and response. The volume when they responded "With you . . ." was almost deafening and a charge of energy ran through the room. One could palpably feel a sense of connection that had not been there moments earlier. In terms of its use in this performance, Roopa stated:

> Why the call and response? Well, out of an ancient tradition comes a new era of African-based call and response. It is the fabric of protest marches, of cheerleading, of crowd pleasing, of preaching, of hip-hop, and popu-lar education workshop technique. I engage the call and response to feed myself in the moment and to get the people moving with me through a paralyzing issue. (Personal interview 2007)

It seems to me this call and response is a rhetorical strategy—one that consciously connects her with other women of color—that builds relations between the speaker and the audience. It is an invitation to participate in the emerging performance—to be a party to the creation of the testimony. It is a moral act and an ethical gesture; as Hyde (2006) would argue, in listen-ing and being-with-others we "open ourselves to all that others have to say about who and how they are and what they need in order to be saved from the pain and suffering of Being . . . help[ing] set the stage for the goodness of acknowledgment" (16). Listening provides the potential for welcome. As the audience listens to the performer and the performer listens to the audience, they are gathered together in a more intimate proximity to one another. As Dolan (2005) observes, such "intersubjectivity extends beyond the binary of performer-spectator (or even performers-audience) into an affective possibility among members of the audience . . . This moment acknowledges that we all came here to do this, to share our attention, to acknowledge our pleasure, and to hope for our mutual, collective transformation" (42).

Passionate Acknowledgment in the Performance of Suffering

Most research on performance and witnessing engages with the theoretical concept of recognition. As chapter 1 discussed, from classical literature to contemporary political thought, recognition is understood as a "social good"; it is a political and ethical aspiration thought to free individuals and societies from prejudice and ignorance (Ricoeur 2004). Indeed, as Markell (2003) notes, "Aristotle famously declared recognition, *anagnorsis*, to be one of the constitutive elements of the best tragedies. Since then, recognition has been a central concept in poetics and has continued to be an important literary device" (62). Within the field of rhetoric, the noted scholar Tom Farrell, uses the term "passionate recognition" to describe the rhetorical process of recognition that takes place in tragic discourse, from testimony to dramatic performance to eulogy. Drawing primarily upon Aristotle, Farrell argues that, in a general sense, an aesthetic of recognition is a mode of seeing that offers audience members the pleasure of learning (Farrell 1993). That is, audiences find enjoyment in seeing likeness and difference because through this process they obtain information about themselves and the world they inhabit, thus leading to increased understanding. To be truly effective, such recognition must also inherently be related to a feeling of public belonging. He writes, "Where tragedy is concerned, recognition must be accompanied by a sense that one's self-discovery or knowledge is embedded in the human condition" (117). Most importantly, according to Farrell, passionate recognition grows from "the sense that the power of individual action is finite and *this finitude is itself universal*" (116). We all are limited in the ways that we can respond to the contingencies of life. Thus, in performance, the depiction of tragic events awakens fear and pity as audience members encounter characters who cause, contest, recognize, and eventually suffer an unwelcome fate. While in real life this suffering would be intensely disturbing, in staged performances, through the rhetorical aspect of the recognition process, these painful feelings are purged. Over the years, similar accounts of the significance of *katharsis* animated by tragedy have been offered repeatedly in scholarship from anthropology and philosophy to theater and cultural studies (Schechner 1988). More recently, however, critical scholars have offered a different perspective of *katharsis*. Many interested in resistive performances by marginalized groups have noted that a focus upon *katharsis* has limited our ability to explore how testifying about suffering through cultural practices often requires audiences to move beyond "fear and relief" to a continued engagement with the tragedy at hand—to connect with another's pain (and remain with that pain) so that social change might begin (Raheja and Gold 1994).

Building from this perspective, I would like to suggest that the call and response elicited a sense of "passionate acknowledgment"—acknowledgment that takes place in staged performances that employ personal testimony to witness tragic events. In performances characterized by suffering, this "passion" might be understood as one that moves us away from mere *katharsis*. Rather, *passionate acknowledgment* may gesture toward a rhetorical aspect of the acknowledgment process that works to help us to engage others through neighborly love or compassion.

"Passion," as Derrida (2000) notes, has at least seven intertwined meanings ranging from Christian passion linked to a history of human rights and democracy, to the experience of amorous and erotic love, to a form of passion that implies martyrdom and testimony. My sense of "passion" in "passionate acknowledgment" grows from a reading of Arendt's (1929, 1958) work and her exploration of care, love, and human rights. From this perspective, at its core, care is a kind of motion—a movement toward something. In this movement, care or love has many forms. When propelled by desire or craving it manifests as *cupiditas*. In contrast, love as neighborly love—or *caritas*—is a form of care or love that is relational.

I believe calls for passionate acknowledgment in performance contexts, like Roopa's, help to facilitate just this type of care by connecting us not only to specific people or allowing us to "see" them, but by showing us how to care for people in communities or care for people as part of humanity. Everyone who stands in some relation to myself is included in this order of care. Care demands mutual help for the sake of this connection, rather than for a particular person's identity—taking note of differences but caring regardless of them.

I find myself attracted to this idea that passionate acknowledgment in performances, such as Roopa's, helps us to move beyond an us/them or friend/enemy dichotomy to a more complicated place that values dialogue—where people handle public matters from a perspective in which an opponent is not considered an enemy. Through rhetorical acts of acknowledgment, performers address the problems from the perspective of "care." Performers like Roopa show audiences how to respond to others' needs and why they should. They point toward ways to build trust, express concern, and forge connections between people. They encourage people to focus upon their humanity as they make judgments about pressing social matters. In the process, performance may become a way of "being-for others" that creates a context in which audiences engage in ethical listening and exhibit a profound wakefulness toward others, the challenges they face, and the suffering they have experienced.

Therefore, passionate acknowledgment can be understood, in my estimation, as a gift. More specifically, drawing from Mifsud's (2007) work, I would like to envision the process of passionate acknowledgment in performance "not so much as a *gift* but as *giving.*" This giving is an open-ended, reciprocal, participatory process. The performer offers their performance, not only as a means of relaying information about an issue, but also as a request for compassion and an invitation for intersubjective connection. But the offering of the gift appears as a request for acknowledgment that is, as Hyde (2006) argues, a sign that there is something moral happening—something related to the "heart." In this way, this form of acknowledgment attends to the *pathos* through which audience members are gathered, so that ethical relationships can be forged, constraints upon conditions for understanding can be overcome, and work toward social change can be started.

To my mind, passionate acknowledgment in performance contexts is fed by a *pathos* that both offers and requests *welcome*. Hannah Arendt argues that this welcome "refers to the risky inclusion of another in a shared activity, without reference to her identity, or state of character, or degree of merit" (Markell 2003, 180). Interestingly, in response to Arendt's reflections, Markell argues that "to welcome someone says more about the welcomer than the welcomed; it represents the slackening of the urge to convert an uncertain activity into a predictable process by setting and enforcing strict boundaries to participation. Equally important, many times it does not necessarily indicate that the welcomer is full of warmth toward the welcomed" (180). However, it does imply a sense of relationality—something that troubles the tensions and distinctions that underlie our understanding of recognition and acknowledgment.

It seems to me this sense of presence and wakefulness allows for Roopa to tell the truth of her existence and enact a mode of self-care as well. The audience, in their response, shows concern for how Roopa is faring—not only with communicating the larger issues at hand, but also how she is managing the difficult work of acknowledgment. Moreover, this "lingering-with" helps her to exceed a confessional structure; she eliminates the expert mediator and creates a context in which it is replaced by a compassionate audience who is invited to understand her as witness, expert, and theorist of her own experience.

In this case, I read Roopa's admission, "I am in pain" as the conduit through which she is able to escape a sense of inexpressible seclusion. This, of course, does not mean that she will be understood. Yet, as Veena Das (2007) argues, "pain in this rendering is not that inexpressible something that destroys communication or marks an exit from one's existence in language. Instead, it makes a claim on the other—asking for acknowledgment that may be given or denied" (40). Indeed, a critical engagement with this trauma, Roopa argues, requires vulnerability—a vulnerability that allows for such an approach or encounter. As Roopa stated in one of our interviews, "performance requires people to feel. Practicing ways of being alive in different ways than you are. And it's hard to be vulnerable . . . . [So] I don't want to talk about incest without making sure that people [in the audience] are breathing, without making sure that people know they are in a room together with other people and they're safe. And I need to get reminded of that too. There is a kind of isolation that comes with torture. It stays with me. So, particularly on stage, it's a place of connection with the world." And this, I contend, is a space with the potential to engender passionate acknowledgment.

A Day of Dialogue: After the Curtains Rise

Unlike *The Vagina Monologues*, performances of *Yoni Ki Baat* do not end without any promise of continuing conversations about such sensitive topics. For those who choose to participate, South Asian Sisters offers the *Day of Dialogue* as a tandem event to *Yoni Ki Baat*. This occasion is designed to answer questions or further explore issues that may have arisen for audience members and performers during the performance.

The philosophy grounding the *Day of Dialogue* grows partially out of the San Francisco sex-positivity movement—a movement that advocates a reversal of sex-negative attitudes—as well as an affirmation of a culture that would support and foster the expression of sexual desire. This approach goes beyond simply affirming sex as a set of practices. Rather, it promotes working toward positive conceptions of self as a sexual being, as well as the positive exploration of desire and sex. While the sex positivity movement is directed toward American culture more generally, members of South Asian

Sisters have recognized the importance of exploring these issues in the context of the South Asian American community. As Vandana Makker, a former organizer of the event, put it to me in an interview following the 2005 *Yoni ki Baat* performance, "For many South Asian women, sexuality and desire are difficult to discuss. It is ironic because, as the *Kama Sutra* shows, sex was considered a real art in places like India. But in everyday life, social norms for women have required us to be modest, sexually naïve or self-sacrificing." These norms become further complicated in the diasporic experience, with South Asian Americans often feeling compelled to maintain a cultural identity that comes at the expense of desire.

Many times, adolescent girls and women are judged for becoming too "Western" in their behaviors if they are interested in discussing sex or engaging in sexual practices. In families and communities, monitoring sexuality and talk about sexuality becomes a way of sustaining cultural identity. The Day of Dialogue offers a safe space in which to discuss the tensions that arise around sexuality for Desi women. It also functions as a space for women to offer testimony about experiences of sexual violence and provide information about South Asian women's shelters in the Bay Area.

South Asian Sisters' *Day of Dialogue*, held in 2005 at the California Institute for Integral Studies in San Francisco, California, was the event at which I first became acquainted with several core members of South Asian Sisters and their organization's mission. This event was devoted to reflecting upon the vocabulary and the topoi South Asian American women use to speak of their own bodies and desires. Sessions at the Day of Dialogue revolved broadly around the two themes of pleasure and violence, and, more specifically, with issues of sexuality, identity politics, law and human rights, violence, and sexual identity. In a session called "Politics and the Yoni," participants were offered a chance to discuss the ways international and domestic policies shape perceptions of gender and sexuality. As the event pamphlet explained,

> Topics of discussion include, but are not limited to policies and reactions that governments and courts make that affect women's bodies and human rights (reproduction rights, pornography, genital mutilation, rape, prostitution, gay marriage, etc.). We will explore the representation of minority groups in politics and exchange inspirational stories of resistance to learn about strategies for community organizing and for defending our human rights.

Here, women are enjoined to go beyond simplistic modes of consciousness raising. Instead, the goal is to reach a place of talk that provides space allowing for divergence and dispute—a space that confronts its own plurality. For example, in the session, "Nurturing the Yoni," participants explored the potential of sexual desire through discussions of masturbation, fantasy, pleasure, sexual relationships with others, as well as sexual health. In "Violence and the Yoni" leaders provided a safe, confidential space to share experiences of violence, ask questions, and gather resources. Participants were encouraged to "learn more from each other about the disturbing epidemic of violence that girls and women face too much in their relationships (parent/child, same-sex relationships, spousal) and how this violence is justified and perpetuated by many of our institutions" (http://sasisters.blogspot.com). Through experiences of witnessing and testimony, women were encouraged not only to build solidarity in a safe space but also to deliberate upon what they might accomplish through community work and political advocacy. The Day of Dialogue concluded with an opportunity for "Open Sharing" in which women performed life narratives, poetry, songs, and readings together—a space and time of artistic testimony and witnessing organized to facilitate both personal growth and political action.

Curtains Rising Again in the Midwest

As events like *Yoni Ki Baat* or the *Day of Dialogue* suggest, they are willing to build upon "old bones" of sisterhood and feminism to gain attention for issues that intrigue, anger, or delight them. Yet, they also are not troubled by the process of critiquing the work of second- and third-wave feminists and inventing new ways of approaching exigencies or events from a diasporic feminist perspective.

Across the country, new productions of *Yoni Ki Baat* are forming. From Chicago to Ann Arbor to Madison, these women are beginning to work together to create time and space that allows for political discourse to emerge, creative invention to be nurtured, issues to be debated, feelings to be expressed, friendships to be formed, and diverse groups of people to be passionately acknowledged. For example, Swati from the University of Wisconsin-Madison noted:

I have spent the last couple of years (specifically within a university setting) organizing around multicultural womyn's issues. However, after spending a majority of my time growing up on stage and two years running and working on the staff of a multicultural art and literature magazine, I still didn't feel like I was in a space or context that really embraced my identity as a South Asian womyn. I spent almost all of my time

Madison Yoni ki Baat
performance. Photo credited
to Madison Yoni ki Baat
directors.

studying, researching and creating platforms for marginalized communities to explore the intersections of their different identities and voices,
but I just couldn't do the same for myself. Working within a system where
Black, Native, East Asian and Latina womyn (of various sexual, socioeco-
nomic and abled backgrounds) have historically been oppressed, I wasn't
sure where my experiences as a second generation Indian womyn fit in.
I tried to pick and choose, like, doing Vagina Monologues and then helping organize a workshop for Asian-Americans, but it felt forced. I was
always fighting for struggles that didn't really feel like they were mine.
And then I found *Yoni Ki Baat*. In almost eight years of performance, and
a lifetime in the Midwest looking for a politically active community of
South Asians, I found the perfect marriage of the two in UW-Madison's
production of YKB. Not only was it an effective grassroots approach to
dealing with social justice issues, but the first-person narrative in many
of the pieces (written and performed by the womyn) were found to be
even more engaging to the audience than Eve Ensler's Vagina Monolgues
(which I had performed in just a few months earlier). Our two nights of
performance were part of the best show I have ever been involved in. As
every womyn took the stage and shared some of her most intimate, funny
and heart-wrenching stories I was proud, embarrassed, and just as hurt
as they were, because every single one of those ladies were my sisters and
talking about problems in our communities. (Personal Correspondence)

Ayeshah, founder and director of Madison's version of *Yoni ki Baat*, elabo-
rates further by relating the following account:

I directed Eve Ensler's *Vagina Monologues* in 2007 and found myself becoming boxed into a specific ethnic category . . . Bosnian, Iraqi, Afghani, Pakistani . . . and interestingly, all these monologues talked of sexual violence.

I could not perform The Vagina Workshop or My Short Skirt or The Little Coochie Snorcher because I wasn't "authentic" enough. Did Arab, South Asian, and Afghani women not experience sexual pleasure or desire? I remember all-women gatherings in my childhood where my grandma, aunts, mom and neighborhood aunties would discuss everything from what kinds of sexual positions to adopt if one wanted the birth of a son or daughter, to their unique methods of birth control to the ways in which they could make themselves more desirable to their husbands. I remember the women only gatherings as being confined to certain spaces . . . rooms where men were not allowed and where they did not even bother or dare to intrude. Some aunties were so blatantly sexual that I would feel embarrassed. Once, I remember one of the aunties disclosing an embarrassing sexual secret about her husband to the other women. At that moment, the husband knocked on the door saying that he was ready to go home. He hadn't heard the conversation, but we all stopped dead in our tracks for a moment. Then everyone exploded into wild laughter. The poor man was perplexed because he couldn't understand what was happening. Little did he know that his wife had disclosed something personal about him to the rest of the women. Anyway, long story short, I wanted to organize a platform where women of color could narrate their own stories.

Yoni Ki Baat was like an answer to a prayer. I was doing my fieldwork in the Bay Area back in 2008 and stayed for a few days with some South Asian gay friends who were members of an LGBT group called Trikone. Trikone had organized an event called Kulture Kulcha, where I first saw a performance of YKB by the South Asian Sisters. I was immediately drawn to it and later got in touch with Vandana, one of the South Asian Sisters. I obtained the rights to organize something similar in Madison . . . and the rest is herstory! The first year that we performed, we had a cast member, Farah, who was second generation Lebanese. As the entire cast was South Asian, except Farah, I felt uneasy about YKB's focus on South Asian narratives not being sensitive to her ethnic identity (which was important to her). The next year, two previous YKB cast members—Amberine and Borna—came on board. We decided to experiment with the idea of making YKB a multiethnic vagina monologues. Our cast members included Hispanic, East Asian, South Asian, African American and African women. Vandana gave me the freedom to experiment with the monologues, for which I am truly grateful. After YKB was a big success in its second year, other women approached. They were not women of color, but they too had stories to share. So Amberine, Borna and I, and later Nathalie, heavily debated over whether YKB should be based on ethnicity or something else. We were all worried about the voices of minorities being marginalized again if primarily "white" women auditioned. Yet, we did not want to exclude women just because they were "white." I suggested that we focus instead on experiences of exclusion and privilege. I think we all face exclusion and privilege in different ways because of ethnicity, gender, sexual orientation, age, class etc, etc. With a name like *Yoni Ki Baat*, my hunch was that more South Asian or women with South Asian connections would be attracted anyway. But I think that at least 70–75% of the cast members should be women of color. My purpose behind YKB is not to give women a voice. They already have it. I see myself as a medium . . . someone who can help channel those voices to others who would benefit from their experiences. I see YKB as an instrument of empowerment. It has been for me, at least.

In many senses, this is no utopian endeavor—these groups are small with scant resources and dauntingly complicated agendas. However, it would be too critical—in that occasionally overly zealous academic fashion—not to allow for the utopian possibilities growing out of the dedication and energy they bring to their efforts. As Dolan (2005) writes, "I see and write about performance with the hope for what it can mean politically, but also affectively, through my faith that emotions might move us to social action. That is, I believe that being passionately and profoundly stirred in performance can be a transformative experience useful in other realms of social life" (15). Her faith in the political potential of performance is one that I share. I believe that performances like *Yoni Ki Baat* offer us important ways to be-with-others—ways that create time and space for deliberation about the exigencies we face in public and domestic spheres. Theater also provides opportunities to envision new ways that justice, equality, peace, and democracy might take root and flourish in our everyday lives. It holds the potential to create moments in which people, as part of an audience, can connect emotionally with those around them. Lastly, the spectators of such performances produce ever-new publics—people who come together briefly and then move out again into the public sphere, perhaps sharing what they have learned or felt during their experience at the theater (Dolan 2005). This, I believe, is the utopian potential the South Asian Sisters offers audiences through performances that foster passionate acknowledgment.

Chapter Six

✦   ✦   ✦

Intertwining Folklore and Rhetoric

Cultural Performance, Acknowledgment, and Social Justice

✦   ✦   ✦

Violence is not merely killing another. It is violence when we use a sharp word, when we make a gesture to brush away a person, when we obey because there is fear. So violence isn't merely organized butchery in the name of God, in the name of society or country. Violence is much more subtle, much deeper . . .

—**Jiddu Krishnamurti** (1969, 51)

As part of the human condition, innumerable manifestations of violence challenge us during the course of our lives. Around the world, people struggle daily to respond with dignity as they are subjected to terrorist acts, war crimes, racist speeches in public forums, physical and sexual abuse in the home, or deafening silence in response to requests for acknowledgment. Diverse as they are, these forms are undeniably interrelated. As I argued in the initial chapters of this book, hate speech performed in everyday contexts has often made exceptional violence—like religious genocide—appear reasoned or just (Das 2007). At the same time, even the threat of exceptional violence raises apprehension that is real and can constitute a climate of fear in daily life that forecloses the promise of relationality and community.

Sometimes, in our struggle to respond to such problems with dignity and ethical awareness, we make a decision to put ourselves at risk. Perhaps we share our own experiences of violence in public forums and make calls for acknowledgment to an unknown audience. Or maybe we risk ourselves by engaging with another's experience of violence, with another's pain. At a certain point, when we are simultaneously confronted by violence and yet

My Silent Cry. Photo credited to Amish Desai.

free to keep silent, we must ask ourselves difficult questions: Will I speak out publicly? Would I say something that compromises my own well-being if I felt it was true? Could I open my heart and mind in front of potentially hostile audience members? Should I risk my reputation in front of an audience of people with whom I already have relationships—family, friends, and community members—in order to provide or support a critical counternarrative? When community activists answer yes to these questions, they not only answer a call of conscience, they also work toward their own freedom and that of others (Hyde 2006).

In this book, I have illustrated the diverse ways in which some contemporary, progressive South Asian American groups endeavor to do just this. Grassroots advocacy groups grounded in the South Asian American community have responded to disparate forms of violence in diverse ways, from political speeches to community forums. This book considers a less conventional, but no less important, means of political activism: community performance. These performances—found within documentaries, progressive community theater, and cultural festivals, among other places—are used to witness transgressions, encourage discussion about contentious issues, and argue for changes in the social environment.

Viewed this way, performances can be understood as "political and ethical means of putting the critical sociological imagination to work" (Denzin and Lincoln 2000, 335). As you have seen, the performances in this book, based on South Asian American women's personal testimony, play with local, national, and transnational cultural forms as they take up key diasporic concerns, including those of memory and cultural loss, violence and exploitation, social justice, and personal healing. Seen as an intervention and embodied struggle, these performances are meant to broaden consciousness. In doing so, they are not necessarily interested in providing information or answers for audiences, although they sometimes do. Instead, they are more concerned with asking questions or requesting acknowledgment from a desired audience.

These performances are distinctive not only in their cultural form but also in the ways that they critically engage issues of oppression. These activists undertake this risky task despite the personal sacrifice and potential for social censure in order to keep trauma visible, testify to the suffering of others, and engage in the rhetorical work of speaking, listening, and deliberating about important social exigencies facing their communities. This diasporic discourse performs important functions, adding to our social knowledge, shaping interpretations of historic events and periods, and influencing political action among immigrant communities throughout the world.

Consequently, my attention in this book has focused upon the autobiographical and semiautobiographical narratives often embedded within diasporic folk performance as a means of political activism. These performances, found within folk festivals, political blogs, and Web sites, as well as progressive community theater, among others, are used to witness transgressions, encourage discussion about contentious issues, and argue for social change. Many grassroots organizations utilize performances of "narratives of personal experience" or "autobiographical testimonials" to advance calls for acknowledgment. These claims are based in oppositional interpretations of identities, histories, and experiences, both in terms of political and cultural struggles within mainstream society and their struggles for diversity and equality within South Asian American communities and families. This book has sought to explore the contours of these competing struggles as part of broader research being done on testimony, witnessing, social justice, and diasporic rhetoric—focusing on the ways that testimonies can be embedded and intertwined within more artistic cultural performances. Taken together, the performances explored in this book—all of which are performed by women—also open a window into the concerns and aspirations of diasporic South Asians exploring issues of gender and justice through appeals to an ethic of care.

I have suggested that this sense of "care" should be conceptualized as a political concept—as a means of working toward a society in which individuals help one another develop and sustain their basic and innate capabilities, their aesthetic appreciation, their pursuit of knowledge, and their opportunities to associate and organize. We can see this manifestation of care in local and international contexts, from community school involvement to global relief activities to activist performances. In my interest in the critical labor of caring, I find myself particularly aligned with and interested in expanding aspects of Robinson (1999) and Sevenhuijsen's (1998) work as described in chapter 1. For Robinson, a critical ethic of care is understood as a way of reflecting on morality and moral responsiveness in our communities and in the world at large. In contexts rife with conflict, an ethic of care becomes a way to examine social structures of power within the activities of caring that are taking place. For example, she argues that international relations depend heavily upon citizens caring about potential victims, wanting to prevent their suffering, and understanding what needs to be done.

Held (2006, 18) also puts it well when she argues that this political conception of care goes beyond simply "caring about" a problem experienced by distant others and toward an orientation in which we bring the same attentiveness, responsiveness, and empathy to those distant others that we would to those near to us. Without question, an ethic of care should take the well-being of all humanity into consideration. But "to be concerned for a friend or for a community with which one is closely identified and of which one is a member is to reach out not to someone or something wholly other than oneself but to what shares a part of one's own self and is implicated in one's own sense of identity. They are caring relations" (Blum 1980, 42).

I have used this sense of an ethic of care to understand the ways various performance forms enable South Asian Americans to protest violence and request acknowledgment in a manner that invites connection with their fellow citizens and community members. In the process, I have sought to tease out the links between the political performance, diasporic rhetoric, the ethic of care, and acknowledgment. It is through the lens of these theoretical concepts that I believe we can gain new understanding of how some South Asian American women are adding their perspectives to the public sphere and responding to violence directed at them from both outside and inside their communities using artistic means.

Specifically, these performances seem to display the following components:

1. Judging with Care

a. Addressing Problems: Through rhetorical acts of acknowledgment, performers address the problems of others and self in ways that exhibit care. They show audiences how to respond to others' needs and why they should. Performers point toward how to build trust, mutual concern, and connectedness between people. They encourage people to focus upon their humanity as they make judgments about pressing social matters.

b. Displaying Competency: Acknowledgment in performance requires a rhetorically competent performer—someone whom Hyde (2006) would call a "linguistic architect" whose symbolic constructions "both imagine and invite others into a place where they can feel at home while thinking about and discussing the truth of some matter" (86). To accomplish this task, it is generally considered useful to draw upon familiar topoi or figures, for example. The more people feel at home with another's arguments and worldviews the more likely they are to open to the other's viewpoint. In this way, a performance both undertakes an epideictic function and displays a communal character (ethos).

c. Dwelling with Difference: Although rhetorical competence is a key element of acknowledgment, one must also take into consideration what it means to live in a community characterized by deep difference. Within inhospitable dwelling places, individuals with complicated worldviews and identities must strategize with rhetorical competency in order to give a compelling account of themselves, while considering conflicting expectations for "well done" public discourse. In this sense, calls for acknowledgment in performance might appear as a much more open-ended and transgressive act—something not so immediately deducible or intelligible to audience members for the purposes of inviting inquiry.[1] Or perhaps, it might be an artistic declaration of personal experience offered by someone who, despite social and cultural taboos, has the courage to speak out and seek acknowledgment of their difference.

2. Creating Caring Communities:

a. Being-For-Others: The act of acknowledgment in performance is a way of "being-for-others." Within performance contexts, acknowledgment (in discursive and nondiscursive modes) creates a context in which audiences engage in ethical listening (i) to allow performers to tell about the truth of their existence and (ii) to allow audiences to witness the problems of others. At a basic level, this sense of presence is an expression of acknowledgment.

b. Being-With-Others: In performances, rhetorical acts of acknowledgment invoke a sense of communal relationships—a "being-with-others" that shows concern for how people are doing in their everyday relationships with others and in relation to issues of importance. Acts of positive acknowledgment in performance exhibit a profound wakefulness toward others, the challenges they face, and the suffering they have experienced. This acknowledgment involves lingering-with-others.

c. Hospitality-For-Others: Acknowledgment in performance is also a form of hospitality. It is a matter of giving of oneself in order to extend to the audience an invitation to inquire. The aporia of hospitality requires risk in that "to be hospitable is to let oneself be overtaken, surprised, and unprepared" (Derrida 2000, 361). Through acts of acknowledgment, care may appear in the direct interaction that takes place in performances. Here, the feelings of self and Other and connections between people are explored and expressed.

3. Caring for Oneself

a. Performers perform acts for the benefit of others but also for themselves. In this sense, acknowledgment is also a form of self-care. Indeed, sometimes caring for oneself in a performance trumps caring for others; for example, traumatic witnessing of sexual violence may necessitate moments of self-care and reflection, and the seeking of support from the audience.

Building Connections of Folklore, Performance, and Rhetorical Studies

Given this framework, as I conclude this book, I want to emphasize the need for scholars to focus on the ways local rhetorical practices and vernacular or traditional culture often intertwine. Roger Abrahams's 1968 article, "Introductory Remarks to a Rhetorical Theory of Folklore," motivated a generation of folklorists to consider the connections between folklore and rhetoric.

Post Natyam Collective. Photo credited to Andrei Andreev.

These scholars have investigated how folk performances create time and space for deliberations about matters of public and personal importance, raise political consciousness, or constitute identity through critical play with a rich heritage of folk forms, figures, or practices, drawing from phi- losophers such as Aristotle, Kenneth Burke, or Mikhail Bakhtin (Garlough 2008; Howard 2008; Oring 2008). In this book, I have been interested in building upon this work. Other scholars with human-rights-centered agen- das are drawn to exploring the social contexts in which injustice or indif- ference arise due to conflicts over difference, identity, and sovereignty (Fraser 2000; Markell 2003; Povinelli 2002; Ricoeur 2005). However, given common interests in issues of nationalism, identity politics, ethnic com- munity development, to name only a few, folklore scholars, for the most part, have remained unusually quiet regarding these topics. In addition, calls for acknowledgment in performances by South Asian Americans have gone relatively unnoticed by scholars in fields of communication, such as rhetoric. Perhaps this should come as no surprise, because—despite signs of improvement in recent years—comparatively there has been a dearth of research that addresses non-Western rhetorical performances or those of racial and ethnic minority communities and individuals in the United States (Garlough 2007; Garrett 1997; Hegde 2005; Oliver 1971; Ono and Sloop 2002; Shome 1996; Watts 2002).[2]

To begin, I believe that in order to better research and understand minority, transnational, and global rhetoric, a renewed commitment to interdisciplinary approaches is necessary. Necessary interdisciplinarity goes beyond simply inserting relevant references from related fields. It means engaging in ongoing conversations with experts in other disciplines in order to draw upon their insights and reconfigure them in novel ways to address the questions at hand. Indeed, Elizabeth and Jay Mechling argue that at its core interdisciplinarity has much to do with our ability to play (Mechling and Mechling 1999). It would seem that as a discipline we risk isolation, if not irrelevance, by not recognizing the connections we have and the scholarly contributions we can make, not only to our own field but to those of others as well.

In my own work, I am interested in forging connections with disciplines that deal with culture, particularly folklore. In doing so, I take Thomas B. Farrell's charge seriously when he argues:

> When one is immersed within a cultural "lifeworld," whether it be that of an urban East Coast street person or that of a Japanese peasant, the rhetorical characteristics of ongoing cultural activities are likely to go unnoticed. This does not mean that they are absent or unimportant, but only that our practices themselves are taken for granted in a way that withholds their partisanship . . . We are drawn into a more public awareness of rhetoric, when the different activities of others must have an impact upon our needs, priorities, and practices. Rhetoric, in its venerable sense of an art form, emerges when we have recognized features of our activities as directional choices from among an array of options . . . this means that rhetorical phronesis (practical reason) cannot be enacted without at least a partial intuition of what is appropriate in each historically specific setting. (Farrell 1993, 279)

Certainly, working within this set of assumptions, excellent research has emerged, particularly with regard to the vernacular and popular culture (Brummett 1994; Cloud 2004; Hauser 1999; Ono and Sloop 2002). Yet in the literature that discusses non-Western, ethnic, or immigrant rhetoric, rarely do we see the discipline of folklore engaged. Many are unclear about what folklore is or why it may constitute an important area of inquiry, despite its 150-year history. Perhaps this is because, as the cliché goes, there are as many definitions of folklore as there are folklorists. Folklore is not simply something that is old fashioned or rooted in rural communities. In sometimes unforeseen ways, we throughout our lives participate in vernacular folk culture, whether we live in an isolated farming town or a crowded urban environment.

To be sure, for many decades, there have been folklorists interested in exploring the ways vernacular culture can be used for persuasive purposes, perhaps as potential *resources* in mobilizing social or political action. However, most are more likely to refer to such communicative forms as strategic or resistive discourse than as rhetoric specifically (Garlough 2008).

For the handful of folklore scholars who have directly engaged with rhetoric, a diverse set of theoretical perspectives has been utilized. Roger Abrahams has focused upon conceptualizing a "rhetorical theory of folklore" that has functionalist undertones but also draws upon Kenneth Burkes's discussion of symbolic form (Abrahams 1968). Others such as Elliot Oring have applied a neo-Aristotelian approach to reimagine the potential of ethos, pathos, and logos for folklore studies (Oring 2008). My colleague Robert Howard has drawn upon Burke and speech act theory to explore the use of vernacular culture by marginalized groups in online environments (Howard 2008). My own work has tapped into hermeneutic, critical, and performance theory to think through the ways South Asian folklore can be used to invent grassroots political rhetoric (Garlough 2007, 2008). Here, culture is not conceptualized as a set of laws or rules that transform chaos into order, and folklore is not merely a way to construct meaning embedded in public symbols (Burke 1931; Geertz 1973). Instead, folklore is viewed as a way of doing—and the work and play of folklore is rhetorical (Oliver 1971).

Folk forms are considered to be potentially powerful rhetorical forms because they are highly iconic and multidimensional, promote self-reflection and identity formation, create ties to other members of the group, define boundaries, and, ultimately, are readily put to use in defense of an in-group against threats by an out-group. Also, due to their performative quality, these forms can be used to reach out to all members of a community, including individuals who are typically disenfranchised (Kumar 1994). Individuals involved in social organizations and movements can engage in the strategic use of folk forms to confront social issues and to persuade others to ascribe to a particular perspective and act upon it. Many folklore scholars focus attention on the emergence of verbal art in social interaction, rather than the study of a text as a reified object. They have shifted their attention away from issues of classification to those of strategic use (Bauman 1977, 1990, 1992, 1993b). This, I believe, is where rhetoric and folklore has much to say to one another.

Folklore, Rhetorical Hermeneutics, and Critical Play

Finally, I would like to pause and reflect for a moment upon what I call "critical play"—its characteristics and its potential as a rhetorical concept. Challenging demands to demonstrate total immersion into American culture or exclusive connections to an ethnic community, I have sought to show in this book the ways performers often display a notable cultural and rhetorical competence in critically playing with cultural and institutional discourses and practices in inventive ways that challenge normative thought or practice. For example, in her autobiographical performance titled *Rise*, Post Natyam performer Shyamala Moorty critically plays with classical Indian Bharatanatyam with ballet and modern dance, along with a toilet plunger, to make visible the ways her diasporic identity puts her at risk for hate crimes immediately following 9/11, while simultaneously drawing parallels to communal violence between Hindus and Muslims in the Indian state of Gujarat. Her work combines a number of the ideas considered in this book—religious divisions, intolerance, and eclectic performances—to challenge norms and preconceptions in inventive ways. Her performance shows the ways that critical play can be conceptualized as an ethical endeavor—one that seeks to facilitate the recovery of a human voice.

In these performances, words and images also work to create the possibility for moments of ethical play *between* people. Through this play, community identities might be constituted, coalitions might be built, and the limits of community might be explored. Indeed, this play between self and an Other encourages a consideration of the stranger at the borders of the spaces to which we belong. It facilitates reflection upon the ways community can be torn apart by the refusal to *acknowledge* or *recognize* others as an integral part of the social fabric. It also shows us the potential connections that can be drawn between everyday folk practices and political performances.

Of course, play is by no means a new concept. In classical Greece, Plato wrote expansively upon the connection between everyday life and play (Krentz 1983). He was one of the first philosophers of rhetoric to observe the importance of play in relationship to the health of the public sphere, civic life, and the creation of a "just city." In fact, in Plato's *Republic* alone, more than sixty citations to play in reference to education can be found (Brandwood 1976). Play, however, is not simply a Western concept. Indeed, Indian classical philosophy is replete with discussions of play (*lila*), although this play takes place on a more transcendental plane (Hansen 1992; Hatcher 1999).[3] Johan Huizinga, the Dutch historian, and one of the founders of modern cultural history also identifies humans as fundamentally playful

Shyamala Moorty. Photo credited
to Michael Burr.

beings. His work, focusing upon art and spectacle's role in public life, grew
from a background in comparative linguistics and Sanskrit, and culminated
in his doctoral thesis on the role of the jester in Indian drama. Later, he
extended this understanding in his influential book *Homo Ludens: A Study
of the Play Element in Culture* (Huizinga 1950) where he argues that play is
the core of every human expression. Indeed, he contended that play is *the*
central component of human culture.

In modern and postmodern scholarship, many scholars have focused
upon play as an inventive activity. This sense of invention can be understood
in a variety of senses, from the invention of self and culture to rhetorical
invention within a text, to the invention that creates space and time for the
performance of subjectivity (Conquergood 1989; Sutton-Smith 1997). Victor Turner in *From Ritual to Theater: The Human Seriousness of Play* (1982)
argues that the *ludic* or play is the essence of invention. Through play with
symbols and meanings in performance, ritual, and narrative, individuals can
generate multiple alternative models for living, that are able to influence the
behavior of those in mainstream social and political roles in the direction of
radical change.

For this reason, many folklorists have found play to be a productive concept to consider, as can be seen in the work of Mechling (1980) and Abrahams. For example, in *Everyday Life: A Poetics of Vernacular Practice*, Abrahams (2005) picks up this thread, asserting that play is a vital dimension of community activity, particularly celebratory gatherings or epideictic events, such as parades, festivals, or commemorative functions with a strong ceremonial component, such as a Fourth of July event. In these events, people assemble to display themselves, often in customary or conventional ways. Abrahams argues that, "from a pragmatic perspective, participants in these shows, displays, and performance events seldom have any problem recognizing and interpreting that something beyond the everyday is taking place" (106). Although these experiences generally rely heavily upon playful mimetic behavior, they also draw considerably upon the vernacular, mimicking it, and then returning participants to the real world. In this vernacular play, participation is key. The greater the involvement, the more potential exists for being carried away by a shared activity. This involves what Mihaly Csikszentmihalyi (1990) has called "flow." Abrahams further contends that, in performance events, this play may consume everyone in its presence, so even if we are not performing ourselves, we are affected sympathetically by body memory or sensations (2005, 110).

Hans Georg Gadamer, building upon the work of Heidegger, also argues that play is such a fundamental function of human life that culture is inconceivable without it. In *Truth and Method* (1977), Gadamer explores play as a hermeneutical phenomenon of interpretation—*the play of understanding*. He maintains that, in our lives, understanding is continually in play and, like Freud, notes that this play is characterized by movement. Understanding is endlessly replenished through play—a rhythmic movement in which past meanings influence our everyday lives. This flow surrounds us and we are part of it from the moment of our existence. Each day, in order to create understanding in a chaotic world, our practices, including those that are rhetorical, are invented from our communities' traditions, histories, norms, and customs. Such hermeneutic rhetorical practice opens us to the imaginary and plays with the always renewable reservoir of memory, history, myth, and desire (Gadamer 2004). Such play extends outward and creates space and time for the potential of dialogue in conversation, literature, speeches, artwork, festivals, ritual practices, and so on. The success of this dialogue relies on the willingness of participants to "give in" to the flow of communication for the "purpose of letting meaning emerge in an 'event' of mutual understanding" (Michelfelder and Palmer 1989, 1). Play requires a "playing along" and so even a spectator is more than just an observer. She is one who takes part (Gadamer 1977). In this exchange between self and Other, Gadamer argues that hermeneutics offers a pathway to speaking and listening ethically by finding a common language so that the speaker can be heard by the Other (Watts 2002).

I have found this approach to play helpful in my own thinking about the ways that diasporic individuals and communities negotiate cultural identity and national/transnational belonging. With this in mind, I would like to extend this scholarship to explore play in diasporic performance as a *rhetorical concept*, especially its critical potential. I wonder, in what ways can we describe critical play as a mode of rhetorical hermeneutics? What comprises its philosophical character, as well as its practical strategies? How can critical play provide conditions for understanding and show where understanding is productively denied? How does it point to where power unfolds?

To begin, I would argue that the concept of critical play calls attention *both* to questions of power in play and the ways we can play with power. All play is inevitably implicated by power dynamics; in play, there are always rules, no matter where it falls on the continuum between freedom from and duty toward recognized cultural practices (Huizinga 1950). Critical play, more specifically, engages with traditional figures and representations, institutional frameworks, and cultural norms to make a rhetorical point. In the case of this book, the play in these performances is critical and rhetorical because it engages the limits and conditions and consequences of truth-telling. In doing so, it contributes to the formation of subjects. It may help people to reinterpret and appropriate signs of violence, perhaps in gestures of defiance. Through discursive and nondiscursive means, it may voice the pain that has been felt. In doing so, it participates in moral acts of acknowledgment and recognition in ways that evoke an awakening and an unsettling, providing an interruption of discourse and sometimes helps to engender, as Jean-Luc Nancy (2002, 78) says, the "we in us."

In addition, I believe critical play is intimately related to rhetorical practices of invention, opening the speaker and the audience to the presence of what is expressive and artful. This requires, in most cases, the display of rhetorical competencies. However, it may also necessitate the refusal of this display in rhetorical situations in order to remain committed (in varying degrees) to engagement, speculation, experimentation, and curiosity. In these performances, rhetors may make language and images foreign for audiences to get at what is difficult, puzzling, or distressing and move toward an embodied affective experience. Critical play asks audiences to participate actively—to read into, follow along, imagine, establish independent flights of thought and offer divergent perspectives. They are performances that often foreground the power of the uncanny.

Beyond this, critical play in performance has much to do with *kairos*—making moments—during which words, images, and bodies interact to create time and space for reflection and deliberation. Critical play is about making the time and space not always available (or welcome) in the public sphere. As the examples in this book illustrate, critical play can take place in a liminal space, at some remove from the mundane in which we live our lives (Turner 1969, 1982; Turner and Schechner 1987). However, I contend that it also can be experienced in the everyday within the vernacular practices. Indeed, in some cases the point of critical play may, in fact, be to challenge the boundaries of the liminal. It contests the power dynamics of social rituals and ceremonies, in order to bring what is supposed to remain in the boundaries into the everyday. In other cases, as we have seen in chapter 2 of this book, critical play makes the flow of time in performance uneven in order to create possibility of understanding.

Drawing upon Gadamer, among others, critical play allows for a way of moving beyond interrogation to a question. In this respect, critical play may do the work of rendering performativity contingent (Doxtader 2011). That is, play is an opening of contingency that blurs the lines between recognizing and acknowledging in contexts of "truth-telling." In this sense, play embodies the work of discovery. This critical play is related to a hermeneutics that is not necessarily based upon understanding or interpreting. Rather, sometimes it has more to do with simply attending to the Other (*Seinlassen*) and of letting others come near or creating an opening for questions to emerge. In this way, critical play is a gift—a means of giving and receiving through rhetorical performances.

In sum, in order to understand how this functions in diasporic rhetorical performances, particularly personal experience stories in festivals, documentaries, and progressive theater productions, it seems important to attend to the ways that critical play in diasporic performances may pose important problems of interpretation. This is particularly the case in contexts driven by concern for authenticity, traditional rhetorical competence, and synthesis. In addition, it appears crucial to reflect upon the ways in which critical play within these performances is constrained by cultural translation, appropriateness, and appropriation. Here I am concerned with how and where constitutive power unfolds within performances and how this is achieved through certain rhetorical strategies. Along these lines, I am interested in the ways that such power might function as a form of violence itself.

This framework responds to the longstanding conception of rhetoric as the art of informing, explaining, and entertaining, and reconceives of it as a way of exploring. Performers play through their performances, learning about themselves at the same time as they are connecting with their audiences. The question is what pushes such play to its limits? When does play as meaning making become challenged by the limits of knowing? How can we understand play as a rhetorical means of addressing not-knowing, including not-knowing oneself? How might critical play engage in the ethical? Examining these issues through a series of illustrative cases, this book traces the range and strategies of critical play in diasporic performance. It also further develops the notion of play as an important rhetorical concept, crucial for understanding the political work of marginalized groups.

This book, then, hopes to contribute to the fields of folklore, women's studies, and rhetoric in numerous ways. It explores how South Asians have responded to the threat and reality of violence, especially since 9/11, during which time a growing number have found themselves the target of prejudice and hate crimes. At the same time, incidents of exclusion, oppression, and abuse remain evident in the South Asian American community, dividing Hindus from Muslims, first generation from second generation, and men from women. As this book documents, South Asian Americans have responded to these challenges by using rhetorical performances to make calls of conscience and invite recognition and acknowledgment from audiences. Emphasizing a politics of difference, the three case studies comprising the core of this book—the development and presentation of a cultural booth at the Minnesota Festival of Nations, the production and content of an eclectic performance drawing attention to hate crimes, and the performance of a feminist spoken-word poetry reading concerning sexual violence within the home—provide a set of portraits of emergent modes of political engagement.

Some employ performance within contexts of conventional engagement, such as large-scale community events like the Minnesota Festival of Nations, events which serve as sites of collective activity and locations of strategic self-presentation. Others emphasize the advocacy work of feminists like the South Asian Sisters. Here, the complexities of a bicultural identity are expressed and demands for tolerance are made through political performances that use everyday culture as a tool for contestation and negotiation. Striving to make the invisible visible, and to foster conversation and deliberation within the South Asian community, these types of performances emanate from the margins of the margins, and offer new ways of understanding the social justice and human rights work of South Asian Americans.

These case studies, then, provide a portrait of contemporary rhetorical practices within the South Asian community, updating a hidden history of immigrant rhetoric in America. This focus on grassroots activism and performance growing out of the borders of a diaspora seeks to trouble essentialized representations of South Asian Americans, redirect attention to intercommunity diversity, and understand the conditions for ethical communication.

Notes

Chapter One

1. Rhetoric, understood most broadly as the art of persuasion, certainly includes the communicative goals of informing, commemorating, and entertaining (Farrell 1993). To my mind, however, one of rhetoric's most important functions is instigating and sustaining processes of critical inquiry. These performances provide a venue for engaged questioning of topics of social importance. As such, they are crucial forms of engagement in the public sphere (Doxtader 2003). Specifically, I am interested in the ways I believe diasporic performances express both local and global knowledge and create alternative spaces of intervention and struggle.

2. The field of communications has long focused on examining how meaning in political performances is created and exchanged. An excellent early example of this type of work was completed by Bordenaue (1979), who studied communities in Northeast Brazil and reported political discourse styles among peasant groups. He observed that when leaflets were distributed to educate individuals about tuberculosis control, the materials were undeniably unsuccessful. The fundamental problem revolved around the language structure; the short sentences, simple words, and concrete meanings were not culturally sensitive to the rhetorical styles of the audience. In response, another pamphlet was created in which the information was explained through *Folhetos*, a traditional form of storytelling commonly used within this group. Given this rhetorical form, the participants memorized the information and later reported it to others orally.

3. Akin to other types of political performance, these street plays create a forum in which to discuss important issues related to sex-selection abortion, sexual violence, or gender discrimination. These works of *imagination* encompass artistry, provide tactics of *intervention*, and create an alternative space for civic struggles where social justice can take place (Garlough 2007, 2008).

4. Braziel and Mannur argue the word "diaspora" can be traced etymologically to the Greek "diasperien" that refers to the scattering and sowing of seeds. This sense of the word suggests a double movement—one of diffusion and another of dwelling and cultivation.

5. As a consequence, many debates on the relationship between care and justice have had much to do with the gendering of ethics and moral responses. Scholars have asked whether care and justice represent two distinct types of moral thinking or whether an approach to ethics must include and integrate both care and justice thinking (Tronto 1993). These debates are interesting to me, as they raise important questions about women's ability to address ethical problems. Close adherents to Habermas's notion of communicative rationality have been critiqued by feminists for pushing aside feeling, aspirations, and anxieties as relevant to debates in the public sphere (Fraiser 1990; Pajnik 2006). An ethic of care counters such justice-centered notions of rationality that Mansbridge (1990) notes "can easily mask subtle forms of control." In addition, it brings private issues, such as domestic abuse or sexual violence, to public consideration. However, here I am not concerned with the historical origins of these debates. Rather, I am interested in how an ethic of care goes beyond the personal and private sphere to critically address large-scale social or global problems.

6. This position, I believe, requires a more encompassing sense of care than scholars like Engster (2007) are willing to grant. That is, reducing the scope of care, as Engster does, to "helping individuals to develop and sustain their basic or innate capabilities, including the abilities for sensation, movement, emotion, imagination, reason, speech, affiliation, and, in most societies today, the ability to read, write, and perform basic math" (27) excludes important categories of human endeavor to which an ethic of care might apply.

7. Critical cultural scholars like Honneth (1995) and Fraser (1997) have asserted that this is particularly problematic because recognition from the dominant culture is necessary; it is needed to build a solid sense of one's own personal and group identity. Our identity is partially shaped by recognition or its lack. Identity is not a given. Rather, it is part of a *struggle* for personal, social, and political recognition. Said another way, oppressed people are obliged to engage in struggles for recognition in response to their lack of recognition from the dominant culture. This need for recognition is an outcome of the pathology of colonial or oppressive cultures.

8. In addition, she challenges notions of recognition and subjectivity by developing a concept of witnessing not grounded in the ocular; rather, subjectivity involves testifying to something that cannot be seen. She argues that through performances of witnessing and testimony, our sights are directed beyond the visible world of the eyewitness. What witnessing testifies to is not a litany of facts but a commitment to understanding subjectivity as addressability and responsibility.

9. This perspective reflects my choice to focus not only on key rhetorical situations in a community but also on the broad range of exigencies and resources available to community members over time. Through this wide lens, I examine closely the ways rhetorical practices evolve, transform, and respond to one another. In addition to providing a deep sense of context, this approach provides the scholar with yet another means of considering power issues. Katriel notes this is particularly important for researchers studying immigrant groups in Western society, because their position vis-à-vis the host majority is often marked by social disadvantage and power disparities.

Chapter Two

1. The American Federation of Labor in the early 1900s was an organization of 2.5 million. Young was a special representative of this organization at the First International Convention of the Asiatic Exclusion League of North America, Seattle, February 3, 1908.

2. See Radha Hegde's (2002) "Postcolonial approaches to communication: Charting the terrain, engaging the intersections" in *Communication Theory*.

3. One of the first records of a South Asian in America appears in a 1670 colonial diary that mentions a sailor from Madras accompanying a sea captain on a visit to Salem, Massachusetts (La Brack 1988; Prashad 2000).

4. For example, the records of Pennsylvania's Abolition Society include a petition by a James Dunn, originally from Calcutta, who was indentured as an eight-year-old boy to the mate of a ship. He was traded many times and severely punished for endeavoring to escape and free himself (Jensen 1988, 13). Many of those who survived married into the black community.

5. The University of Wisconsin was considered a progressive institution and enrolled the largest number of Indian students in the United States at this time. In 1912, there were

eleven Hindu students: nine from Bengal, one from Bombay, and one from the United Provinces. The students included Nabin Chandra Das, Baneswar Das, Rajani Kanto Das, M. S. Birendranath Das Gupta, Raghubar Dayal Gupta, Barendra Kumar Palit, Rajendra Narayan Chowdhury, Shankar Pagar, Khagendra Narayan Mirta, Hemendra Kisore Rakshit, and Basanta Kumar Roy.

6. Both of these perspectives assume that women would have migrated if the opportunity were present. That is, the decision to migrate was an individual decision rather than a collective household strategy. By contrast, Mazumdar argues that it is unlikely that large numbers of married women would have immigrated, even if the laws had allowed it. This has much to do with the economic system that was built around women's labor on farms and in homes. At the turn of the century, one-third of the land in Punjab was used for farming and women were often in charge of weeding fields, milking cattle, churning, and cleaning stalls, as well as household chores, child rearing, and caring for the elderly. Consequently, women's labor was very difficult to replace. However, the labor of sons, especially second and third sons, was dispensable on a farm. This goes a long way toward explaining, in addition to cultural and legal reasons, why so few women migrated to America.

7. This aesthetic practice, an important part of the discursive repertoire of many Indians in colonial, nationalist, and postcolonial contexts, involved a sense of play (*lila*) that provided speakers and audiences in these complex social situations a means for flexible transformation that has enabled the coexistence of rich and historically diverse cultural traditions. It allowed Indian reformers and intellectuals during the colonial era to appropriate foreign forms of knowledge and argue for socioreligious reforms, while at the same time guarding a sense of cultural authenticity and tradition (Hatcher 1999).

8. This movement drew into its midst a group of wealthy individuals interested in neo-transcendentalism and communal living. Lecture series and yoga classes were organized at Unitarian churches, philosophical societies, and community groups. Vedanta centers or "peace retreats" opened from California to Connecticut. There is no doubt that the success of the Vedanta movement had much to do with its flexibility in negotiating themes of tradition and modernity, mysticism and social action through an eclectic discourse that drew upon both South Asian and Western rhetorical traditions.

9. Proceedings of the Asiatic Exclusion League, San Francisco, March 1908: 13.

10. Ct. Curry, secretary of state, wrote this in a June 30, 1910, letter to A. E. Voell, secretary-treasurer of the Asiatic Exclusion League. The letter can be found in the correspondence from Candidates for Federal and State Offices, Farmer's Co-op and Educational Societies of California on the Asiatic Question, 1910.

11. Indeed, at the First International Convention of the Asiatic Exclusion League, Chairman Tveitmaoe states: "God Almighty placed certain barriers around different races. He has given to each a special locality for a home. Mongolians and whites never have camped under the same fig tree and never can dwell together in peace" (Proceedings of the first International Convention of the AEL, 4).

12. Asiatic Exclusion League Proceedings, September 1910: 10–11.

13. The first federal laws restricting immigration were enacted in 1875 and 1882.

14. In order to limit South Asians' liberties—the very ones it was argued they could not understand—this group advocated a series of limitations upon civil rights and asked politicians to put these into law. During election seasons, pamphlets were published that explicitly listed these demands and the names of public officials who had committed to them. So we find letters like the following:

... I beg to state that I am heartily in favor of forbidding and prohibiting Asiatics for owning or acquiring real property in the state of California and I shall favor all legislation that can be enacted to that end ... I believe that no Asiatic child or Oriental should be permitted to sit in our schools with our white children ... the intermarriage of white persons with Chinese, Japanese, Hindus or any other colored race is, to my mind, a positive menace to our civilization, and can have no other effect than to break down our American ideals and institutions, and I would strongly urge an extension of our present law so as to prohibit all such intermarriages.

15. Census records show that Roy lived in New York in 1918 and registered for the draft in WWI and WWII.

16. *Wisconsin Alumni Magazine*, vol. 13, no. 8.

17. *Wisconsin Alumni Magazine*, vol. 13, no. 8.

18. Das had fled India in 1905 to avoid imprisonment for political agitation, made his way to Japan, and stayed there disguised as a Hindu ascetic until he was extradited by British officials. Escaping to Canada, Das founded the Swadesh Sevek Home, a boarding school for the children of South Asian immigrants that also held evening classes teaching English and math for adults. In 1907, he established the Hindustani Association in Vancouver. Then, in 1908, he began the journal *Free Hindustan*, written in English—one of the first South Asian publications in North America. Its motto was "To protest against all tyranny is a service to humanity and the duty of civilization." In articles like *A Direct Appeal to the Sikhs* (September–October 1909) he wrote, "Coming into contact with free people and institutions of free nations, some of the Sikhs, though laborers in the North American Continent, have assimilated the idea of liberty and trampled the medals of slavery." This discourse was not well received and he was deported from Canada in 1908. Das took this opportunity to enroll in the University of Washington's political science department.

19. *Gadar* is an Urdu/Punjabi word that means "mutiny" or "rebellion" or "revolt." The Gadar movement was housed at 436 Hill Street, San Francisco. Its original home was known as Yugantar Ashram.

20. Specifically, Ramnath (2005) argues the Bengalis in Gadar approached the problem of British colonialism from a position of Western-influenced rationalism, a Bengali tradition of *Kropotkinism*, spiritual nationalism, and leftist radicalism. In contrast, the Punjabis advocated for a more liberal democratic nationalism or anticolonial form of communism that seemed to pair well with the traditions of Sikhism. "Inspired by the nationalist movements of the previous century, particularly Mazzini's Italian Risorgimento, [the Gadar movement] had close ties of solidarity with Irish and Egyptian opponents of British colonialism, as well as with Pan-Asianist and, more problematically, with Pan-Islamist movements against Western imperialism" (Ramnath 2005, 8). Together, the elite members of the Gadar movement were associated with networks of socialists and anarchists in North America, Japan, and Europe.

21. Har Dayal's political philosophy, according to Don Dignan, "was a distinctive amalgam of western anarchism and Hindu revivalism, [which] did not prevent him from welding together into the first purely secular Indian revolutionary organization a cross-section of very disparate groups and individuals who comprised the hitherto unorganized and sporadic revolutionary movement" (18).

22. On November 1, 1913, members of Gadar began printing a self-titled paper, with the goal of stirring debate about India's freedom in diasporic South Asian communities around the world. Published in the Punjabi, Hindi, Urdu, Bengali, Gujarati, and Pushto languages,

this paper was sent to South Asians living in the United States, Canada, Fiji, Sumatra, Shanghai, Hong Kong, Hankow, Java, Singapore, Malaya, Siam, Burma, East Africa, and, of course, throughout the Indian subcontinent. In it, Har Dayal wrote: "Today there begins in foreign lands, but in our country's tongue, a war against the British Raj . . . . What is our name? Mutiny. What is our work? Mutiny. Where will mutiny break out? In India."

23. http://www.sukh-history.com/sikhist/personalities/sarabha.html.

24. Pressured by the British, the U.S. Government began a series of investigations that alleged Gadar members violated U.S. laws and engaged in secret negotiations with German leaders. They also claimed Gadar members sought to incite rebellion against the British, our allies in World War I. In April 1918, a conspiracy trial was held in San Francisco (La Brack 1988; Shah 1999).

25. During this time, when there was very little social support, Gadar leaders found kinship in the Irish revolutionary brotherhood. It could be argued that their work paved the way for the coming of Indian independence.

26. Wilson had vetoed the bill on January 28, 1915, stating that the legislation would "undoubtedly enhance the efficiency and improve the methods of handling immigration," but that his duty to the Constitution left him no choice but to dissent.

27. Dr. Bhagat Singh Thind (letter to the Editor, "The Mahratta" Poona from Linton, Oregon, January 22, 1922). In Varma 1995, 125.

28. Thind had come to the United States in 1913 to pursue university education. On July 22, 1918, he was recruited by the U.S. Army to fight in World War I and was quickly promoted to the rank of acting sergeant. He received an "honorable discharge" on December 16, 1918, with full commendations. Nevertheless, five years later he found his citizenship rights being revoked. In a letter to the editor in a Linton, Oregon, newspaper, Thind wrote, it is "a battle for recognition we Indians are fighting in this country!"

29. At this time, Associate Justice Sutherland wrote the opinion of the Court, declaring that although "Caucasian" and the words "White person" often are treated as synonymous: "'Caucasian' is a conventional word of much flexibility, as a study of the literature dealing with racial questions will disclose, and while it and the words of 'white persons' are treated as synonymous for the purposes of that case, they are not identical meaning idem per idem . . . . The intention was to confer the privilege of citizenship upon that class of persons whom the fathers knew as white, and to deny it to all who could not be so classified."

30. Thind applied for and received U.S. citizenship through the state of New York a few years after his original U.S. citizenship was revoked by the U.S. Supreme Court.

31. See "Hindus Here Burn Miss Mayo's Book," *New York Times*, January 22, 1928, and "Forgive Miss Mayo," Jan Kothanda Ram, Letter to the Editor, February 22, 1928.

32. Baroda: Laxmi Printing Press, 1934.

33. Bose cites a newspaper article from the *Chattanooga Daily Times*, February 13, 1918, titled "Tortured and Then Burned."

34. Reprinted from *On Common Ground: World Religions in America*, Columbia University Press, CD-ROM, 3rd ed.

35. See "Racial Attacks Evoke Self-Scrutiny," *Hinduism Today*, January 1989.

36. See Michelle Marriot, "In Jersey City: Indians Protest Violence," *New York Times*, October 12, 1987: B1.

37. In 1996, immigration law changed again, compromising the rights of longtime South Asian residents in the United States. Under this new legislation, South Asian Americans could be detained and deported without proper representation in court. Even relatively

minor misdemeanors committed twenty years prior, including shoplifting, could lead to one's deportation from the United States.

38. Congress, in Section 280003(a) of the Violent Crime Control and Law Enforcement Act of 1994 (28 U.S.C. 994 note), defines a hate crime as "a crime in which the defendant intentionally selects a victim, or in the case of a property crime, the property that is the object of the crime, because of the actual or perceived race, color, national origin, ethnicity, gender, disability, or sexual orientation of any person."

39. Government policies such as the U.S. patriot act, the Absconder Initiative, and Special Registration program have resulted in mass deportations and detentions. Indeed, the Asian American Legal Defense and Education Fund (AALDEF) claims that the special registration program is "the worst in a series of counter-productive and increasingly draconian policies implemented in the name of national security." Although it has now ended, Special Registration was the most visible and systematic government-instituted program to detain members of specific ethnic groups in the United States since the internment of Japanese Americans during World War II.

40. These types of sentiments show no signs of abating. For example, in response to the assassination of Benazir Bhutto, former Arkansas governor and one-time Republican front-runner Mike Huckabee stated: "We ought to have an immediate, very clear monitoring of our borders and particularly to make sure if there is any unusual activity of Pakistanis coming into the country. We just need to be very, very thorough in looking at every aspect of our own security internally because again, we live in a very, very dangerous time." Huckabee's senior advisor, James Pinkerton, who worked in the White House under presidents Ronald Reagan and George H. W. Bush, warned in September 2007 of a "Muslimization" of America—reminiscent of sentiments expressed a century earlier by members of the Asiatic Exclusion League—and concluded that "to keep the peace, we must separate our civilizations." In a January 2008 interview with *Mother Jones* editor David Corn, Pinkerton stated that America needs "a cop in front of every mosque," flatly assuming threat and danger on the basis of religion and nationality. In July 2012, five Republican members of the House of Representatives, including Michele Bachman, alledged that longtime aid to Secretary of State Hillary Clinton, Huma Abedin, has ties to the Muslim Brotherhood through her late father, mother, and brother. In response, Republican senator John McCain took the Senate floor to refute these allegations, stating, "Ultimately, what is at stake in this matter is larger even than the reputation of one person. This is about who we are as a nation, and who we aspire to be. What makes America exceptional among the countries of the world is that we are bound together as citizens not by blood or class, not by sect or ethnicity, but by a set of enduring, universal, and equal rights that are the foundation of our constitution, our laws, our citizenry, and our identity. When anyone, not least a member of Congress, launches specious and degrading attacks against fellow Americans on the basis of nothing more than fear of who they are and ignorance of what they stand for, it defames the spirit of our nation, and we all grow poorer because of it" (http://www.theatlanticwire.com/politics/2012/07).

41. The population of India alone is more than a billion people, the second highest national population in the world after China and nearly one-sixth of the planet's population. India is the world's largest democracy, with twenty-three official languages and more than one thousand dialects spoken. Within the nation's twenty-eight states, there exists a rich variety of regional and tribal cultures, in addition to a wide array of religious affiliations including Buddhism, Christianity, Hinduism, Jainism, Judaism, Islam, Sikhism, and Zoroastrianism. Consequently, South Asian American community identities now exhibit a

notable degree of variance within worldviews and lifestyles. Indeed, as Khilnani reminds us, "India—contrary to the BJP [Bharatiya Janata Party] dream of a homogeneous nation—daily becomes more, not less, diverse as ideas proliferate about what it should be" (Khilnani 1999, xiv). The situation becomes even more complex when you add in the migrant situations of the Trinidanian Indians, East African Indians, Malaysian Indians, British Indians, or Indians coming from the Middle East.

Yet, for many, their identity refers not so much to national affiliations, but to an elaborate network of regional culture, dialect, and custom. This fragmentation, of course, is not surprising given that India was composed of separate and distinct princely states prior to and during British rule and did not become a nation in the formal sense of the term until slightly more than fifty years ago. Indeed, India is still developing a sense of what it means to be "Indian." Many individuals connect much more closely to regional or religious identities than to some national loyalty. Thus, it is relatively easy to understand how adopting a South Asian American identity might be challenging for some immigrants, particularly those in the first generation. Loyalties to an Indian homeland unite this diverse group on many levels, providing a collective sense of identity. But like all groups, they must struggle against their own discrepancies, "which lie precisely in the fact that they are composed of individuals, self-conscious individuals, whose differences from each other have to be resolved and reconciled to a degree which allows the group to be viable and cohere" (Cohen 1985, 11). For these reasons, the answer to the question, "Who are you?" is markedly negotiable for many South Asian Americans. While in a group of other South Asians, a person might identify himself or herself regionally, as a Gujarati. Yet, while at work, surrounded by non-South Asians, a person might choose the label South Asian, South Asian American, Indian, Pakistani, Indian American, Asian American, Asian, or just American. Strategically with the response provided, the answer often depends upon who is asking the question and why.

42. This is largely a function of the secondary immigration of extended family members that resulted from sponsorship by established "brain drain" immigrants, which drew more economically heterogeneous individuals yet ethnically homogeneous communities of South Asians to the United States during the 1990s. In post-9/11 America, religious divisions have also become starker. Indeed, the multiple ways of being "South Asian" has much to do with the diversity of South Asia itself, which has frequently experienced bouts of communal violence between Hindus and Muslims, sometimes involving other social groups like upper caste and Dalits.

43. From the group's Web site: http://www.samarmagazine.org/.

44. Other notable groups include the Asian Pacific Americans for Progress—a national grassroots group that facilitates progressive political action through political dialogue on Internet blogs—and the South Asian American Voting Youth (SAAVY)—an organization committed to guaranteeing the equal and full participation by South Asians in the civic and political life of the United States. In an attempt to connect minority groups, the Coalition for an Egalitarian and Pluralistic India has sponsored parades to simultaneously mark the anniversaries of the assassination of Mahatma Gandhi and MLK.

45. Indeed, South Asian women residing in the United States appear to be at particularly high risk for intimate partner violence. In recent studies, 35 percent of South Asian American women report intimate partner violence in their current relationship (Dasgupta 2007, 3). Of even more concern, some within the South Asian community report an increase in domestic violence after 9/11 due to high levels of stress, fear, a weakened economy, and intense scrutiny by law enforcement and locals (Ebrahhim 2001). Yet, in recent years, many South Asian

domestic violence victims are deterred from seeking public services or leaving battering spouses, for fear of jeopardizing their immigration status and/or custody of their children.

Chapter Three

1. The names of performers have been changed to protect their anonymity.

2. In SILC Yearbook 1994, 9.

3. This legislation allowed up to 20,000 people from India to enter the United States annually. In 1990, the Minnesota South Asian community comprised a little more than 8,000 individuals, nearly 75 percent of them living in Hennepin County or Ramsey County. This number increased 200 percent from 1980 to 1990. According to the 2000 census, in the Minneapolis/St.Paul community the number has reached 14,535.

4. Polly Sonifer, "Interview with Neena Gada," 2002. *SILC Oral History Project*, Minnesota State Historical Society, 27.

5. Polly Sonifer, "Interview with Preeti Mathur," 2002. *SILC Oral History Project*, Minnesota State Historical Society, 21.

6. From 1979 to 1988, SILC used the Commonwealth Community Center; from 1988 to 1992, they reserved St. Anthony Park Elementary. Currently, the school is located at Como Park Senior High School and meets every Saturday after Labor Day through early May.

7. Polly Sonifer, "Interview with Neena Gada," 2002. *SILC Oral History Project*, Minnesota State Historical Society, 17.

8. Polly Sonifer, "Interview with Rama Padamnashan," 2002. *SILC Oral History Project*, Minnesota State Historical Society, 20.

9. During the time I was working at SILC, students participated in the Minnesota Asian American festival and marched in a parade with two dozen other Asian American organizations that concluded with a festival that included food, entertainment, and an information booth. SILC students also celebrated India's fiftieth anniversary of independence with the India Association of Minnesota. Here, students sang the Indian national anthem and heard older community members recount their personal stories relating India's independence movement. These performance experiences encouraged deliberation and debate, broadened the students' critical consciousness, and taught them the value of participating in the public sphere. During Diwali, students and teachers celebrated with a traditional Indian shadow puppet show and students made diyas in art class to display for parents. Later in the year, many students participated in a Festival of India celebration performing in a Mohini Attam dance.

10. Polly Sonifer, "Interview with Neena Gada," 2002. *SILC Oral History Project*, Minnesota State Historical Society, 17.

11. However, it is easy to see how an event predicated upon the issue of ethnic and national identity could also kindle political, economic, social, or cultural antagonisms and rivalries. In response to such potential conflict, festival organizers work to avoid points of contention that may divide or antagonize other groups. As I learned in a Festival of Nations organizational meeting, this orientation is maintained through a series of rules and regulations that are strictly enforced. No symbolism or logos of an inflammatory nature may be displayed and no items containing political or racial statements or slogans can be displayed, reproduced, or sold. To avoid controversy, no maps or names of countries are used in the booths, only the names of the people from a given area and one flag no larger than 3x5.

Further, exhibits at the Festival of Nations may only involve the display of cultural articles "worthy of the culture" and "typical and in keeping with the theme" (Festival of Nations Procedures and Policies 2000, 29). Finally, no title of a specific organization or club representing an ethnic community may be displayed. All of these rules, strictly enforced, function to contain and control festival discourse. Yet, despite all the attempts to neutralize discourse, the political nature of the festival is simply unavoidable. From the focus upon nationalism to questions of cultural domain, the issues at the heart of the festival naturally breed controversy. Even the rules, meant to diffuse potential conflict, can be construed as problematic. That is, while festival organizers have an opportunity to help disenfranchised individuals and groups be heard, their role as culture brokers sometimes leads them to ignore some practices and peoples while promoting others. Therefore, while it might be the festival organizers' intent to downplay political speech, the festival is without a doubt a political venture as has been noted by folklore scholars from Bauman and Sawin (1991) to Kirshenblatt-Gimblett (1991).

Chapter Four

1. Shyamala, of course, is just one of a growing number of South Asian and South Asian American women who use dance as a medium for public activism (Garlough 2007, 2008). In the South Asian American community, Ananya Chatterjea, a University of Minnesota assistant professor of dance, recently founded "Women in Motion." This performing company of South Asian artists creates political theater and performs in community-based and other artistic forums. Chatterjea explains, "I do political theater, using dance to tell ordinary stories about ordinary people and to address violence. I am interested in being someone who has something to say, to inspire social change, to invite people into political thought . . . The world is a mess and I thought 'How can I dance this dance about beauty and spirituality when I see what is going on around me: violence, patriarchy, class hierarchy?'" (Minnesota "Body Language," July/August 2003, 32). Chatterjee notes that the reaction to her work from the South Asian community is mixed; "Some say, 'Where were you all these years?' But some said, 'You're washing our dirty laundry in public.' They thought people would think that India is terrible. I said, 'No, I'm showing how Indian women resisted violence'" (Minnesota "Body Language," July/August 2003, 33).

2. Shyamala and Sandra had worked together on a project called InnerDiVisions before collaborating with Anjali. Soon after, Sangita added the dimension of video/film for dance.

3. See Post Natyam Web page, http://www.postnatyam.net/.

4. See Post Natyam Web page, http://www.postnatyam.net/.

5. See Post Natyam Web page, http://www.postnatyam.net/. Through their performances and research interests, Post Natyam Collective members hope to develop "a critical awareness of the politics surrounding South Asian dance forms and our contemporary realities." The research of Post Natyam Collective members takes many forms. It often "blends the line between art-making and academic scholarship." Their scholarly output includes published academic papers, conference presentations, lectures, copy editorial work, art books, and archival documentation of the collective's creative processes. In doing so, the Post Natyam Collective engages in "scholarly research that reflects its critical, border-crossing approach to contemporary South Asian performance" (http://www.postnatyam.net/).

6. In addition, Post Natyam commitment to an egalitarian or democratic approach to organizing has had a significant impact upon the work they produce. They note, "We have

chosen the collective as an organizational model because it gives voice to different perspectives, allows us to pool resources, and encourages democratic dialogue. This model contrasts with a traditional western dance company model, which embodies a single choreographer's artistic vision, and from the classical guru-shisya model, where students are dedicated to only one teacher" (http://www.postnatyam.net/).

7. Because Post Natyam is a collective, the members "often work in modular fashion, assembling our repertoire in different ways to create various thematically related evening length performances. This means solos, duets, or ensemble pieces are available and can be booked individually or together as determined by the presenting organization in conjunction with the choreographers" (http://www.postnatyam.net/).

8. Moreover, the "racial profiling, long under attack in some parts of the United States, became acceptable to many who might earlier have objected to the practice. Along with that, detentions by the state were widespread and undertaken without any shred of evidence. Sikh men, with turbans and beards, bore a special burden of 'looking Muslim' given that Osama bin Laden who was accused by the United States of masterminding the attacks also had a turban and a beard" (Grewal 2005, 210).

9. It seems important to note that being misidentified as a terrorist is a real problem even now.

10. SAALT also adds the following: "We would be remiss, however, if we didn't mention that in addition to tales of terror were many of hope. In many communities throughout the United States, Americans were responsive and even pro-active in reassuring their Muslim, Sikh, Arab, and South Asian American neighbors that they would stand with them. Acts of kindness and compassion included public statements and vigils, editorials denouncing stereotypes, interfaith worship, and simply patronizing the businesses owned by Middle Eastern and South Asian entrepreneurs" (SAALT 2008).

11. Of course, this does not mean that there were no differences in South Asian Americans' post-9/11 experiences. It is clear that some communities had better experiences than others. However, as Cainkar points out, it also seems clear that most communities faced some degree of challenge post-9/11, with regard to how they lived their lives in a state of "homeland insecurity" (116).

12. As Katrak (2007) notes, "There are positive nurturing aspects of practicing traditional arts, there are also disturbing resonances of nationalist deployments of the dance for fundamentalist ideologies. Specifically, Bharata Natyam . . . . is given exclusionary connotations as though no other forms do not exist apart from those practiced by the Hindu majority" (219).

13. The concept of intersectionality has deep roots in the early work of Anna Julia Cooper and W. E. B. Du Bois.

14. In addition, the concept of intersectionality also has been developed by communications and rhetoric scholars. For example, Enck-Wanzer (2006) has used the notion of "intersectional rhetoric" to describe "a rhetoric that places multiple rhetorical forms (in this case speech, embodiment, and image) on relatively equal footing, is not leader centered, and draws from a number of diverse discursive political or rhetorical conventions" (177). Here, there is a commitment to studying the complicated ways that bodies, words, and silences can draw upon and combine cultural traditions and popular culture. This puts rhetoric scholars in dialogue with performance studies scholars, who research body rhetoric in order to understand the ways that nonverbal forms serve to bolster testimony and political discourse. Interestingly, scholars from other disciplines have used a variety of metaphors to describe this type of discourse and performance. These metaphors range from borderland, "mestizaje," hybridity, strategic essentialism, or a third space.

15. Eclecticism has a deeply rooted intellectual history in India; examples can be seen in a variety of philosophical and religious texts written as early as 1000 BCE. Eclecticism is evident in the Jain view of truth known as *anakantavada*, the Hindu *Vedas*, *Puranas*, and *Yogasastras*, and Nagarjuna's *Mahayana* Buddhist dialectic. Far from being a monolithic phenomenon rooted in ancient texts, eclecticism exists in many varieties, its differences often being based upon the other philosophical perspectives with which it comes into contact. So, one might speak of a democratic eclecticism that seeks to build consensus, as seen in the discourse of Rammohun Roy during the Indian Renaissance or the postmodern eclecticism of Salman Rushdie that calls attention to the hybridity and disjunctures within postcolonial and transnational identities (Garlough 2007; Hatcher 1999).

Chapter Five

1. The last names of participants have been omitted to protect their anonymity, unless requested otherwise.

2. For example, like *The Vagina Monologues*, *Yoni Ki Baat* works toward ending the silence around violence against women in South Asian culture. Here, women confront difficult issues that range from domestic abuse to incest to rape. In doing so, these women draw upon a long legacy of feminist activists and scholars who advocate for the power of speaking the truth in public places—not only because it brings issues of importance to the fore, but also because it works to connect women through discourses of care and concern. As Lorde so eloquently argued, "My silences did not protect me. Your silence will not protect you. But for every real word spoken, for every attempt I ever made to speak those truths for which I am still seeking, I had made contact with some women while we examined words to fit a world in which we all believed, bridging our differences. And it was the concern and caring of all those women which gave me the strength and enabled me to scrutinize the essentials of my living" (81–82).

3. In addition to being performed at *Yoni ki Baat*, this poem was later published on Roopa's blog, political poet(ry) on July 10, 2007 (http://politicalpoet.wordpress.com/?s=surviving+sexual+abuse). Here she recounts her experience, the reasons she composed the poem, and why she feels it is important to share her story with others. The intent of this chapter is not to attest to the veracity of her story of sexual violence but to focus attention on how she uses performance for political purposes.

4. *The Vagina Monologues* has been translated into over forty-five languages, appearing in theaters around the globe and hailed as a "feminist classic" although it is only a decade old (Bell and Reverby 2005). Indeed, as Cooper (2007) notes, "By now *The Vagina Monologues* is a worldwide phenomenon. Much more than a dramatic script, the play is a mass culture event, performed hundreds of times each year" (727). A testament to its popularity, HBO aired an original documentary of the play in 2002 that generated high ratings. Many attribute the power of *The Vagina Monologues* to its transgressive content and carnivalesque public nature. Performing the personal publicly, women's private experiences are played out on a stage and celebrate typically disparaged expressions of desire, fantasies, or physical body parts, such as the vagina (Bell and Reverby 2005). In doing so, *The Vagina Monologues* draws from a long history of feminist political practices or what could be called the "old bones" of sisterhood (Bell and Reverby 2005, 431). In a sense, it is a reclamation project that relates closely to work on the women's health movement that "takes back" the female body for women in the same spirit as the feminist text *Our Bodies Ourselves*. It also bears close resemblance to work done in early self-help movements and consciousness-raising groups. For example, in terms

of feminist performances, Bell (2005) notes, that it is not unusual for feminist performers to conduct interviews with other women and use this material to deliver "other women" on stage in addition to themselves.

5. The proceeds funded two shelters for women and girls and the extensive national and local press coverage put a news spotlight on Indian women's experience of violence and local efforts to confront it. The V-day events hosted by Jagon and Sangat (two leading South Asian feminist organizations) also included a three-day conference in Delhi entitled "Confronting Violence, Recounting Resistance, Envisioning Justice." Here, women from India, Pakistan, Bangladesh, Afghanistan, Sri Lanka, Nepal, Germany, France, Sweden, the Netherlands, and the United States presented research on violence against women in South Asia and its relationship to militarism, fundamentalism, and globalization (http://www.vday.org).

Chapter Six

1. My thinking about the importance of "questions" to rhetorical performances owes much to my participation in USC's Rhetorical Theory Conferences.

2. What is surprising, however, is that very few scholars seek to consider the more important question of why such rhetorical work has gone understudied. Certainly, language barriers often make such research particularly challenging for those who are not a part of the cultural group under consideration (Blake 1979). Further, studying contemporary non-Western, ethnic, or immigrant rhetoric often requires an understanding of present-day politics as well as thoughtful investigation of historical, economic, and societal contexts. For example, in chapter 2, I argued that in order to understand Sudhindra Bose's calls for recognition and acknowledgment in his Chautauqua lectures and books addressing South Asian immigration and anti-British rule, a rhetorical analysis should also pay attention to the historical and economic context of pre-independence India, the diverse rhetorical strategies of Indian intellectuals and politicians, as well as the anti-immigration rhetoric in the United States. Another important reason that non-Western, immigrant, or ethnic rhetoric often goes unnoticed is because the rhetorical practices are not in a *form* that scholars of rhetoric traditionally recognize. Studying rhetorical modes, media, and situations—some of them significantly different from those found in the West—requires not only a firm grasp on rhetorical theory but also a thorough grounding in the target group's culture (Blake 1979). As Starosta suggests, such rhetoric often "remains invisible to the untrained eye and lies beneath the surface of culture" (Starosta 1979). Researchers must be prepared to analyze both discursive and nondiscursive texts, attending to both local and popular variation upon forms. For example, in this book I have shared how Indian folk songs, appropriated by members of the Gadar movement, were used rhetorically to publicly perform critiques of British violence and the suffering it inflicted upon Indian people. These songs were strategically employed to stir support for rebellion and what would later be a fight for independence.

3. In Hinduism, for example, as the gods and goddesses play, the invention and destruction of the world is their game. This sense of creation as play is apparent in vernacular religious performances, such as the *Rasa lila* (translated literally as "performance of play," or as it is more widely known, the Dance of Divine Love).

4. For these reasons, critical play, to my mind, is best characterized by a sense of wandering and ambiguity, as suggested by Dotader (2007). Indeed, as Caputo notes, the word ambiguity itself is derived from the Latin *agere* "to act" and comes from the verb *ambigere* "to

wander" (*ambi*—around—and *agere*—to do). In critical play, the audience is asked to wander with the rhetorical performance, tolerate disjunctures, ruptures of context, and apparent betrayals of meaning, as they learn to become at home in a world that is plural. This play attempts to deliver a message without covering or explaining away what remains baffling about it and the other in it. It invites a "poetically rigorous attentiveness to language, a reading of words against themselves . . . working language against itself, delivering its silence" (Ziarek 1994, 10). In doing so, it brings language close to Otherness, showing forth strangeness and foreignness for political purposes.

References

Abbott, D. 1987. The ancient word: Rhetoric in Aztec culture. *Rhetorica* 5: 251–64.

Abbott, D. 1989. Aztecs and orators: Rhetoric in New Spain. *Texte* 8 (9): 353–65.

Abbott, D. 1996. *Rhetoric in the New World: Rhetorical theory and practice in colonial Spanish America*. Columbia: University of South Carolina Press.

Abrahams, R. 1968. Introductory remarks to a rhetorical theory of folklore. *Journal of American Folklore* 81: 144–58.

Abrahams, R. 2005. *Everyday life: A poetics of vernacular practices*. Philadelphia: University of Pennsylvania Press.

Abu-Lughod, L. 1986. *Veiled sentiments: Honor and poetry in a Bedouin society*. Berkeley and Los Angeles: University of California Press.

Appadurai, A. 2003. Disjuncture and difference in the global cultural economy. In *Theorizing diaspora: A reader*. Ed. J. E. Braziel and A. Mannur. Oxford: Blackwell Publishing.

Arendt, H. 1929. *Love and Saint Augustine*. Chicago: University of Chicago Press.

Arendt, H. 1958. *The human condition*. Chicago: University of Chicago Press.

Arnold, B. 1983. *Imagined communities: Reflections on the origin and spread of nationalism*. London: Verso.

Asen, R., and D. Brouwer. 2001. *Counterpublics and the state*. Albany: State University of New York Press.

Assisi, F. 2007. Yoni ki Baat spotlights desi diaspora women's sexuality. http://www.indolink .com.

Bahr, D. 1988. *Pima and Papago ritual oratory: A study of three texts*. San Francisco: Indian Historical Press.

Bakhtin, M. 1990. *Art and answerability: Early philosophical essays*. Ed. M. Holquist and V. Liapunov. Trans. V. Liapunov and K. Borstrom. Austin: University of Texas Press.

Balgooyen, T. 1968. The Plains Indian as public speaker. *Landmarks in Western Oratory*. Ed. David H. Grover, 213–43. Laramie: University of Wyoming Publications.

Basch, L., N. Schiller, and C. Blanc. 1994. *Nations unbound: Transnational projects, postcolonial predicaments, and deterritorialized nation-states*. New York: Gordon & Breach.

Bateson, G. 1972. *Steps to an ecology of mind*. New York: Ballantine.

Bauman, R. 1977. *Verbal art as performance*. Prospect Heights, IL: Waveland Press.

Bauman, R. 1986. *Story, performance, and event: Contextual studies of oral narrative*. Cambridge: Cambridge University Press.

Bauman, R. 1992a. Contextualization, tradition, and the dialogue of genres: Icelandic legends of the *Kraftaskald*. In *Rethinking context: Language as an interactive phenomenon*. Ed. C. Goodwin and A. Duranti, 125–45. Cambridge: Cambridge University Press.

Bauman, R. 1992b. *Folklore, cultural performances and popular entertainments: A communication-centered handbook*. Oxford: Oxford University Press.

Bauman, R. 1992. Disclaimers of performance. In *Responsibility and evidence in oral discourse*. Ed. Jane H. Hill and Judith T. Irvine, 182–96. Cambridge: Cambridge University Press.

Bauman, R. 1993. The nationalization and internationalization of folklore: The case of Schoolcraft's "Gitshee Gauzinee." *Western Folkore* 52: 247–69.

Bauman, R., ed. 1993. *Folklore and culture on the Texas-Mexican border.* Austin, TX: CMAS Books.

Bauman, R., and C. Briggs. 1990. Poetic and performance as critical perspectives on language and social life. *Annual Review of Anthropology* 19: 59–88.

Bauman, R., and P. Sawin. 1991. The politics of participation in folklife festivals. In *Exhibiting cultures: The poetics and politics of museum display.* Ed. S. D. Lavine and I. Karp. Washington: Smithsonian Institution Press.

Beach, J. 2007. Yours, not mine: Contested notions of Americanism and Americanization. Paper presented at International Globlization, Diversity and Education Conference, Spokane, Washington.

Behar, R. 1996. *The vulnerable observer.* Boston: Beacon Press.

Behar, R., and D. A. Gordon. 1995. *Women writing culture.* Berkeley and Los Angeles: University of California Press.

Bell, S. E., and S. M. Reverby. 2005. Vaginal politics: Tensions and possibilities in *The Vagina Monologues. Women's Studies International Forum* 28: 430–44.

Bhabha, H. K. 1980. Of mimicry and man: The ambivalence of colonial discourse. In *Race critical theories.* Ed. P. Essed and D. T. Goldberg. Oxford: Blackwell Publishing.

Bhabha, H. K. 1990. DissemiNation: Time, narrative, and the margins of the modern nation. In *Nation and narration.* Ed. Homi Bhabha. London: Routledge

Bhabha, H. K. 1994. *The location of culture.* New York: Routledge.

Bharati, A. 1970. The Hindu renaissance and its apologetic patterns. *Journal of Asian Studies* 39: 267–87.

Bhargqva, S. 2012. Yoni ki Baat: Talk of the vagina. *Brown Girl Magazine*, April 10, 2012. http://browngirlmagazine.com/2012/04.

Bhattacharya, M. 1979. The second Kasauli seminar on aesthetics. *Social Scientist* 10 (8): 64–71.

Bhattacharya, M. 1983. The IPTA in Bengal. *Journal of Arts and Ideas* 2: 9.

Biesecker, B. A. 2002. Remembering World War II: The rhetoric and politics of national commemoration at the turn of the 21st century. *Quarterly Journal of Speech* 88 (4): 393–409.

Bingham, C. 2006. Before recognition and after: The educational critique. *Educational Theory* 56: 325–44.

Blair, C., M. S. Jeppeson, and E. J. Pucci. 1991. Public memorializing on postmodernity: The Vietnam Veterans Memorial as prototype. *Quarterly Journal of Speech* 77: 263–88.

Blake, C. 1979. Rhetoric and intercultural communication. In *Handbook of intercultural communication.* Ed. H. Kotthoff and H. Spencer-Oatey. Beverly Hills, CA: Sage Publications.

Blank, T. J. 2009. Folklore and the Internet: Vernacular expression in a digital world. *All USU Press publications.* Book 35. Logan: Utah State University Press.

Blum, L. 1980. *Friendship, altruism, and morality.* London: Routledge.

Blythin, E. 1990. *Huei Tlatoani: The Mexican speaker.* Lanham, MD: University Press of America.

Bordenaue, P. 1979. Intercultural communication. In *Handbook of intercultural communication.* Ed. Molefi Kete Asante, Eileen Newmark, and Cecil A. Blake. Beverly Hills: Sage Publications.

Bose, S. 1920. *Fifteen years in America.* Calcutta: Kar, Majumder & Co. Publishers.

Bose, S. 1923. Indians barred from American citizenship. *Modern Review* 33: 691–95.

Bourdieu, M. 1990. *The logic of practice*. Stanford: Stanford University Press.

Bourdieu, P., and J. B. Thompson. 1991. *Language and symbolic power*. Cambridge, MA: Harvard University Press.

Bradunas, E., and B. Topping. 1988. *Ethnic heritage and language schools in America: Studies in American folklife No. 4*. Washington: American Folklife Center.

Brah, A., and A. Phoenix. 2004. Ain't I a woman? Revisiting intersectionality. *Journal of International Women's Studies* 5 (3): 75–86.

Brandwood, L. 1976. *A word index to Plato*. Leeds: W. S. Macy and Son.

Braziel, J., and A. Mannur. 2003. *Theorizing diaspora: A reader*. Oxford: Blackwell Publishing.

Britzman, D. 1998. Queer pedagogy and its strange techniques. In *Lost subjects, contested objects*. Albany: State University of New York Press.

Bronner, S. 2002. *Folk nation: Folklore in the creation of American tradition*. New York: Rowman and Littlefield Publishers.

Brown, J. M. 2006. *Global South Asians: Introducing the modern diaspora*. Cambridge: Cambridge University Press.

Brummett, B. 1991. *Rhetorical dimensions of popular culture*. Tuscaloosa: University of Alabama Press.

Brummett, B. 1994. *Rhetoric in popular culture*. New York: St. Martin's Press.

Bruner, M. 2002. *Strategies of remembrance: The rhetorical dimensions of national identity construction*. Columbia: University of South Carolina Press.

Burke, K. 1931. *Counterstatement*. Los Altos, CA: Hermes Publishing.

Burke, K. 1931. *Counter-statement*. Berkeley and Los Angeles: University of California Press.

Burke, K. 1950. *A rhetoric of motives*. Berkeley and Los Angeles: University of California Press.

Butler, J. 1987. *Subjects of desire: Hegelian reflections in twentieth-century France*. New York: Columbia University Press.

Butler, J. 1993. *Bodies that matter*. New York: Routledge.

Butler, J. 2004. *Precarious life: The powers of mourning and violence*. London: Verso.

Butler, J. 2005. *Giving an account of oneself*. New York: Fordham University Press.

Caillois, R. 2001. *Man, play and games*. Trans. M. Barash. Chicago: University of Illinois Press.

Cameron, D., and D. Kulick. 2003. *Language and sexuality*. Cambridge: Cambridge University Press.

Camp, C. 1978. American Indian oratory in the white image: An analysis of stereotypes. *Journal of American Culture* 1: 811–17.

Canning, C. M. 2005. *The most American thing in America: Circuit Chautauqua as performance*. Iowa City: University of Iowa Press.

Caputo, J. D. 1987. *Radical hermeneutics: Repetition, deconstruction, and the hermeneutic project*. Bloomington: Indiana University Press.

Caputo, J. D. 2000. *More radical hermeneutics*. Bloomington: Indiana University Press.

Case, S. E. 1990. *Performing feminisms: Feminist critical theory and theatre*. Baltimore: Johns Hopkins University Press.

Case, S. E. 1990. Introduction. In *Performing feminisms: Feminist critical theory and theatre*. Ed. S. E. Case. Baltimore: Johns Hopkins University Press.

Case, S. E. 2001. Feminism and performance: A post-disciplinary couple. *Theatre Research International* 26 (2): 145–52.

Case, S. E. 2008. *Feminism and theatre*. New York: Palgrave Macmillan.

Cavell, S. 1987. *Must we mean what we say? A book of essays*. Updated ed. New York: Cambridge University Press.

Cavell, S. 2005. *Philosophy the day after tomorrow*. Cambridge, MA: The Belknap Press of Harvard University Press.

Chatterjee, P. 1993. *The nation and its fragments*. Princeton, NJ: Princeton University Press.

Cheng, M. 2002. *In other Los Angeleses: Multicentric performance art*. Berkeley and Los Angeles: University of California Press.

Chitnis, S. 1988. Feminism: Indian ethos and Indian convictions. In *Women in Indian society. A reader*. Ed. R. Ghadially. New Delhi: Sage Publications.

Choo, H. Y., and M. M. Ferree. 2010. Practicing intersectionality in sociological research: A critical analysis of inclusions, interactions, and institutions in the study of inequalities. *Sociological Theory* 28 (2): 130–49.

Cloud, D. L. 2004. To veil the threat of terror: Afghan women and the "clash of civilizations." *Quarterly Journal of Speech* 90: 285–306.

Coaltion against Genocide. 2005. Genocide in Gujarat: The Sangh Parivar, Norendra Modi and the Government of Gujarat. March 2, 2005. www.coaltionagainstgenocide.org.

Coe, C. 1999. The education of the folk: Peasant schools and folklore scholarship. *Journal of American Folklore* 113 (447): 20–43.

Cohen, A. 1985. *The symbolic construction of community*. London: Routledge.

Cohen-Cruz, J. 2006. The problem democracy is supposed to solve. In *The Sage handbook of performance studies*. Ed. D. Soyini Madison and Judith Hamera, 427–45. London: Sage Publications.

Conquergood, D. 1989. Books in review: Poetics, play, progress, and power: The performative turn in anthropology. *Text and Performance Quarterly* 1: 82–95.

Conquergood, D. 1992. Ethnography, rhetoric, and performance. *Quarterly Journal of Speech* 78: 80–123.

Conquergood, D. 2000. Rethinking evolution: The trope of the talking book and other figures of speech. *Text and Performance Quarterly* 20 (4): 325–41.

Conquergood, D. 2002. Legal theatre: Performance, punishment, and the death penalty. *Theatre Journal* 54: 339–67.

Conquergood, D. 2002. Performance studies interventions and radical research. *Drama Review* 46 (2): 145–56.

Conquergood, D. 2006. Rethinking ethnography: Towards a critical cultural politics. In *The Sage handbook of performance studies*. Ed. D. S. Madison and J. Hamera. London: Sage Publications.

Cooper, C. M. 2007. Worrying about vaginas: Feminism and Eve Ensler's *The Vagina Monologues*. *Journal of Women in Culture and Society* 32: 727–58.

Coorlawala, U. A. 2003. It matters for whom you dance: Audience participation in Rasa theory. In *Audience participation: Essays on inclusion in performance*. Ed. S. Kattwinkel, 37–54. London: Praeger.

Cornell, D. 1992. The ethical significance of the Chiffonnian. In *The philosophy of the limit*. New York: Routledge.

Crenshaw, K. 1989. Demarginalizing the intersection of race and sex: A black feminist critique of antidiscrimination doctrine, feminist theory and antiracist politics. *University of Chicago Legal Forum*, 139–68.

Crenshaw, K. 1995. Mapping the margins: Intersectionality, identity politics, and violence against women of color. In *Critical race theory: The writings that formed the movement*. Ed. Kimberle Crenshaw et al. New York: New York University Press, 357–83.

Csikszentmihalyi, M. 1990. *Flow: The psychology of optimal experience*. New York: Harper Perennial.

Cvetkovich, A. 2003. *An archive of feelings: Trauma, sexuality, and lesbian public cultures.* Durham, NC: Duke University Press.

Dall, C. 1888. *The life of Dr. Anandabai Joshee: A kinswoman of the Pundita Ramabai.* Boston: Roberts Brothers.

Darder, A. 1991. *Culture and power in the classroom: A critical foundation for bicultural education.* Westport, CT: Greenwood Publishing Group.

Darnovsky, M., B. L. Epstain, and R. Flacks. 1995. *Cultural politics and social movements.* Philadelphia: Temple University Press.

Das, V. 2007. *Life and words: Violence and the descent into the ordinary.* Berkeley and Los Angeles: University of California Press.

Das, V., A. Kleinman, M. Lock, M. Ramphele, and P. Reynolds, eds. 2001. *Remaking a world: Violence, social suffering, and recovery.* Berkeley and Los Angeles: University of California Press.

Das, V., A. Kleinman, M. Ramphele, and P. Reynolds, eds. 2000. *Violence and subjectivity.* Berkeley and Los Angeles: University of California Press.

Dasgupta, M. 2006. *Unruly immigrants: Rights, activism, and transnational South Asian politics in the United States.* Durham, NC: Duke University Press.

Dasgupta, S. D. 2007. *Body evidence: Intimate violence against South Asian women in America.* New Brunswick, NJ: Rutgers University Press.

Davis, C. 2008. Pond-women revelations: The subaltern registers in Maithil women's expressive forms. *Journal of American Folklore* 121: 286–318.

Davis, D. 2000. *Breaking up (at) totality: A rhetoric of laughter.* Carbondale: Southern Illinois University Press.

Davis, S. 1986. *Parades and power: Street theatre in the nineteenth century.* Berkeley and Los Angeles: University of California Press.

de Bary, W. 1958. *Sources of Indian tradition.* New York: Columbia University Press.

Degh, L. 1968. Approaches to folklore research among immigrant groups. *Journal of American Folklore* 77: 167–91.

Dehejia, H. 2004. Kalasha: A living visual metaphor. In *Sabda: Text and interpretation in Indian thought.* Ed. Santosh Sareen and Makarand Paranjape, 199–214. New Delhi: Mantra Books.

Dehejia, H., and P. Makarand. 2003. *Saundarya: The perception and practice of beauty in India.* New Delhi: Samvad India Foundation.

Del Negro, G. 2004. *The Passeggiata and popular culture in an Italian town: Folklore and the performance of modernity.* Montreal: McGill-Queen's University Press.

Delgado, F. 1998. Chicano ideology revisited: Rap music and the (re)articulation of Chicanismo. *Western Journal of Communication* 62: 95–113.

Denzin, N. 2006. The politics and ethics of performance pedagogy: Toward a pedagogy of hope. In *The Sage handbook of performance studies.* Ed. D. S. Madison and J. Hamera. London: Sage Publications.

Denzin, N., and Y. Lincoln, eds. 2000. *The handbook of qualitative research.* 2nd ed. London: Sage Publications.

Derrida, J. 1978. *Writing and difference.* Trans. A. Bass. Chicago: University of Chicago Press.

Derrida, J. 1981. *Dissemination.* Trans. B. Johnson. Chicago: University of Chicago Press.

Derrida, J. 1985. *The ear of the other: Autobiography, transference, translation.* Trans. P. Kamuf, C. McDonald, C. Levesque, and A. Ronell. Lincoln: University of Nebraska Press.

Derrida, J. 1994. *The politics of friendship.* Trans. G. Collins. New York: Verso.

Derrida, J. 2000. Demeure: Fiction and testimony. In *The instant of my death.* Trans. E. Rottenberg. Stanford: Stanford University Press.

Derrida, J. 2001. *On cosmopolitanism and forgiveness*. New York: Routledge.

Derrida, J. 2005. *On touching Jean-Luc Nancy*. Trans. C. Irizarry. Stanford: Stanford University Press.

Derrida, J., and A. Dufourmantelle. 2000. *Of hospitality*. Stanford: Stanford University Press.

Diamond, E. 1997. *Unmaking mimesis: Essays on feminism and theater*. New York: Routledge.

Dirik, A. 1994. The postcolonial aura: Third world criticism in the age of global capitalism. *Critical Inquiry* 20: 328–56.

Divakaruni, C. 2002. Being dark-skinned in a dark time. *Good Housekeeping*, January 2002, 89–90.

Dolan, J. 1993. *Presence and desire: Essays on gender, sexuality, performance*. Ann Arbor: University of Michigan Press.

Dolan, J. 2005. *Utopia in performance: Finding hope at the theater*. Ann Arbor: University of Michigan Press.

Dolan, J. 2005. The polemics and potential of theatre studies and performance. In *The Sage handbook of performance studies*. Ed. D. S. Madison and J. Hamera, 508–26. Thousand Oaks: Sage Publications.

Dorst, J. 1990. Tags and burners, cycles and networks: Folklore in the telectronic age. *Journal of Folklore Research* 27: 179–90.

Doxtader, E. 2001. Loving history's fate, perverting the beautiful soul: Scenes of felicity's potential. *Cultural Studies* 15: 206–21.

Doxtader, E. 2001. In the name of reconciliation: The faith and works of counterpublicity. In *Counterpublics and the state*. Ed. Robert Asen and Daniel Brower, 59–86. Albany: State University of New York Press.

Doxtader, E. 2003. Reconciliation—a rhetorical concept/ion. *Quarterly Journal of Speech* 89: 267–92.

Du Toit, F., and E. Doxtader. 2010. *In the balance: South Africans debate reconciliation*. Auckland Park: Jacana Media.

Dugger, C. 2002. Religious riots loom over Indian politics. *New York Times*, July 27. http://www.genocide atach.org/Indiariots27July2002.htm.

Dundes, A. 1980. *Interpreting folklore*. Bloomington: Indiana University Press.

Ebrahhim, N. 2001. *Annual report 2001: Muslim women's helpline*. Retrieved April 2, 2005, from http://www.mwhl.org/fnfor.htm.

Ek, R. 1966. Red Cloud's Copper Union address. *Central States Speech Journal* 16: 252–62.

Enck-Wanzer, D. 2006. Trashing the system: Social movement, intersectional rhetoric, and collective agency in the Young Lords Organization's Garbage Offensive. *Quarterly Journal of Speech* 92: 174–201.

Engster, D. 2007. *The heart of justice: Care ethics and political theory*. Oxford: Oxford University Press.

Ensler, E. 1998. *The vagina monologues*. New York: Villard.

Fabian, J. 1983. *Time and the other: How anthropology makes its object*. New York: Columbia University Press.

Farrell, T. B. 1993. *Norms of rhetorical culture*. New Haven, CT: Yale University Press.

Felman, S., and D. Laub. 1992. *Testimony: Crises of witnessing in literature, psychoanalysis, and history*. New York: Routledge.

Fessenden, T. 2007. *Culture and redemption: Religion, the secular, and American literature*. Princeton, NJ: Princeton University Press.

Fishman, J. A 1980. Minnesota ethnic language schools: Potential for the 80s. Conference proceedings, 9.

Flores, L. 1996. Creating discursive space through a rhetoric of difference: Chicana feminists craft a homeland. *Quarterly Journal of Speech* 82: 142–56.

Foucault, M. 1979. *Discipline and punish: The birth of the prison*. New York: Vintage.

Foucault, M. 1986. *The history of sexuality: Volume 3, The care of the self*. New York: Random House.

Foucault, M., and J. Pearson. 2001. *Fearless speech*. Los Angeles: Semiotext(e).

Fraser, N. 1990. Rethinking the public sphere: A contribution to the critique of actually existing democracy. *Social Text* 25: 56–80.

Fraser, N. 1997. *Justice interruptus*. New York: Routledge.

Fraser, N. 2000. *Rethinking recognition*. London: New Left Review.

Frueh, J. 2003. Vaginal aesthetics. *Hypatia* 18: 137–58.

Gadamer, H.-G. 1976. *Philosophical hermeneutics*. Berkeley and Los Angeles: Unversity of California Press.

Gadamer, H.-G. 1977. *The relevance of the beautiful and other essays*. Trans. N. Walker. Cambridge: Cambridge University Press.

Gadamer, H.-G. 2004. *Truth and method*. Trans. J. Weinsheimer and D. G. Marshall. 2nd rev. ed. New York: Continuum.

Garlough, C. 2007. Transfiguring criminality: Eclectic representations of a female bandit in Indian nationalist and feminist rhetoric. *Quarterly Journal of Speech* 93: 253–78.

Garlough, C. 2007. The life-giving gift of acknowledgment by Michael Hyde. *Philosophy and Rhetoric* 40: 434–38.

Garlough, C. 2008. On the political uses of folklore: Performance and grassroots feminist activism in India. *Journal of American Folklore* 121 (480): 167–91.

Garlough, C. 2008. The risks of acknowledgement: Performing the sex-selection identification and abortion debate. *Women Studies in Communication* 31 (3): 368–94.

Garlough, C. 2008. Playing with boundaries: Self and dialogue in an Indian-American fatana performance. *Folklore* 39: 63–94.

Garlough, C. 2011. Folklore and the potential of acknowledgment: Representing "India" at the Minnesota Festival of Nations. *Western Folklore* 70 (1): 69–98.

Garrett, M. 1997. How far we've come: How far we have to go. In *Making and unmaking the prospects for rhetoric*. Mahwah, NJ: Lawrence Erlbaum Associates, Publishers.

Geertz, C. 1973. *Interpretation of cultures*. New York: Basic Books.

Geertz, C. 2001. *Available light: Anthropological reflections on philosophical debates*. Princeton, NJ: Princeton University Press.

Gilligan, C. 1993. *In a different voice: Psychological theory and women's development*. 2nd ed. Cambridge, MA: Harvard University Press.

Gopinath, G. 2005. *Impossible desires: Queer diasporas and South Asian public cultures*. Durham, NC: Duke University Press.

Gould, H. 2006. *Sikhs, Swamis, students and spies: The Indian lobby in the United States, 1900–1946*. New Delhi: Sage Publications.

Grewal, I. 2005o. *Transnational America*. Durham, NC: Duke University Press.

Gronbeck, B. B. 1979. Celluloid rhetoric: On genres of documentary. In *Form and genre: Shaping rhetorical action*. E. K. K. Campbell and K. H. Jameson. Fallschurch, VA: Speech Communication Association.

Gupta, C. 2002. *Sexuality, obscenity, community: Women, Muslims, and the Hindu public in colonial India*. New York: Palgrave.

Gupta, M. 2006. *Unruly immigrants: Rights, activism, and transnational South Asian politics in the United States*. Durham, NC: Duke University Press.

Hall, S. 1997. The local and the global: Globalization and ethnicity. In *Dangerous liaisons: Gender, nation, and postcolonial perspectives*. Ed. A. McClintock, 173–87. Minneapolis: University of Minnesota Press.

Hamer, L. 1999. Folklore in schools and multiculturale: Toward institutionalizing noninstitutional knowledge. *Journal of American Folklore* 113: 44–69.

Hamera, J. 2002. An answerability of memory: "Saving" Khmer classical dance. *Drama Review* 46: 65–85.

Hamera, J. 2006. Performance, performativity, and cultural poiesis in practices of everyday life. In *The Sage handbook of performance studies*. Ed. D. S. Madison and J. Hamera. London: Sage Publications.

Hamera, J., ed. 2006. *Opening acts: Performance in/as communication and cultural studies*. London: Sage Publications.

Hamera, J., and D. Conquergood. 2006. Performance and politics: Themes and arguments. In *The Sage handbook of performance studies*. Ed. D. S. Madison and J. Hamera. London: Sage Publications.

Hammerback, J., and R. Jensen. 1994. Ethnic heritage as rhetorical legacy: The plan of Delano. *Quarterly Journal of Speech* 80: 53–70.

Handler, R. 1983. In search of the folk society: Nationalism and folklore studies in Quebec. *Canadian Ethnology Society Outremont* 3 (1): 103–14.

Handler, R. 1988. *Nationalism and the politics of culture in Quebec*. Madison: University of Wisconsin Press.

Handler, R., and J. Linnekin. 1984. Tradition, genuine, or spurious? *Journal of American Folklore* 97: 273–90.

Hansen, K. 1992. *Grounds for play: The Nautanki Theatre of North India*. Berkeley and Los Angeles: University of California Press.

Harriman, R., and J. L. Lucaites. 2002. Performing civic identity: The iconic photograph of the flag raising at Iwo Jima. *Quarterly Journal of Speech* 88: 363–92.

Hart, L., and P. Phelan. 1993. *Acting out: Feminist performances*. Ann Arbor: University of Michigan Press.

Hartman, G. 2006. The humanities of testimony: An introduction. *Poetics Today* 27 (2): 249–60.

Hashmi, S. 1998. From "The right to perform." In *Radical street performance: An international anthology*. Ed. J. Cohen-Cruz. New York: Routledge.

Hatcher, B. 1999. *Eclecticism and modern Hindu discourse*. Oxford: Oxford University Press.

Hauser, G. 1999. Incongruous bodies: Arguments for personal sufficiency and public insufficiency. *Argumentation and Advocacy* 36: 1–8.

Hauser, G. 1999. *Vernacular voices: The rhetoric of publics and public spheres*. Columbia: University of South Carolina Press.

Hawes, L. 2006. Becoming other-wise: Conversational performance and the politics of experience. In *Opening acts: Performances in/as communication and cultural studies*. Ed. J. Hamera. London: Sage.

Hay, S. 1974. Rabindranath Tagore in America. *American Quarterly* 14: 578.

Hazen, M., and D. Williams. 1998. Introduction: Argument and identity. *Argumentation and Advocacy* 34: 5–8.

Hegde, R. 2005. Disciplinary spaces and globalization: A postcolonial unsettling. *Global and media communication* 1 (1): 59–62.

Hedge, R. 2011. Introduction. *Circuits of visibility: Gender and transnational media cultures.* New York: New York University Press. 1–20.

Heidegger, M. 1965. *Der satz vom grund.* 3rd ed. Pfullingen: Neske.

Heidegger, M. 1971. *Poetry, language, thought.* New York: Perennial Classic.

Heidegger, M. 1996. *Being and time: A translation of Sein und zeit.* Trans. J. Stambaugh. Albany: State University of New York Press.

Held, V. 2006. *The ethics of care: Personal, political, and global.* New York: Oxford University Press.

Hess, G. R. 1974. The forgotten Asian Americans: The East Indian community in the United States. *Pacific Historical Review* 43: 576–96.

Honneth, A. 1995. *The struggle for recognition: The moral grammar of social conflicts.* Cambridge: MIT Press.

hooks, b. 1990. *Yearning: Race, gender, and cultural politics.* Boston: South End Press.

Howard, R. 1997. Apocalypse in your in-box: End-times communication on the Internet. *Western Folklore* 56: 295–315.

Howard, R. 2005. A theory of vernacular rhetoric: The case of the "sinner's prayer" online. *Folklore* 116 (2): 172–88.

Howard, R. 2008. Electronic hybridity: The persistent process of the vernacular web. *Journal of American Folklore* 121: 192–218.

http://www.samarmagazine.org/archive.

http://www.southasiansisters.org.

http://www.vday.org.

Huizinga, J. 1950. *Homo lundens: A study of the play-element in culture.* Boston: Beacon Press.

Huyler, S. 1994. *Painted prayers: Women's art in village India.* New York: Rizzoli.

Hyde, M. J. 1979. Hermeneutics and rhetoric: A seen and unobserved relationship. *Quarterly Journal of Speech* 65 (4): 347–63.

Hyde, M. J. 2006. *The life-giving gift of acknowledgment: A philosophical and rhetorical inquiry.* West Lafayette, IN: Purdue University Press.

Inwood, M. 1992. *A Hegel dictionary.* Oxford: Blackwell.

Jackson, C. 1981. *The Oriental religions and American thought: Nineteenth-century explorations.* Westport, CT: Greenwood Publishing Group.

Jackson, C. 1994. *Vedanta for the West: The Ramakrishna movement in the United States.* Bloomington: Indiana University Press.

Jensen, J. M. 1988. *Passage from India: Asian Indian immigrants in North America.* New Haven, CT: Yale University Press.

Jiwani, S. 2002. NY Desis protest Hindu right. *Samar* 15(1).

Jones, L. 1965. *Aboriginal American oratory: The tradition of eloquence among the Indians of the United States.* Los Angeles: Southwest Museum.

Jost, W., and M. Hyde. 1997. *Rhetoric and hermeneutics in our time: A reader.* New Haven, CT: Yale University Press.

Kadende-Kaiser, R., and P. Kaiser. 1997. Modern folklore, identity, and political change in Burundi. *African Studies Review* 40: 29–54.

Kapchan, D. 1996. *Gender on the market: Moroccan women and the revoicing of tradition.* Philadelphia: University of Pennsylvania Press.

Katrak, K. 2004. Cultural translation of Bharata Natyam into contemporary Indian dance: Second-generation South Asian Americans and cultural politics in diasporic locations. *South Asian Popular Culture* 2:2 (October): 79–102.

Katrak, K. 2008. The gestures of Bharata Natyam: Migrating into diasporic contemporary Indian dance. In *The migration of gesture: Art, film, dance, writing*. Ed. Carrie Noland and Sally Ann Ness, 217–40. Minneapolis: University of Minnesota Press.

Katrak, K. 2009. The arts of resistance: Arundhati Roy, Denise Uyehara, and the ethno-global imagination. In *Violence performed: Local roots and global routes of conflict*. Ed. P. Anderson and J. Menon, 244–63. London: Palgrave Macmillan.

Katrak, K. 2009. Toward defining contemporary Indian dance: A global form. *Proceedings of the 2008 Congress of Research on Dance Conference*. Chicago: University of Illinois Press.

Katriel, T. 1995. Sites of memory: Discourses of the past in Israeli pioneering settlement museums. *Quarterly Journal of Speech* 80: 1–20.

Kennedy, G. 1998. *Comparative rhetoric: A historical and cross- cultural introduction*. Oxford: Oxford University Press.

Khandelwal, M. 1995. India immigrants in Queens, New York City: Patterns of spatial concentration and distribution 1965–1990. In *Nation and migration: Politics of space in the South Asian diaspora*. Ed. P. Van der Veer. Philadelphia: University of Pennsylvania Press.

Khilnani, S. 1999. *The idea of India*. New York: Farrar, Straus and Giroux.

Kirkwood, W. G. 1983. Storytelling and self-confrontation: Parables as communication strategies. *Quarterly Journal of Speech* 69 (1): 58–74.

Kirkwood, W. G. 1985. Parables as metaphors and examples. *Quarterly Journal of Speech* 71 (4): 422–40.

Kirkwood, W. G. 1990. Shiva's dance at sundown: Implications of Indian aesthetics for poetics and rhetoric. *Text and Performance Quarterly* 10: 93–110.

Kirkwood, W. G. 1992. Narrative and the rhetoric of possibility. *Communication Monograph* 59 (1): 30–47.

Kirshenblatt-Gimblett, B. 1983. Studying immigrant and ethnic folklore. In *Handbook of American folklore*. Ed. Richard M. Dorson, 39–47. Bloomington: Indiana University Press.

Kirshenblatt-Gimblett, B. 1991. Objects of ethnography. In *Exhibiting culture: The poetics and politics of museum display*. Ed. L. Steven. Philadelphia: Smithsonian.

Kirshenblatt-Gimblett, B. 1995. Theorizing heritage. *Ethnomusicology* 39 (3): 367–80.

Kirshenblatt-Gimblett, B. 1996. The electronic vernacular. In *Connected: Engagements with the media*. Ed. G. Marcus, 21–65. Chicago: University of Chicago Press.

Kirshenblatt-Gimblett, B. 1998. *Destination culture: Tourism, museums, and heritage*. Berkeley and Los Angeles: University of California Press.

Klumpp, James F. 1997. The rhetoric of community at century's end. In *Making and unmaking the prospects for rhetoric: Selected papers from the 1996 Rhetoric Society of America conference*. Ed. R. Enos. Mahwah, NJ: Erlbaum Publishers.

Knudsen, S. V. 2005. Intersectionality: A theoretical inspiration in the analysis of minority cultures and identities in textbooks. In *Caught in the Web or lost in the textbook?* Ed. E. Bruillard, B. Aamotsbakken, S. V. Knudsen, and M. Horsley, 61–76. Eighth International Conference on Learning and Educational Media.

Korom, F. 2003. *Hosay Trinidad: Muharram performances in an Indo-Caribbean diaspora*. Philadelphia: University of Pennsylvania Press.

Korom, F. 2006. *South Asian folklore: A handbook*. Santa Barbara: Greenwood Press.

Korom, F. 2006. *Village of painters: Narrative scrolls from West Bengal*. Santa Fe: Museum of New Mexico Press.

Kristeva, J. 1982. *Powers of horror: An essay on abjection*. New York: Columbia University Press.

Kumar, N. 1994. *Women subjects: South Asian histories*. Charlottesville: University Press of Virginia.

Kumar, R. 1993. *The history of doing*. London: Verso Publishing.

La Brack, B. 1988. *The Sikhs of Northern California, 1904–1975*. New York: AMS Press.

Lal, V. 1999. A political history of Asian Indians in the United States. *Live like the Banyan tree*. Philadelphia: Balch Institute for Ethnic Studies. 42–48.

Langellier, K. M. 1999. Personal narrative, performance, performativity: Two or three things I know for sure. *Text and Performance Quarterly* 19: 125–44.

Leonard, K. 1997. *The South Asian Americans*. Westport, CT: Greenwood Press.

Lepecki, A. 2004. *Of the presence of the body*. Middletown: Wesleyan University Press.

Leshkowich, A. M., and C. Jones. 2000. What happens when Asian chic becomes chic in Asia? *Fashion Theory* 7 (3): 281–300.

Levinas, E. 1998. *Otherwise than being: Or beyond essence*. Pittsburgh, PA: Duquesne University Press.

Lorde, A. 2001. The transformation of silence into language and action. In *Identity politics in the women's movement*. Ed. B. Ryan. New York: New York University Press.

Lucaites, J., and R. Hariman. 2002. Performing civic identity: The iconic photograph of the flag raising at Iwo Jima. *Quarterly Journal of Speech* 88: 363–92.

Lyons, S. 1997. Crying for revision: Postmodern Indians and rhetorics of tradition. In *Making and unmaking the prospects for rhetoric: Selected papers from the 1996 Rhetoric Society of America Conference*. Ed. T. Enos and R. McNabb. Mahwah, NJ: Lawrence Erlbaum Associates.

Madison, D. S. 2005. *Critical ethnography: Method, ethics, and performance*. London: Sage Publications.

Madison, D. S. 2005. Staging fieldwork, Performing human rights. In *The Sage handbook of performance studies*. Ed. D. S. Madison and J. Hamera, 397–418. London: Sage Publications.

Madison, D. S. 2006. Staging fieldwork/performing human rights. In *The Sage handbook of performance studies*. Ed. D. S. Madison and J. Hamera, 397–418. London: Sage Publications.

Madison, D. S., and J. Hamera. 2005. *The Sage handbook of performance studies*. London: Sage Publications.

Madison, D. S., and J. Hamera, S. 2006. Introduction: Performance studies at the intersection. In *The Sage handbook of performance studies*. Ed. D. S. Madison and J. Hamera. London: Sage Publications.

Maharishi, A. 2000. *A comparative study of Brechtian and classical Indian theatre*. New Delhi: Bahavalpur House.

Maira, S. 2002. *Desis in the house: Indian American youth culture in New York City*. Philadelphia: Temple University Press.

Maira, S. 2009. *Missing: Youth, citizenship, and empire after 9/11*. Durham, NC: Duke University Press.

Makker, V. 2004. "If my vagina could speak . . ." *Samar Magazine*, May 29. http://samarmagazine.org.archive.

Mannur, A. 2005. Culinary fictions: Immigrant foodways and race in Indian American literature. In *Asian American studies after critical mass*. Ed. K. O. Ono. Oxford: Blackwell Publishing.

Mansbridge, J. 1990. *Beyond self-interest*. Chicago: University of Chicago Press.

Marcus, G. 1995. Ethnography in/of the world system: The emergence of multi-sited ethnography. *Annual Review of Anthropology* 24: 95–117.

Markell, P. 2003. *Bound by recognition*. Princeton, NJ: Princeton University Press.

Markula, P. 2006. The dancing body without organs: Deleuze, femininity, and performing research. *Qualitative Inquiry* 12 (1): 3–27.

Mayo, K. 1927. *Mother India*. New York: Blue Ribbon Books.

Mazumdar, S. 2003. What happened to the women: Chinese and Indian male migration to the United States in global perspective. In *Asian/Pacific Islander American women*. Ed. S. Hune and G. Nomura. New York: New York University Press.

McGee, M. 1980. The "Ideograph": A link between rhetoric and ideology. *Quarterly Journal of Speech* 66: 1–16.

Mechling, E., and J. Mechling. 1999. American cultural criticism in the pragmatic attitude. In *At the intersection: Cultural studies and rhetorical studies*. Ed. T. Rosteck. New York: Guilford Press.

Michelfelder, D., and R. Palmer. 1989. *Dialogue and deconstruction: The Gadamer-Derrida encounter*. Albany: State University of New York Press.

Mieder, W. 1987. *Tradition and innovation in folk literature*. London: University Press of New England. Burlington, VT: University Press of New England.

Mies, M. 1980. *Indian women and patriarchy: Conflict and dilemmas of students and working women*. New Delhi: Concepts Publishing Co.

Mifsud, M. 2007. On rhetoric as gift/giving. *Philosophy and Rhetoric* 40: 89–107.

Mills, M. 1985. Sex role reversals, sex changes, and transvestite disguise in the oral traditions of a conservative Muslim community in Afghanistan. In *Women's folklore, women's culture*. Ed. Rosan A. Susan J. Kalcik. Philadelphia: University of Pennsylvania Press.

Mills, M. 1991. *Rhetorics and politics of Afghan traditional storytelling*. Philadelphia: University of Pennsylvania Press.

Mills, M. 1993. Feminist theory and the study of folklore: A twenty-year trajectory toward theory. *Western Folklore* 32: 173–92.

Minh-ha, T. 1989. *Woman, native, other*. Bloomington: Indiana University Press.

Mirzoeff, N., ed. 1999. *Diaspora and visual culture: Representing Africans and Jews*. London: Routledge.

Mitchell, T. 1992. Orientalism and the exhibitionary order. In *Colonialism and culture*. Ed. N. B. Dirks. Ann Arbor: University of Michigan Press.

Mohanty, C. 1980. *Cartographies of struggle: Third world women and the politics of feminism*. Oxford: Blackwell Publishing.

Mohanty, C. 1988. Under western eyes: Feminist scholarship and colonial discourse. *Feminist Review* 30: 61–88.

Mohanty, C. 1993. Defining genealogies: Feminist reflections on being South Asian in North America. In *Our feet walk the sky: Women of the South Asian diaspora*. San Francisco: Aunt Lute Books.

Mohanty, C. 2003. *Feminism without borders: Decolonizing theory practicing solidarity*. Durham, NC: Duke University Press.

Mohl, R. A. 1981. Cultural assimilation versus cultural pluralism. *Educational Forum* 45: 323–30.

Mookherjee, M. 2005. Affective citizenship: Feminism, postcolonialism and the politics of recognition. *Critical Review of International Social and Political Philosophy* 8 (1): 31–50.

Morris, R., and P. Wander. 1990. Native American rhetoric: Dancing in the shadows of the ghost dance. *Quarterly Journal of Speech* 76: 164–91.

Mukherjee, T. 1998. *Taraknath Das: Life and letters of a revolutionary exile*. Bengal: National Council of Education.

Mumukshananda, S. 1979. *The life of Swami Vivekananda*. Calcutta: Advaita Ashrama.

Nancy, J-L. 2002. *Hegel: The restlessness of the negative*. Trans. J. Smith and S. Miller. Minneapolis: University of Minnesota Press.

Narayan, K. 1986. Birds on a branch: Girlfriends and wedding songs in Kangra. *Ethos* 24 (1): 47–75.

Narayan, K. 1993. Refractions of the field at home: Hindu holy men in America in the nineteenth and twentieth centuries. *Cultural Anthropology* 8: 476–509.

Noddings, N. 2000. The challenge to care in schools: An alternative approach to education. In *Philosophical documents in education*. Ed. Tony W. Johnson and Ronald F. Reed. Reading: Longman Press.

Oliver, K. 2001. *Witnessing: Beyond recognition*. Minneapolis: University of Minnesota Press.

Oliver, K. 2004. Witnessing and testimony. *Parallax* 10 (1): 79–88.

Oliver, R. 1971. *Communication and culture in Ancient India and China*. New York: Syracuse University Press.

Olneck, M. R. 1993. Terms of inclusion: Has multiculturalism redefined equality in American education? *American Journal of Education* 101: 234–60.

Ono, K. O., and J. M. Sloop. 2002. *Shifting borders: Rhetoric, immigration, and California's Proposition 187*. Philadelphia: Temple University Press.

Oring, E. 2008. Legendry and the rhetoric of truth. *Journal of American Folklore* 121 (480): 127–68.

Pajnick, M. 2006. Feminist reflections on Habermas's communicative action: The need for an inclusive political theory. *European Journal of Social Theory* 9 (3): 385–404.

Paredes, A. 1993. *Folklore and culture on the Texas-Mexican border*. Ed. Richard Bauman. Austin: University of Texas Press.

Park-Fuller, L. M. 2000. Performing absence: The staged personal narrative as testimony. *Text and Performance Quarterly* 20: 20–42.

Patraka, V. 1993. Split britches in *Split britches: Performing histories, vaudeville and the everyday*. In *Acting out: Feminist performances*. Ed. L. Hart and P. Phelan. Ann Arbor: University of Michigan Press.

Patraka, V. 1999. *Spectacular suffering: Theatre, fascism, and the holocaust*. Bloomington: Indiana University Press.

Pezzullo, P. C. 2007. *Toxic tourism: Rhetorics of pollution, travel, and environmental justice*. Tuscaloosa: University of Alabama Press.

Phelan, P. 1993. White men and pregnancy: Discovering the body to be rescued. In *Acting out: Feminist performances*. Ed. L. Hart and P. Phelan. Ann Arbor: University of Michigan Press.

Phelan, P. 1993. *Unmarked: The politics of performance*. London: Routledge.

Phillips, K. R. 2007. *Rhetorical maneuvers: Subjectivity, power, and resistance*. College Station: Penn State University Press.

Plummer, K. 1995. *Telling sexual stories: Power, change and social worlds*. London: Routledge.

Pollock, D., ed. 1998. *Exceptional spaces: Essays in performance and history*. Chapel Hill: University of North Carolina Press.

Pollock, D. 1999. *Telling bodies, performing birth*. New York: Columbia University Press.

Pollock, D. 2005. *Remembering: Oral history performance*. New York: Palgrave Macmillan.

Pollock, D. 2006. Memories, remembering, and histories of change: A performance praxis. In *The Sage handbook of performance studies*. Ed. D. S. Madison and J. Hamera, 87–105. London: Sage Publications.

Poore, G. 2007. Silences that prevail when the perpetrators are our own. In *Body evidence: Intimate violence against South Asian women in America*. Ed. S. Dasgupta. New Brunswick, NJ: Rutgers University Press.

Portes, A., and R. Rumbaut. 1996. *Immigrant America: A portrait*. Berkeley and Los Angeles: University of California Press.

Povinelli, E. A. 2002. *The cunning of recognition: Indigenous alterities and the making of Australian multiculturalism*. Durham, NC: Duke University Press.

Prasad, L. 1999. *Live like the Banyan tree: Images of the Indian American experience*. Philadelphia, PA: The Balch Institute for Ethnic Studies.

Prashad, V. 2000. *The karma of brown folk*. Minneapolis: University of Minnesota Press.

Prashad, V. 2001. *Everybody was Kung Fu fighting: Afro-Asian connections and the myth of cultural purity*. Boston: Beacon Press.

Prosser, M. 1978. *The cultural dialogue: An introduction to intercultural communications*. Boston: Hougton Mifflin.

Purkayastha, B. 2005. *Negotiating ethnicities: Second-generation South Asians transverse a transnational world*. New Brunswick, NJ: Rutgers University Press.

Putnam, R. 2000. *Bowling alone: The collapse and revival of American community*. New York: Simon and Schuster.

Rabinow, P. 1977. *Reflection on fieldwork in Morocco*. Berkeley and Los Angeles: University of California Press.

Radhakrishnan, R. 2003. Ethnicity in an age of diaspora. In *Theorizing diaspora: A reader*. Ed. J. Braziel and A. Mannur. Oxford: Blackwell Publishing.

Radner, J., and S. Lannser. 1993. Strategies of coding in women's culture. In *Feminist messages: Coding in women's folk culture*. Ed. Joan Radner, 1–29. Chicago: University of Illinois Press.

Raheja, G. G., and A. Gold. 1994. *Listen to the heron's words: Reimagining gender and kinship in North India*. Berkeley and Los Angeles: University of California Press.

Ramnath, M. 2005. Two revolutions: The Gadar movement and India's radical diaspora, 1913–1918. *Radical History Review* 92: 7–30.

Ranciere, J. 1995. Politics, identification, and subjectivization. *The identity in question*. Ed. John Rajchman, 63–70. New York: Routledge.

Richman, P., ed. 1991. *Many Ramayanas: The diversity of a narrative tradition in South Asia*. Oxford: Oxford University Press.

Ricoeur, P. 2004. *Memory, history, forgetting*. Trans. K. Blamey and D. Pellauer. Chicago: University of Chicago Press.

Ricoeur, P. 2005. *The course of recognition*. Trans. D. Pellauer. Cambridge, MA: Harvard University Press.

Robinson, F. 1999. *Globalizing care: Ethics, feminist theory, and international relations*. Boulder, CO: Westview Press.

Rosteck, T., ed. 1999. *At the intersection: Cultural studies and rhetorical studies*. New York: Guilford Press.

Ryan, B. 2001. *Identity politics in the women's movement*. New York: New York University Press.

Sastri, P. S. 1989. *Indian theory of aesthetic*. Delhi: Bharatiya Vidya Prakashan.

Sawin, P. 2002. Performance at the nexus of gender, power, and desire: Reconsidering Bauman's *Verbal Art* from the perspective of gendered subjectivity as performance. *Journal of American Folklore* 115 (455): 28–61.

Schaffer, K., and S. Smith. 2004. *Human rights and narrated lives: The ethics of recognition*. New York: Palgrave Macmillan.

Schechner, R. 1985. *The Future of ritual: Writings on culture and performance*. New York: Routledge.

Schechner, R. 1988. *Performance theory*. New York: Routledge.

Schechner, R. 2003. The street is the stage. In *Performance Studies*. Ed. E. Striff. New York: Palgrave Macmillan.

Schiappa, E. 2001. Second thoughts on the critiques of big rhetoric. *Philosophy and Rhetoric* 34: 260–74.

Schiappa, E. 2008. *Beyond represenational correctness: Rethinkng criticism of popular media.* Albany: State University of New York Press.

Schrag, C. 2002. *God as otherwise than being: Toward a semantics of the gift.* Evanston, IN: Northwestern University Press.

Sevenhuijsen, S. 1998. *Citizenship and the ethic of care: Feminist considerations on justice, morality, and politics.* London: Routledge.

Shah, H. 1999. Race, nation, and citizenship: Asian Indians and the idea of whiteness in the US press 1906–1923. *Howard Journal of Communication* 10: 249–69.

Shankar, S. 2008. *Desi land: Teen culture, class, and success in Silicone Valley.* Durham, NC: Duke University Press.

Sharma, N. 2010. *Hip-hop desis: South Asian Americans, blackness, and a global race consciousness.* Durham, NC: Duke University Press.

Shome, R. 1996. Postcolonial interventions in the rhetorical canon: An "other" view. *Communication Theory* 6: 40–59.

Shukla, S. 2003. *India abroad: Diasporic cultures of postwar America and England.* New Delhi: Orient Longman Private Limited.

Shuman, A. 2005. *Other people's stories: Entitlement claims and the critique of empathy.* Chicago: University of Illinois Press.

Sickels, A. 1945. *Around the world in St. Paul.* Minneapolis: University of Minnesota Press.

SILC Yearbook. 1994.

Sims, M. C., and M. Stephens. 2005. *Living folklore: An introduction to the study of people and their traditions.* London: Muse Publishing.

Sinha, M. 2006. *Spectors of Mother India: The global restructuring of an empire.* Durham, NC: Duke University Press.

Smith, A. 1971. Markings of an African concept of rhetoric. *Communication Quarterly* 19: 13–18.

Snyder, G. 2011. *Multivalent Recognition: A Politics of Recognition for Late Modern America.* Unpublished.

Sommer, D. 1995. *Sacred secrets: A strategy for survival.* In *Women, autobiography, theory: A reader.* Ed. S. Smith and J. Watson. Madison: University of Wisconsin Press.

Song, C. C. 2006. South Asians put on monologues. *Michigan Daily,* February 13, 2006.

South Asian Sisters. 2004. If my vagina could speak . . . *Samar.* http://samarmagazine.org/archive/articles/157.

Stacey, J. 1988. Can there be a feminist ethnography? *Women's Studies International Forum* 11 (1): 21–27.

Starosta, W. 1979. Roots of an older rhetoric: On rhetorical effectiveness in the third world. *Western Journal of Speech Communication* 43: 278–87.

Stein, J. 2010. My own private India. *Time.* July 5, 2010.

Stoeltje, B. 1983. Festivals. *Handbook of American folklore.* Ed. R. Dorsen. Bloomington: University of Indiana Press.

Stoeltje, B. 1992. *Folklore, cultural performances, and popular entertainments.* Oxford: Oxford University Press.

Striff, E. 2003. *Performance Studies.* New York: Palgrave Macmillan.

Suleiman, S. 1990. *Subversive intent: Gender politics and the avante-garde.* Cambridge, MA: Harvard University Press.

Suleri, S. 1992. *The rhetoric of English India*. Chicago: University of Chicago Press.

Sutton-Smith, B. 1997. *The ambiguity of play*. Cambridge, MA: Harvard University Press.

Taylor, C. 1992. *The ethics of authenticity*. Cambridge, MA: Harvard University Press.

Taylor, C. 1992. *Multiculturalism and the politics of recognition: An essay*. Princeton, NJ: Princeton University Press.

Taylor, C. 1994. *Multiculturalism: Examining the politics of recognition*. Princeton, NJ: Princeton University Press.

Taylor, V., and L. Rupp. 2005. When the girls are men: Negotiating gender and sexual dynamics in a study of drag queens. *Signs* 30: 2115–39.

Tedlock, D., and B. Mannheim. 1995. *The dialogic emergence of culture*. Urbana: University of Illinois Press.

Townsend-Bell, E. 2009. Intersectional praxis. Paper given at the American Political Science Association Annual Meeting, Toronto, Canada.

Tronto, J. 1993. *Moral boundaries: A political argument for an ethic of care*. London: Routledge.

Tsing, A. L. 1993. *In the realm of the diamond queen: Marginality in an out-of-the-way place*. Princeton, NJ: Princeton University Press.

Turner, V. 1969. *The ritual process: Structure and anti-structure*. New York: Aldine De Gruyer.

Turner, V. 1982. *From ritual to theatre: The human seriousness of play*. New York: PAJ Publications.

Turner, V., and R. Schechner. 1987. *The anthropology of performance*. New York: PAJ Publications.

Tyagi, S. 2007. In *Body evidence: Intimate violence against South Asian women in America*. Ed. S. Dasgupta. New Brunswick, NJ: Rutgers University Press.

Vatuk, V. P. 1969. *Thieves in my house (four studies in Indian folklore of protest and change)*. Bhairavnath: Vishvavidyalaya Prakashan.

Varma, P. 1995. *Indian immigrants in USA: Struggle for equality*. New Delhi: Heritage Publishers.

Visweswaran, K. 1994. *Fictions of feminist ethnography*. Minneapolis: University of Minnesota Press.

Volpp, L. 2009. The citizen and the terrorist. In *American studies: An anthology*. Ed. K. G. Janice Radway, Barry Shank, Penny Von Eschen, 78–85. Oxford: Wiley-Blackwell.

Watts, E. K. 2001. "Voice" and "voicelessness" in rhetorical studies. *Quarterly Journal of Speech* 87: 179–96.

Watts, E. K. 2002. African American ethos and hermeneutical rhetoric: An exploration of Alain Locke's *The New Negro*. *Quarterly Journal of Speech* 88 (1): 19–32.

Whisnant, D. 1985. *All that is native and fine: The politics of culture in an American region*. Chapel Hill: University of North Carolina Press.

Wiesel, E. 1984. *Souls on fire: And somewhere a master*. London: Penguin Books.

Wikan, U. 1992. Beyond the words: The power of resonance. *American Ethnologist* 19: 460–81.

Williams, L., Y. Malhotra, S. Kohli, and A. Kalawar. 2004, October. Elements of racial crime and prejudice: Religion or jealousy. Speech presented at The Pluralism Project, Harvard University.

Ziarek, K. 1994. *Inflected language: Toward a hermeneutics of nearness: Heidegger, Levinas, Stevens, Celan*. Albany: State University of New York Press.

Zipes, J. 1983. *Fairy tales and the art of subversion: The classical genre for children and the process of civilization*. New York: Routledge.

Zipes, J. 1995. *Creative storytelling: Building community, changing lives*. New York: Routledge.

Index

www.ingramcontent.com/pod-product-compliance
Lightning Source LLC
Chambersburg PA
CBHW031128270326
41929CB00011B/1542